Twilight of Majesty

Occasional Papers, Number 4

Middle East Center
Jackson School of International Studies
University of Washington

CARL F. PETRY

Twilight of Majesty

The Reigns of the Mamlūk Sultans al-Ashrāf Qāytbāy and Qānṣūh al-Ghawrī in Egypt

Distributed by
University of Washington Press
Seattle • London

This book has been published with
the support of a grant from the
Office of Research and Sponsored Programs of
Northwestern University, Evanston, Illinois

Printed in the United States of America

Library of Congress Cataloging-in-Publication Data

Petry, Carl F., 1943–
Twilight of majesty : the reigns of the Mamlūk Sultans al-Ashrāf Qāytbāy and Qānṣūh al-Ghawrī in Egypt / Carl F. Petry.
p. cm. – (Occasional papers : no. 4)
Includes bibliographical references (p.) and index.
ISBN 0-295-97307-2 (alk. paper)
1. Egypt—History—1250–1517. 2. Qāytbāy al-Maḥmūdī, Sultan of Egypt and Syria, 1412–1496. 3. Qānṣūh al-Ghūrī, Sultan of Egypt and Syria, d. 1516. I. Title. II. Series: Occasional papers (Henry M. Jackson School of International Studies. Middle East Center) : no. 4.
DT96.7.P48 1993
962′.02–dc20 93-4632
CIP

The paper used in this publication meets the minimum requirements of American National Standard for Information Sciences—Permanence of Paper for Printed Library Materials, ANSI Z39.48-1984. ♾

CONTENTS

ACKNOWLEDGEMENTS

THE initial research from which these biographies emerged was funded by a grant from the United States Information Agency in 1985, administered through the American Research Center in Egypt. The latter institution has played a fundamental role in supporting informed inquiry into every aspect of Egyptian history and culture, and I can only echo the praise of so many others for its services. Over a period of five months, I examined several hundred endowment deeds (*awqāf*) kept in the Egyptian National Archives (Dār al-Wathā'iq al-Qawmīya) and the Ministry of Pious Endowments (Wizārat al-Awqāf), both in Cairo. The deeds drawn up by Qāytbāy referred to in the text were but two documents in this archival trove I studied. I am indebted to Madame Sawsan 'Abd al-Ghānī and Ustādh Ḥusām al-Dīn Kenj 'Uthmān, curators of the respective collections, who so graciously facilitated my search.

In 1987, I received a fellowship from the John Simon Guggenheim Foundation that enabled me to spend a year reading through the chronicles that provide the narrative data in the biographies. Two months of that year I spent in Istanbul examining manuscripts from the Mamlūk period housed in the Sulaymānīya Library. The staff of that repository, and in particular its director Dr. Muammer Ülker, exceeded any assistance I could have reasonably expected by temporarily transferring texts from other libraries not readily accessible to foreigners. The productivity of this all-too-brief sojourn I owe to their hospitality.

These biographies form part of a larger analysis of the decline of Egypt as a major power at the end of the Middle Ages. While my thoughts on this topic are still evolving, I have benefited enormously from comments and suggestions of colleagues who have followed the project as it developed. In particular I should mention Muḥammad M. Amīn, Jere L. Bacharach, Bruce D. Craig, R. Stephen Humphreys, John O. Hunwick, Donald P. Little, Ivor Wilks and John E. Woods—whose advice has been more valuable to me than they may realize. While I bear responsibility for any infelicities appearing in the following work, they certainly can claim credit for many of its insights.

Finally, production of this monograph in a format affordable to students as well as scholars was aided by a generous subvention from the Office of Research and Sponsored Programs at Northwestern University. Its quality is due in large measure to the editorial counsel offered by Theodora S. MacKay, of the Middle East Center at the University of Washington, whose collegiality proved to be one of the unexpected pleasures of the enterprise.

A brief statement on transliteration. The Library of Congress system has been used for most Arabic terms. Words common in English usage, such as Mecca, Medina, and Koran, appear in their more conventional forms. The reader will note a high frequency of Turkish, and to a lesser extent Persian, personal names and places. These have been consistently rendered as they were written in the Arabic chronicles.

The plans of the Citadel of Cairo and the City of Cairo were drawn from William Popper's book *Egypt and Syria under the Circassian Sultans, 1382–1468 A.D.* (Berkeley and Los Angeles, University of California Press, 1955).

REIGNS OF MAMLŪK SULTANS CITED IN TEXT

al-Ẓāhir Barqūq (784–801/1382–1392, with interregnum 791/1389)
al-Nāṣir Faraj ibn Barqūq (801–815/1399–1412, with interregnum 808/1405)
al-Mu'ayyad Shaykh (815–824/1412–1421)
al-Ashraf Barsbāy (825–841/1422–1437)
al-Ẓāhir Jaqmaq (842–857/1438–1453)
al-Manṣūr 'Uthmān ibn Jaqmaq (857/1453)
al-Ashraf Īnāl (857–865/1453–1461)
al-Mu'ayyad Aḥmad ibn Īnāl (865/1461)
al-Ẓāhir Khushqadam (865–872/1461–1467)
al-Zāhir Yilbāy (872/1467)
al-Ẓāhir Timurbughā (872/1468)
al-Ashraf Qāytbāy (872–901/1468–1496)
al-Nāṣir Muḥammad ibn Qāytbāy (901–903/1496–1498)
al-Ẓāhir Qānṣūh (Khamsmi'a) (903–905/1498–1500)
al-Ashraf Jānbalāt (905–906/1500–1501)
al-'Ādil Tūmānbāy (906/1501)
Qānṣūh al-Ghawrī (906–922/1501–1517)
al-Ashraf Tūmānbāy (922/1517)

ABBREVIATIONS

BIE	*Bulletin de l'Institut d'Egypte* (Cairo)
BSOAS	*Bulletin of the School of Oriental and African Studies* (University of London)
EI[1]; *EI*[2]	*Encyclopedia of Islam*, first and second editions (Leiden, 1913–1938; 1954–)
GAL, Suppl.	*Geschichte der arabischen Literatur*, two volumes with three-volume supplement by Carl Brockelmann (Leiden, 2d ed. of original two vols., 1943–1949; Supplement, 1937–1942)
IJMES	*International Journal of Middle East Studies* (New York)
IFAO	*Institut français d'archéologie orientale du Caire* (Cairo)
JESHO	*Journal of the Economic and Social History of the Orient* (Leiden)
JAOS	*Journal of the American Oriental Society* (New Haven)
JRAS	*Journal of the Royal Asiatic Society* (London)
REI	*Revue des études islamiques* (Paris)

Abbreviations of sources will be found in the Bibliography.

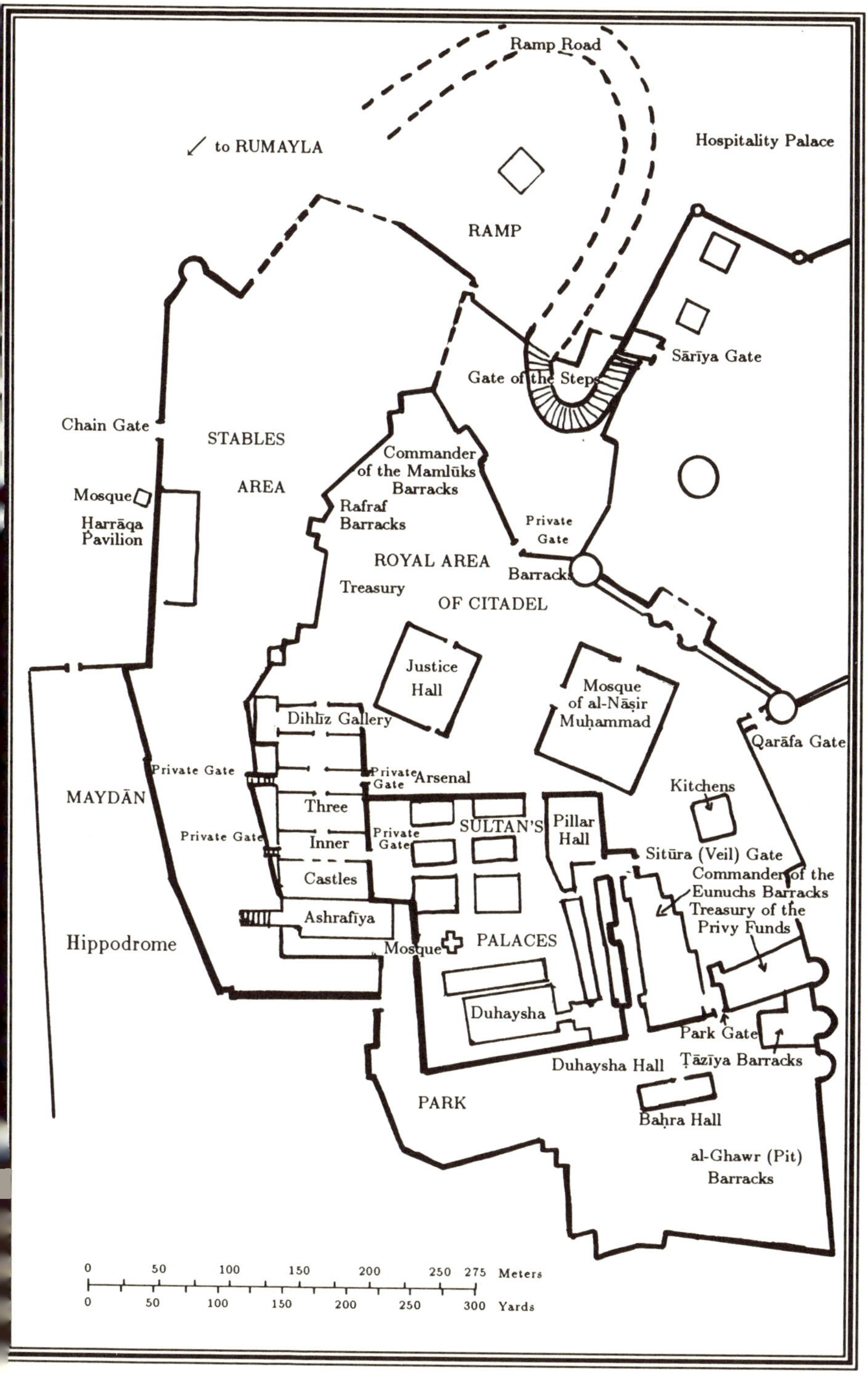

The Citadel of Cairo

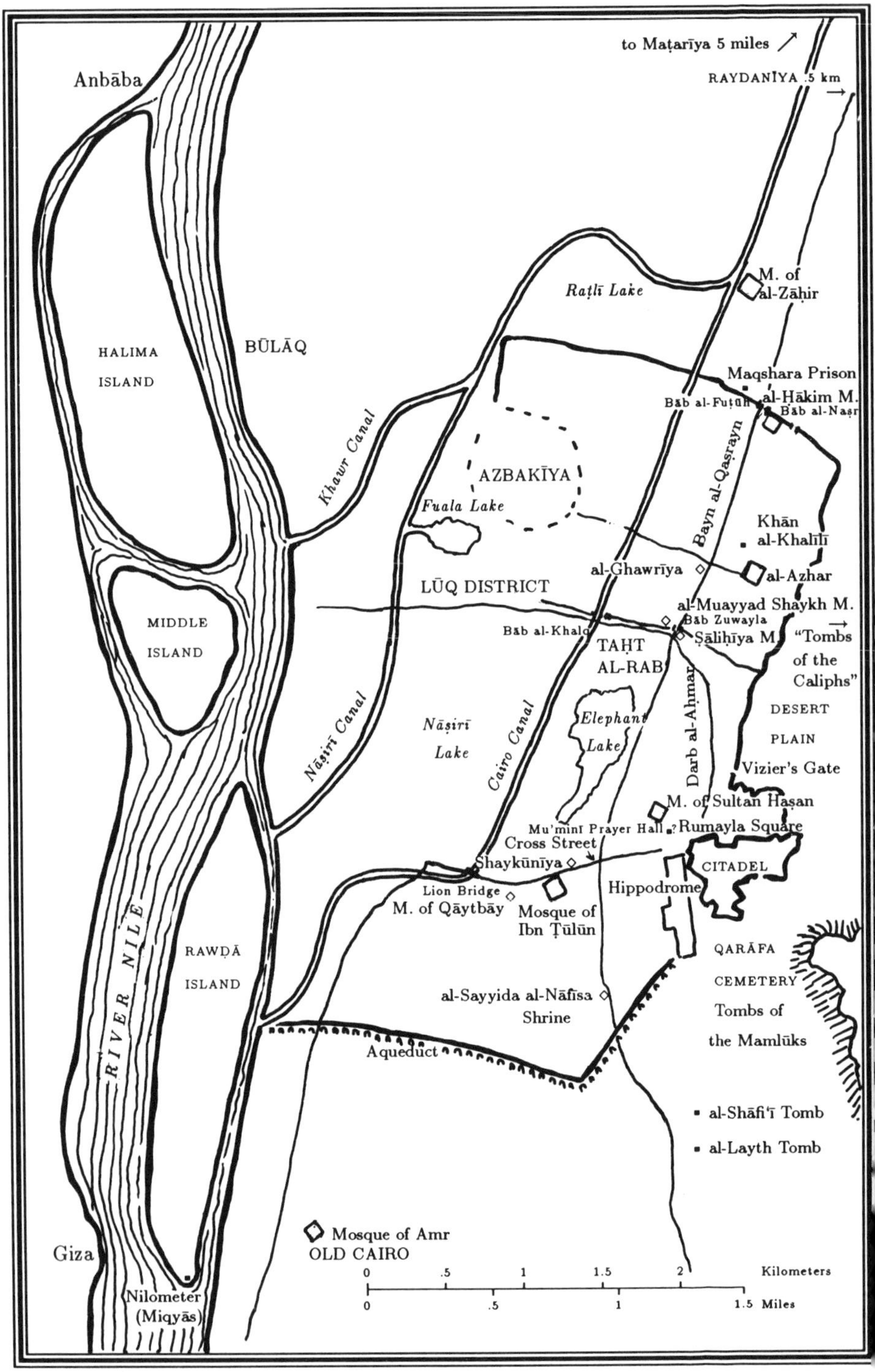

The City of Cairo

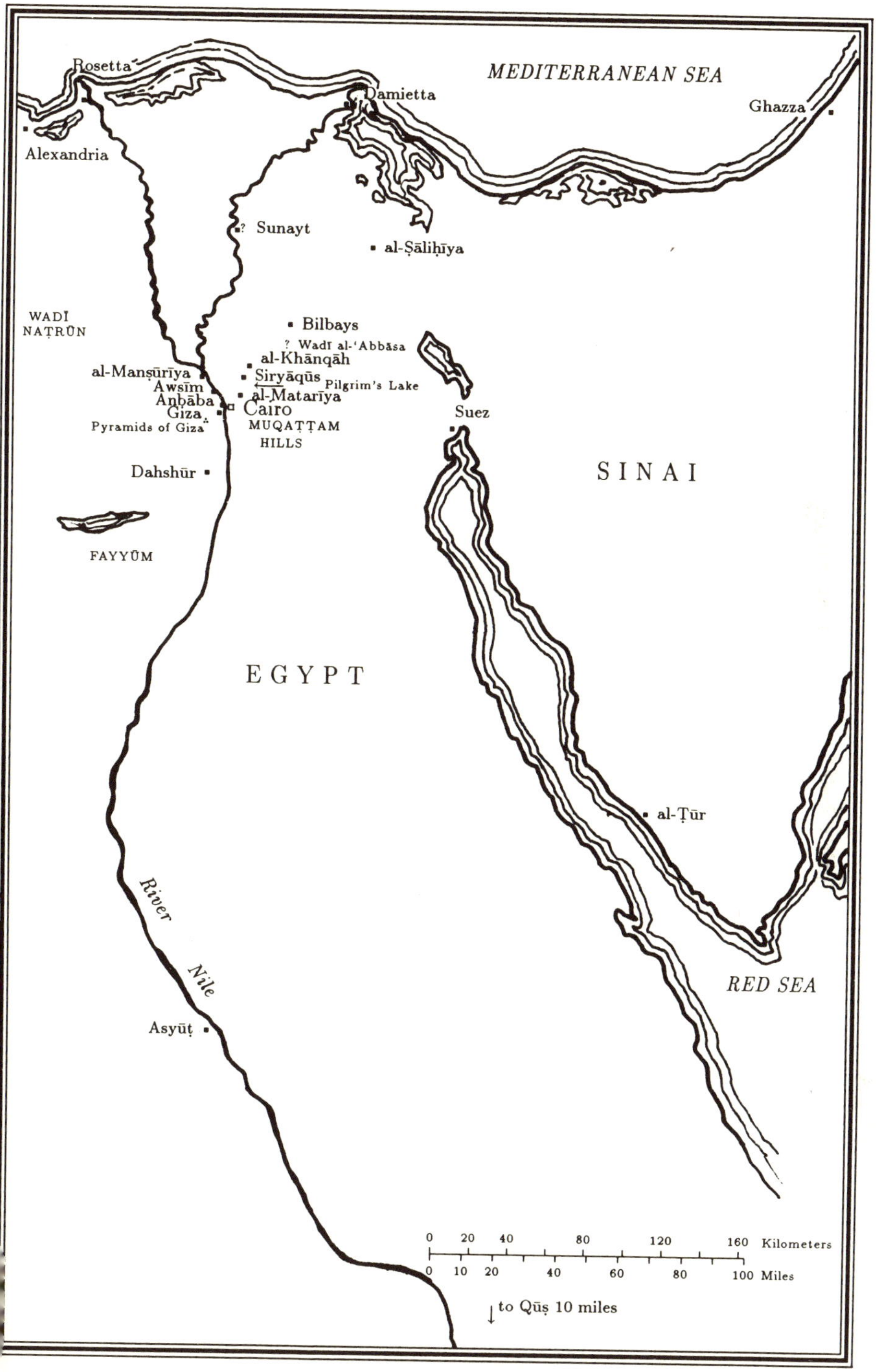

Egypt and Sinai

Southeast Anatolia, Syria, and Palestine

Twilight of Majesty

Chapter One

Introduction

THE following biographies weave a rich, on occasion labyrinthine, tapestry of court intrigues, interstate relations, and power politics played out during the final decades of the Mamlūk sultanate in Cairo. This regime, governed by senior officers who rose from the ranks of military slaves imported from the Caucasus or Central Asia, united Egypt and Syria, heartland of the Arab world, for some two hundred and seventy years (A.H. 648–922/1250–1517 C.E.). The sultanate, centered in Cairo, profoundly affected the course of this region's development. The Mamlūk state left an indelible stamp on the exercise of power, function of the bureaucracy, and resilience of the economy in Egypt.[1] The lurid details of

[1] To date, no comprehensive analysis of the Mamlūk sultanate has been written that incorporates contemporary scholarship. Robert Irwin has completed a useful study of its first or Baḥrī period in his *The Middle East in the Middle Ages: the Early Mamluk Sultanate, 1250–1382* (London 1986). David

these biographies enable a modern reader to relive the exciting events of this era (872–922/1468–1517), beset as it was by external threats and internal dissension, and to ponder the vicissitudes of a regime in its twilight. So far, this pivotal episode in Egypt's history, the country's last phase as an independent power before the Modern Age, remains largely untold.[2] In addition, the narratives, by their sequence of incidents, disclose the tactics adopted by the sultanate's bureaucracy to meet its autocrats' fiscal demands under straitened circumstances, while fattening purses of its more adroit members.

These biographies portray the reigns of two monarchs: al-Ashraf Qāytbāy (r. 872–901/1468–1496) and Qānṣūh al-Ghawrī (r. 906–922/1501–1516). Despite their status at the summit of society, neither of these individuals inherited a self-sustaining sinecure. As absolute heads of state, they exhibited qualities more akin to those found in the practical administration of modern chief executives than in the symbolic suzerainty of titular kings. Both were seasoned professional soldiers who advanced to the top by a combination of martial talent, political acumen, and inscrutable fate. While the two differed markedly, each was a high achiever in the military caste he entered as a slave cadet. Their careers thus convey those values their peers regarded as essential for distinction.

Ayalon has compiled a series of articles covering many aspects of the military institution in myriad detail. See in particular "Aspects of the Mamluk Phenomenon," pts. 1, 2, *Der Islam* 53 (1976) 196–225; 54 (1977) 1–32. For outlines of the sultanate's institutional and political development, consult P. M. Holt, *The Age of the Crusades: The Near East from the Eleventh Century to 1517* (London 1986).

[2] This era has yet to be analyzed as a distinctive period. Neither Qāytbāy nor Qānṣūh al-Ghawrī has been the subject of monographs. Brief articles in the *Encyclopedia of Islam* remain the essential sources of reference. See *EI*[1] 2: M. Sobernheim, "Ḳā'itbey," 663–664, and "Ḳānṣūh," 720–721; *EI*[2] 4: E. Ashtor, "Ḳā'it Bāy," 462–463, and P. M. Holt, "Ḳānṣawh al-Ghawrī," 552–553. Gaston Wiet's remarks in his survey of Islamic Egypt are still the most coherent statement after five decades. See *L'Égypte arabe*, vol. 4 of G. Hanotaux's *L'histoire de la nation égyptienne* (Paris 1937) 589–636.

Both monarchs interacted closely with a host of associates: Mamlūk comrades, civilian clients, and grasping subordinates who rose from diverse levels of society and virtually all its categories. The two therefore accumulated intimate knowledge about those they admitted to their retinues. Although each can justifiably be castigated as a tyrant, neither was ignorant of the burdens his policies imposed on the masses who footed the bills. Most other personalities who figured in the contemporary sources were discussed primarily as they were tied to one of these individuals. A study centered on these rulers' careers thus illuminates the aspirations and machinations of all those who consorted with them, high or low. Their exploitative mentality had a powerful conditioning effect on every social group that came in contact with them. The two autocrats' biographies expose stark contrasts in character within the common attitudes of caste both shared. Qāytbāy's celebrated image as his realm's conservator is assessed as a last revival of traditions venerated from bygone days. The sultan's invigoration of the Mamlūk corps, guardianship of his empire, and manifestations of piety are weighed against the draconian methods he used to ward off bankruptcy. Al-Ghawrī's peculiar path toward his dubious status as a despised innovator is explored against the backdrop of his image as the man who "lost" Egypt's independence to the Ottomans. Attention is paid his paranoia over survival, his love of luxury, and his willingness to contemplate experimental means of financing his novel goals.

The Sources

These biographies are compiled from views of several chroniclers who left detailed accounts of the regime's activities. Of the contemporary authors, four contributed the majority of this monograph's narrative data: Jamāl al-Dīn Yūsuf ibn

Taghrī-Birdī (813/1411–874/1469), Nūr al-Dīn ʿAlī ibn Dā'ūd al-Jawharī al-Ṣayrafī (819/1416–ca. 900/1495), Zayn al-Dīn ʿAbd al-Bāsiṭ ibn Khalīl al-Malaṭī (844/1440–920/1514) and Abū'l-Barakāt Muḥammad ibn Iyās (852/1448–930/1524). The first was the son of a Mamlūk amīr who died in the author's infancy.[3] Ibn Taghrī-Birdī was raised in the households of his two sisters' husbands. He enjoyed the status of a second-generation member of the military caste and the income from his father's estates. His brothers-in-law assured him a savant's education, in which the youth excelled. Showing an early flair for history, the young man studied with the eminent chronicler and topographer al-Maqrīzī. Capitalizing on his family connections at court, Ibn Taghrī-Birdī specialized in elucidating the intricacies behind regime policies and foreign events. Although the polymath al-Sakhāwī criticized him for chronological, factual, and grammatical errors, Ibn Taghrī-Birdī's opinions reflected sober judgments of crises and shrewd assessments of character.

An author of numerous compositions, Ibn Taghrī-Birdī concentrated his major efforts on a biographical dictionary of court notables: *Al-manhal al-ṣāfī wa'l-mustawfī ba'd al-wāfī* (The pure spring and fulfillment after the completion [of al-Ṣafadī]), a comprehensive chronicle extending from the origins of Islam to the year 857/1453 and the death of Sultan Jaqmaq: *Al-nujūm al-zāhira fī mulūk Miṣr wa'l-Qāhira* (Stars that shine among the kings of Egypt and Cairo), and a continuation of Maqrīzī's History, the *Kitāb al-sulūk*, beginning in 845/1441 and terminating in 873/1469, several months before the author's death: *Ḥawādith al-duhūr fī madā al-ayyām wa'l-shuhūr* (Episodes of the epochs that pass in days and months). The third work, despite its chronological brevity, contains Ibn Taghrī-Birdī's observations about his own generation, the musings of a mature thinker whose opinions were tinged with the cynicism of old age. A peer of

[3] *GAL* 2, 41, no. 10; *Ḍaw'* 10, 305, no. 1178; *Badā'i'* 3, 45, l. 23.

Qāytbāy in years and stature, Ibn Taghrī-Birdī earned the monarch's confidence as a learned adviser. Qāytbāy openly shared his aspirations, doubts, and fears, which the historian painstakingly preserved. Because he died early in Qāytbāy's reign, while the sultan was still quelling opponents intent on deposing him, Ibn Taghrī-Birdī could have predicted neither Qāytbāy's successful consolidation of power nor his longevity. He therefore dwelt on the monarch's anxieties and greed, in marked contrast with the adulation of his colleagues—who lived to see the end of a glorious reign in which largesse was copiously distributed. His interpretations of Qāytbāy's actions offer a rare critical view of the deportment of an otherwise venerated figure.

The second chronicler was from a markedly different class background. Al-Ṣayrafī's father served as a moneychanger in the royal dīwāns, who supplemented an embarassingly meager income by trading in the Jewelers' Market of Cairo.[4] Al-Ṣayrafī remained acutely conscious of his father's penury and mediocre status as a minor bureaucrat. Yet the father supervised his son's early education personally before sending him off to the care of more eminent authorities. Al-Ṣayrafī attracted the notice of Cairo's learned luminary Ibn Ḥajar al-ʿAsqalānī. With the esteemed shaykh's encouragment, al-Ṣayrafī tried his hand at historical writing, producing the first works of the so-called "Cairo narrative style," a blending of colloquial and formal language unique to the second half of the ninth/fifteenth century.[5] Prestige eluded al-Ṣayrafī all his days. He coveted appointment to a senior Ḥanafī judgeship, but never received more than a deputy's bench—and this in his fiftieth year at a colleague's behest. Al-Ṣayrafī took up manuscript copying to support his growing family, selling editions of his famous mentor's works with his own appendices and commentaries (dismissed by al-Sakhāwī

4 *GAL* Suppl. 2, 41, no. 12; *Ḍaw'* 5, 217, no. 738; *Badā'i'* 3, 309, l. 23.
5 Ḥasan Ḥabashī, introduction to *Inbā'*, 18–19.

as a blight on the great sage's treatises). But al-Ṣayrafī's judicial marginality served his journalistic bent well. Attending sessions of both the religious (*Sharīʿa*) and appeals (*maẓālim*) courts with few magisterial duties, he took copious notes on proceedings. These he recorded for posterity in his second chronicle.

Al-Ṣayrafī produced two significant historical tracts: *Nuzhat al-nufūs wa'l-abdān fī tawārīkh al-zamān* (A diversion spiritual and corporeal in the annals of time) and *Inbā' al-ḥaṣr fī abnā' al-ʿaṣr* (Deeds of the lion among scions of the age). The first surveyed Egyptian politics from 786/1384 to 879/1475, following a hagiographic depiction of the prophetic era in Medina (of which only fragments remain). The latter was conceived as a celebration of Qāytbāy's reign (the "lion" of its title). The author hoped to secure a place in the sultan's entourage by presenting his work as a gift, but no record of its completion has survived. The extant section covers only the years 873/1468 to 877/1473, albeit in minute detail. Portions of the years 885/1480 and 886/1481 are appended. Nonetheless, the four complete annals offer insights into judicial controversies available in few contemporary works. Since al-Ṣayrafī never deviated from his endorsement of the "court line," Qāytbāy emerges from his folios as a hero without blemish. Yet the sultan's judicial avocation is praised in the setting of its ambivalent reception among legal authorities compelled to abide the monarch's interference. Al-Ṣayrafī's remarks about their discomfiture are illuminating.

The third author claimed descent from a Mamlūk house, but one rung further down than Ibn Taghrī-Birdī.[6] Al-Malaṭī's father occupied the vizierate in Egypt and served as a provincial governor in Syria. Although his son excelled in Ḥanafī studies, he never aspired to the legal profession. He became an eminent physician and traveled to North Africa

[6] *GAL* 2, 54, no. 17, Suppl. 2, 52, no. 17; *Badā'iʿ* 4, 373, l. 23.

on a Genoese galley in the 1460s. Active in Cairo's Ṣūfī orders, to which many among the military elite were attracted, al-Malaṭī "enjoyed wide influence among the Turks and amīrs," having translated numerous works into their language. In his later years, he won al-Ghawrī's favor. When he fell ill of consumption, the sultan saw to his family's needs. Al-Malaṭī compiled a handbook on Scriptural devotions, which he bestowed on his patron in gratitude: *Majmū' al-bustān al-nūrī li-ḥaḍrat mawlānā sulṭān al-Ghūrī* (Anthology of the luminous garden presented to our lord sultan al-Ghūrī). Yet his historical corpus addressed the reign of al-Ghawrī's predecessor. Al-Malaṭī's large chronicle *Al-rawḍ al-bāsim fī ḥawādith al-'umr wa'l-tarājim* (Gardens smiling upon events of lifetimes and life-stories) deals with the period between 872/1468 and 890/1485. Unedited at present and extant in a single autograph, the work charts a middle course between Ibn Taghrī-Birdī's skepticism and al-Ṣayrafī's effusion.

The last member of this primary group casts a long shadow in Islamic historiography. Ibn Iyās belonged to the third generation of the Mamlūk elite.[7] His grandfather held several vice-regencies in Syria and left his progeny rights to the fief (*iqṭā'*) he received for his services. When Sultan al-Ghawrī attempted its expropriation, Ibn Iyās fought a grueling battle in court to reclaim his patrimony. Although he succeeded, his brush with destitution scarred him to the core. He never forgave al-Ghawrī, and fulminated against him repeatedly for his spoliation of the propertied classes in Egypt. But despite his bias, Ibn Iyās stands as a towering figure among chroniclers of the later Middle Ages in Egypt. His vast tract *Badā'i' al-zuhūr fī waqā'i' al-duhūr* (Marvels blossoming among incidents of the epochs) commences with the pre-Islamic period, but addresses specific events upon

7 *GAL* 2, 295, no. 1, Suppl. 2, 405, no. 1; *Badā'i'* 4, 47, l. 11 (obituary of author's father).

Qāytbāy's enthronement. Extending to the year 928/1522, the *Badā'i'* remains the sole firsthand survey of al-Ghawrī's reign. For all his pent-up hostility toward the autocrat, Ibn Iyās attempted to detach his emotions from his reporting. He witnessed many of the sultan's altercations with his sullen troops and devious counselors. Keenly aware of the august tradition of chroniclers to which he fell heir, Ibn Iyās took pains to maintain his predecessors' studied objectivity, even when he besmirched al-Ghawrī. Ibn Iyās sought to justify his castigations with solid facts and accordingly left a trove of evidence for later generations to ponder. Admitting our dependence on one man's point of view, a perspective possibly slanted by his survival into the regime of Egypt's conquerors, we nonetheless possess data sufficient for an informed impression of al-Ghawrī's actions.[8]

Several other writers complement the versions of these chroniclers. While the names of some elude us, their works offer summations composed in hindsight after the passage of decades and reflect judgments of later generations. An onsite commentator in this secondary category was Aḥmad ibn Muḥammad al-Anṣārī, known as Ibn al-Ḥimṣī.[9] Resident in Damascus during Qāytbāy's early years, Ibn al-Ḥimṣī joined the train of the sultan's ambassador, who was returning

[8] Ibn Iyās's comments on the defensive posture adopted by al-Ghawrī's successor, Ṭūmānbāy, and policies of incorporation imposed by Selim I's governors occupy the bulk of volume five in the *Badā'i'*. There is little evidence that Ibn Iyās recast his assessment of al-Ghawrī's actions to any significant degree either to vent his pent-up spleen with even more intensity or to curry favor with Egypt's new authorities. See Michael Winter, *Society and Religion in Early Ottoman Egypt: Studies in the Writings of 'Abd al-Wahhāb al-Sha'rānī* (New Brunswick 1982) 5–6, 13–14, 18, who notes that the chronicler's dismay over the Ottoman Conquest neither disposed him to disparage deceased rulers unduly nor to exaggerate disruptions accompanying the change of government. Annemarie Schimmel focuses on Ibn Iyās's depiction of post-conquest changes in judicial proceedings but not his castigation of al-Ghawrī. See "Kalif und Kadi im spätmittelalterlichen Ägypten," *Die Welt des Islams* 24 (1942) 84–93.

[9] *GAL* Suppl. 2, 41, no. 12a.

from negotiations with the Ottomans, and relocated in Cairo. Stipended from a trust endowed to free scholars for composition, he wrote his *Ḥawādith al-zamān wa-wafayāt al-shuyūkh wa'l-aqrān* (Events of the age with necrologies of savants and sages) in 900/1495. The chronicle was conceived as an extension of Ibn Ḥajar's *Inbā' al-Ghumr*, but was written in an exceedingly colloquial style bordering on the vulgar. Yet Ibn al-Ḥimṣī captured the ethos of Qāytbāy's viceregal establishment in Damascus, and commented at length on the monarch's visits. The *Ḥawādith* is a goldmine for tidbits on bureaucratic carpetbaggery in this second city of the Empire.

Of greater stature but comparable importance to our topic is the polymath Muḥammad ibn 'Abd al-Raḥmān al-Sakhāwī (d. 902/1497).[10] Author of the huge biographical dictionary *Al-ḍaw' al-lāmi'*, al-Sakhāwī wrote a continuation of al-Dhahabī's history during his retirement in Mecca: *Al-dhayl al-tāmm 'alā duwal al-Islām* (The consummate appendix to the nations of Islam). While hardly duplicating the former historian's breadth, Sakhāwī's *Appendix* is valuable for its portrayal of elite doings in the holy cities of the Ḥijāz. The interminable rebellions of Bedouin chiefs are reported with details omitted by chroniclers using secondary evidence in Cairo. Sakhāwī's descriptions of pilgrimage rites and arrivals of eminent personages from the capital read like a gossip column and recover the festive atmosphere of the Ḥajj season.

A member of the wealthy Cairene house of Jī'ān, Badr al-Dīn Abū'l-Baqā' ibn Yaḥyā (fl. 899/1494), who served as deputy to Qāytbāy's Confidential Secretary Zayn al-Dīn ibn Muzhir, participated in the sultan's trip through Syria to the Euphrates frontier in 882/1477.[11] He describes conditions of rural life as well as receptions accorded the royal

10 *GAL* 2, 43, no. 1, Suppl. 2, 31–32.

11 *GAL* 2, 38, no. 1, Suppl. 2, 26, no. 1; *Ḍaw'* 11, 8, no. 8. Not perused for this study but noted here is the account of the Amīr Yashbak al-Ẓāhirī's embassy to Uzun Ḥasan in 880/1475 penned by Shams al-Dīn Muḥammad ibn Ajā, edited by 'Abd al-Qādir Aḥmad Ṭulaymāt (Cairo 1973).

guests by provincial officials in the log of his journey, *Al-qawl al-mustaẓraf fī safar mawlānā al-malik al-ashraf* (The elegant report recounting the voyage of our lord the esteemed monarch).

Among the swarms of admirers eulogizing Qāytbāy was Muḥammad ibn Yūsuf al-Bā'ūnī, who wrote in rajaz metre *Al-lamha al-ashrafīya wa'l-bahja al-sanīya* (The noble glow, the sublime resplendence).[12] Amidst its flowery verses, one can discern the pious beneficence that so endeared Qāytbāy to the 'ulamā' and masked his avarice. Two anonymous authors wrote précis of Qāytbāy's reign: *Ta'rīkh al-malik al-ashraf Qāytbāy* (History of the honored sovereign Qāytbāy)[13] and *Jawāhir al-sulūk fī'l-khulafā' wa'l-mulūk* (Gems of deportment about caliphs and kings).[14] While neither yields any original information, each tallies up Qāytbāy's military expenses according to campaigns. Their focus on vast sums bespeaks the favorable impression made by the sultan's defensive stance and his willingness to pay for it that remained long after the Ottoman Conquest.

Al-Ghawrī received nothing comparable to the multiple coverage granted Qāytbāy. But one tenth/sixteenth-century Syrian necrologist penned an intriguing obituary of him. Muḥammad ibn Ibrāhīm al-Ḥalabī al-Ḥanbalī wrote *Durr al-ḥabab fī ta'rīkh a'yān ḥalab* (Loving pearls embellishing the history of Aleppo notables), which included a savage decrial of al-Ghawrī's greed and love of luxury.[15] An unnamed courtier left a history of Qāytbāy's hapless heir, al-Nāṣir Muḥammad, that elaborates on the shabby treatment he received as powerful amīrs maneuvered for power in the five-year period before al-Ghawrī's succession: *Kitāb ithbāt dalālāt Muḥammad ibn al-marḥūm al-malik al-Ashraf*

12 *GAL* 2, 54, no. 18, Suppl. 2, 67, no. 3; *Ḍaw'* 10, 89, no. 290.

13 *GAL* 2, 38, Suppl. 2, 26.

14 *GAL* 2, 42, Suppl. 2, 53.

15 *GAL* 2, 368; M. Sobernheim, "Ḳānṣūh," *EI*² 2, 721. The work is dated 11 Dhū'l-Qa'da 972/10 June 1565 on the colophon.

Qāytbāy (A book confirming evidence about Muḥammad, son of the deceased monarch al-Ashraf Qāytbāy).[16] The biography of al-Ghawrī composed by the necrologist Abū'l-Makārim Muḥammad al-Ghazzī (977/1570–1061/1651) in his *Al-kawākib al-sā'ira bi-manāqib 'ulamā' al-mi'a al-'ashira* (Lingering luminaries among the virtues of tenth-century savants) relies on earlier evidence and reveals nothing new.[17] Nor does the Damascene chronicler Shams al-Dīn Muḥammad ibn Ṭūlūn (884/1479–935/1529) appreciably expand upon Ibn Iyās's comments. His *I'lām al-warā bi-man wulliya min al-Atrāk bi-Dimashq* (Men of distinction among the Turks appointed viceroys in Damascus) focuses primarily on imbroglios plaguing governors in that city.[18] His episodic tract *Mukāfaha al-khillān fī ḥawādith al-zamān* (Boon banter over anecdotes of the age) qualifies few facets of the sultan's image as Ibn Iyās left it.[19]

These authors, several of whom personally observed the events they described, were fully aware of the heady drama being played out in their days. The two autocrats who presided over Egypt's waning hegemony as an independent power, in consort with their swarms of aides, clients, confidants, and rivals, also keenly appreciated the stakes lurking behind the challenges they faced. The following surveys of their reigns touch upon matters of lofty statecraft and crafty schemes to preserve an antiquated international order,

16 Not listed in *GAL*; Istanbul: Topkapi Saray, no. 2960.

17 *GAL* 2, 291, no. 8.

18 Edited by 'Abd al-'Aẓīm Ḥāmid Khaṭṭāb (Cairo 1973).

19 Edited by Muḥammad Muṣṭafā, 2 vols. (Cairo 1962, 1964). Another noteworthy work not utilized in this monograph bears mention. Aḥmad ibn 'Alī ibn Zunbul al-Shāfi'ī (d. 926/1520) wrote *Ta'rīkh al-Sulṭān Salīm al-'uthmānī ma'a al-Sulṭān Qānṣūh al-Ghūrī* (History of Sultan Selim the Ottoman and Sultan Qānṣūh al-Ghūrī), a detailed log of al-Ghawrī's last campaign, culminating in his defeat and death at Marj Dābiq (*GAL* 2, 43, no. 19, Suppl. 2, 298, no. 1). Exploiting his post in the (Ottoman?) war office, Ibn Zunbul perused eyewitness versions of the dramatic battle. Because this analysis addresses al-Ghawrī's domestic policies, it omits this manuscript. Whether Ibn Iyās knew of it remains indeterminate since he makes no mention of it.

interminable troop unrest and innovative stratagems to diffuse it, probity of personal belief versus cynical yet clever exploitation of religious sentiments cherished by both elites and masses. The disparate images of ruling style in the Mamlūk sultanate during its closing years that emerge show two distinctive approaches to sovereignty in one of the most prominent militarist states of the Muslim world at the end of the Middle Ages. They tell us much about both strengths and weaknesses inherent in a regime of this kind. However a contemporary reader elects to judge these sultans, along with their host of associates, she or he will be struck by their ingenuity in the face of formidable odds. How creative were the responses concocted by the two men to the daunting events of their times will be interpreted differently according to the biases of those who reflect on their actions. But whatever the assessment, these men were fated to rule at a critical moment. The decisions they took, for good or ill, helped shape the future of their country—still a major actor in the maelstrom of Middle Eastern politics. Ever plagued by seemingly insurmountable difficulties, Egypt remains as vibrant a player in the game of nations as she was some five centuries ago. Sultans al-Ashraf Qāytbāy and Qānṣūh al-Ghawrī left their successors an abiding legacy because they influenced an attitude toward authority and bureaucracy that remains peculiarly Egyptian. Their perspective should not be ignored by anyone seeking to probe the essence of this fascinating society.

Chapter Two

Al-Ashraf Qāytbāy
Revered Conservator

HIS career developed in glory and majesty.... He was serene and dignified, correct in decorum, invariably respected, projecting an aura of majesty to official ceremonies. Highly intelligent, sound of judgment, skilled in state affairs, talented in administration. Never indecisive, particularly when [corrupt] officials warranted dismissal. Yet he always reflected carefully before implementing a decision.

Renowned for his bravery, adept as a cavalier ... [he was] proficient in all military arts, and yet obsessed with a lust for money.

His lifestyle was correct. He never drank wine, nor indeed any inebriating substance. He was learned in religious science, widely read. He even authored pious litanies that are recited in mosques to this day. He had faith in mystics, honored scholars, respected rights of the people—acknowledging the status each merited. He particularly admired the self-effacing life of ascetics.

After violent fits of temper, he calmed rapidly. His fury always dissipated—an attractive trait.

Overall, the good qualities outweighed the bad; he was the best of the Turkish monarchs, especially when compared with those who followed him. Although tainted by greed, he was the noblest of Circassian rulers, their finest.[1]

THESE exerpts from Ibn Iyās's obituary for the last Mamlūk autocrat of the ninth Hijrī/fifteenth Christian century might strike an uninitiated reader as routine flattery, prudently offered by a chronicler keenly aware of how fickle an absolute ruler's whims might be. Respected, if not admired, for his caustic appraisal of powerful contemporaries, Ibn Iyās rarely lavished fawning praise to enhance his own position at court. Indeed, the qualities listed in these excerpts are remarkable, since so few of Qāytbāy's peers embodied them. Al-Malik al-Ashraf Abū'l-Naṣr Qāytbāy al-Maḥmūdī was genuinely revered by many of his subjects high and low because of his sense of justice, evenness of temper, and noble mien. His reign inspired nostalgia on the part of chroniclers, who compared it favorably with the administrations of his successors. Historians ultimately acclaimed Qāytbāy as the rejuvenator of his caste, an individual who galvanized the military apparatus he inherited to achieve victories reminiscent of glories won more than two centuries earlier.[2]

Why was this man so uniformly respected? In an age deplored for its decline of moral probity, how did he personify so many respected values? And were these values solely the product of wistful yearning for better days when Egypt reigned supreme over the eastern Mediterranean—her economic hegemony and political dominance uncontested? Since medieval Muslim chroniclers focused their works on the reigns of monarchs, these figures dominate the historiography of

1 *Badā'i'* 3, 325–326, 332.

2 Carl F. Petry, *The Civilian Elite of Cairo in the Later Middle Ages* (Princeton 1981) 27; Gaston Wiet, *L'Egypte arabe*, 606–607.

their eras. Even admitting biases on the part of the chroniclers, we are given more information about the rulers' character than the traits of any other individuals from the period, although their behavioral traits were not routinely enumerated. As one reflects on the mass of detail provided on Sultan Qāytbāy's policies, we behold a mortal quite capable of error and excess. Yet the impression of balance remains, and Qāytbāy radiates an aura of majesty unique in his age. His capacity to imbue his subordinates with confidence won him universal esteem because the regime he was called to command had convinced many of its inherent morbidity, its imperviousness to rejuvenation.

But what did the chroniclers have in mind when they deemed Qāytbāy a rejuvenator? Ibn Iyās's obituary dwells on dignity, intelligence, justice, and serenity—all laudable traits, yet hardly indicative of genius. Nowhere does the historian note exceptional military sagacity, administrative creativity, or an aggressive imperial vision. Fully a creature of his caste, Qāytbāy invariably looked back to policies of his notable predecessors as models for his own attempts to shore up his regime and to restore the confidence of its defenders. The acclaim accorded Qāytbāy is directly linked to this fundamental yet regressive orientation of purpose. The political traditions of Mamlūk Egypt had evolved in ways peculiar to its unique milieu. In its essentials, the Mamlūk sultanate was committed to preserving both an ideological and a territorial heritage with as little change as possible. Change itself entailed risk, the danger of charting a course through the unknown. Achievements accomplished during the formative era back in the mid-seventh/thirteenth century imparted to the Mamlūk regime a legacy of renown and prosperity that served it well in an unstable universe.[3] Why tamper with

[3] David Ayalon, "Studies on the Structure of the Mamlūk Army," pts. 1–3, *BSOAS* 15 (1953) 203–228, 448–476; 16 (1954) 57–90; P. M. Holt, "The Position and Power of the Mamlūk Sultan," *BSOAS* 38 (1975) 237–249; id., "The Structure of Government in the Mamlūk Sultanate," in *The Eastern*

proven patterns of commercial stasis or military equilibrium when the consequences of experimentation were unforeseen? That the international order of the late ninth/fifteenth century was rapidly altering escaped the notice of no one placed high in government, but the response of Qāytbāy and his subordinates invariably centered on attempts to revive earlier precedents that had evolved in radically different circumstances.

And to be sure, the regime Qāytbāy inherited would have taxed the ingenuity of an autocrat far more insightful than he. The Mamlūk sultanate during the Burjī or Circassian period (784–922/1382–1517) was riven with chronic factionalism. Of the twenty-one sultans enthroned, only eight consolidated their authority and built a coherent power structure. Every succession precipitated a crisis since there was no formalized process of transition. Historians disagree whether this condition of endemic crisis should be regarded as an aberration in the evolution of militarist authority throughout the central Islamic lands or should be interpreted as a system of advancement uniquely suited for the competition habitual among Mamlūk elites.[4] Chroniclers of the fifteenth century certainly concurred on the deleterious effects of this phenomenon. Succession crises sapped the ruling class's energies, compelling them to invest their creative efforts on personal survival rather than a comprehensive strategy for long-term

---

Mediterranean Lands in the Period of the Crusades, ed. P. M. Holt (Warminster 1977) 44–61; R. S. Humphreys, "The Emergence of the Mamlūk Army," *Studia Islamica* 45 (1977) 67–100; 46 (1977) 147–182; Robert Irwin, *The Middle East in the Middle Ages: The Early Mamluk Sultanate, 1250–1382* (London 1986) 33–34, 47–58, 64–76; Hassanein Rabie, "Ḳalāwūn," *EI*² 4, 484–486; Peter Thorau, *The Lion of Egypt: Sultan Baybars I and the Near East in the Thirteenth Century* (New York 1992) 251–255; Gaston Wiet, "Baibars I," *EI*² 1, 1124–1126.

4 David Ayalon, "Discharges from Service, Banishments and Imprisonments in Mamlūk Society," *Israel Oriental Studies* 2 (1972) 25–50; Ahmad Darrag, *L'Egypte sous le règne de Barsbay* (Damascus 1961) 11–32; Robert Irwin, "Factions in Medieval Egypt," *JRAS* 1986, 228–246; Petry, *Civilian Elite*, 19–25.

growth.[5] When Qāytbāy secured his own position at the age of fifty-four and went on to govern his empire for almost three decades, his contemporaries regarded him as a savior from chaos. Qāytbāy's restoration of Egypt's traditional grandeur, his devotion to religious orthodoxy, and depth of personal piety enormously impressed the religio-scholastic class, who saw in their sovereign the reincarnation of idealized figures from the formative Islamic age, when leadership ability was defined as much by spiritual purity as by military prowess. Nonetheless, the crises endemic to the Burjī era did little to encourage political innovation. Qāytbāy acquired his reputation as a respected monarch precisely because he typified the best of past reigns. The sultan personified security in an era that feared its termination.

The crisis prefacing Qāytbāy's accession commenced on the death of Sultan al-Ẓāhir Khushqadam (865–872/1461–1467), when his successor, the field marshal (*atābak*) Yilbāy,[6] failed to secure the loyalty of his predecessor's soldiers. Yilbāy had been imported into Egypt in the year 820/1417 and was manumitted soon thereafter.[7] He advanced steadily, was promoted to the rank of royal bodyguard (*khāṣṣakī*), and

[5] Critical statements on the instability of the Circassian regime abound in chronicles of the fifteenth century, but summary assessments of individual rulers' success or failure in coping with it were offered in necrologies of prominent sultans. For al-Ẓāhir Barqūq (784–801/1382–1399): al-Maqrīzī, *Kitāb al-sulūk li-ma'rifa duwal al-mulūk* (Cairo 1934–1973) 3, 943–947; Ibn Ḥajar al-'Asqalānī, *Inbā' al-ghumr bi-anbā' al-'umr* (Cairo, 1969) 2, 66–69; Ibn Taghrī-Birdī, *Al-nujūm al-zāhira fī mulūk Miṣr wa'l-Qāhira* (Cairo 1929–1956) 12, 107–115. For al-Mu'ayyad Shaykh (815–824/1412–1421): Maqrīzī 4, 550–551; Ibn Ḥajar 3, 256–257; Ibn Taghrī-Birdī, *Nujūm* 14, 109–113. For al-Ashraf Barsbāy (825–841/1422–1437): Maqrīzī 4, 1065–1066; Ibn Taghrī-Birdī, *Nujūm* 15, 107–111. For al-Ẓahir Jaqmaq (842–857/1438–1453): Ibn Taghrī-Birdī, *Nujūm* 15, 454–460. Al-Suyūṭī provides a list of all sultans with their dates of accession, death, deposition, or exile. See *Badā'i' al-'umūr fī waqā'i' al-duhūr*, ms. Aya Sofya 2987, f. 151b, l. 14.

[6] Although listed as Bilbāy in other sources, the Muṣṭāfā edition of *Badā'i'* uses the *yā* consistently.

[7] On Sultan Yilbāy: Ibn Taghrī-Birdī, *Nujūm*, 16, 352–360; Ibn Iyās, *'Uqūd al-jumān fī waqā'i' al-azmān*, ms. Aya Sofya, 3311, f. 217, l. 1; al-Sakhāwī,

then to the post of court page (*sāqī*) at the behest of Sultan Jaqmaq (842–857/1438–1453). Yilbāy reached the summit of the Mamlūk hierarchy and joined the elite group of grand amīrs (commanders of a thousand: *muqaddamū alf*) during the reign of al-Ashraf Īnāl (857–865/1453–1461). A close associate of Sultan Khushqadam, Yilbāy held the executive offices of grand chamberlain (*ḥājib al-ḥujjāb*) and chief fodderer (*amīr akhūr kabīr*) before assuming the marshalship (*atābakīya*) in 870/1465–1466. Appointment to this office was tantamount to designation for the sultanate itself, and Yilbāy's peers accepted him as supreme autocrat without resistance upon Khushqadam's death. He was sworn in on 10 Rabī' I 872/8 October 1467. Although his abilities as an officer were denied by no one, Yilbāy made fatal errors of judgment upon his enthronement that precipitated his own deposition fifty-seven days later. He alienated his predecessor's troops, conspired against colleagues of his own station who should have formed the core of his new coalition, and sentenced some 120 Bedouin captured in the Ḥijāz to death by drawing and quartering—an act revolting to his comrades less for its cruelty than its assurance of rebellion in western Arabia.[8] Yilbāy plotted against prominent officers from the previous reign on the advice of his executive secretary (*dawādār*) Khayrbak. When he delayed the customary accession bonus to all but his own bodyguards, Mamlūks of previous sultans rose in rebellion. Yilbāy was deposed on the seventh of Jumādā I 872/4 December 1468, and placed in confinement prior to his imprisonment in Alexandria. He died there of plague less than a year later.[9] Al-Sakhāwī and Ibn Iyās both observed that, although Yilbāy's forceful but erratic personality had served him well as an officer, his

---

Al-ḍaw' al-lāmi' fī a'yān al-qarn al-tāsi' (Cairo 1934) 10, 287, no. 1131; al-Sakhāwī, *Shajarat al-khulafā'*, ms. Aya Sofya 3266, f. 62, l. 3.

8 Ibn Iyās, *'Uqūd*, f. 217, l. 14.

9 *Ḥawādith* 4, 679, l. 5; *Inbā'*, 17, l. 15; *Rawḍ*, f. 204, l. 18; *Badā'i'* 3, 31, l. 7.

conspiratorial impulses disqualified him for the monarchy. His indecisiveness, coupled with excessive reliance on a corrupt adviser, plunged the realm into disorder.

Yilbāy's marshal, al-Ẓāhir Abū Sa'īd Timurbughā, was immediately installed as his successor. An Anatolian by birth, he had been purchased by Jaqmaq while the latter was a grand amīr.[10] Timurbughā revealed an ambition for high office early in his career. Consequently, his rise to the top was interrupted by several arrests and exiles. Promoted to the rank of commander of a thousand (*muqaddam alf*) by Jaqmaq at the end of his reign, Timurbughā assumed the executive secretaryship (*dawādārīya*) to Jaqmaq's heir, al-Manṣūr 'Uthmān, who was installed as a puppet while powerful amīrs jockeyed for eventual succession. Upon 'Uthmān's deposition, Timurbughā was imprisoned in Alexandria, where he remained six years. Released by Sultan Īnāl, he was allowed to reside in Mecca on his promise of abstinence from politics. But Timurbughā kept close tabs on rivalries in Cairo, and when Īnāl died he returned to accept an appointment as captain of the guard by his former comrade (*khushdāsh*)[11] Sultan Khushqadam. The reunion of these two close colleagues soon soured, however, when Khushqadam suspected Timurbughā of plotting treason. Once again, Timurbughā was packed off to Alexandria. Khushqadam permitted Timurbughā back late in his reign, granting him the posts of presiding officer (*amīr majlis*) and the marshalship in exchange for his sworn oath of fealty. Timurbughā supported Yilbāy's accession in exchange for his retention in the atābakīya. His support paid off when the oligarchy of grand amīrs approved his succession on the day of Yilbāy's deposition.

[10] *Ḥawādith* 4, 615–617; *Nujūm* 16, 373; *'Uqūd*, f. 219, l. 17.

[11] The term *khushdāsh*, Persian in origin, meant literally "good colleague" or "companion," and referred to fraternal bonds cemented by Mamlūk recruits during their barracks training under a patron's sponsorship. See R. Dozy, *Supplément aux dictionnaires arabes* (Leiden 1881) 1, 353; R. Irwin, *The Middle East*, 88–90.

Timurbughā was initially popular with both the Mamlūk elite and jurist-scholars. The Caliph and chief justices unanimously legitimized his acclamation. His colleague, Qāytbāy, carried the parasol and bird, ancient symbols of imperial authority,[12] over his head as he proceeded to the throne room of the Citadel from the royal stable. There was every reason to assume that Timurbughā enjoyed enough respect to consolidate his grip on the autocracy. Regarded as both decisive and just, he seemed to restore stability to the chain of command down through the various levels of officers to the ranks of troopers. But in fact, he failed to counter the influence of veterans who had served previous rulers. In particular, he insulted their most powerful faction, the Mamlūks of Sultan Īnāl (857–865/1453–1461), by advancing soldiers promoted by Khushqadam. Whether Timurbughā planned to disperse the Īnālīya Mamlūks is impossible to ascertain, since his own executive secretary, Khayrbak al-Khushqadamī, plotted with several associates to seize power. Khayrbak arrested Timurbughā on the fifth of Rajab 872/30 January 1468 and claimed the sultanate.

Neither the Caliph nor the senior qāḍīs acknowledged this act of usurpation. The judges recognized the tenuousness of Khayrbak's position and prudently awaited the outcome of an inevitable power struggle. It was not long in coming. Qāytbāy, whom Timurbughā had made his atābak, had convened the Īnālīya and warned them of the imminent threat to their status, if not their persons, posed by Khayrbak's coup. Ibn Iyās noted that the Īnālīya were prepared to trust Qāytbāy's word primarily because he had married a relative of Īnāl's wife.[13] Qāytbāy's reputation for good faith

[12] William Popper, *Egypt and Syria under the Circassian Sultans, 1382–1468 A.D.: Systematic Notes to Ibn Taghri-Birdi's Chronicles of Egypt* (Berkeley and Los Angeles 1955) 84, no. 6.

[13] *'Uqūd*, f. 220b, l. 10. In the turbulent world of Mamlūk rivalries, marital ties often counted for more than personal pledges of fealty. See Aḥmad 'Abd al-Rāziq, *La femme au temps des Mamlouks en Égypte* (Cairo 1973) 268, who

notwithstanding, a connubial tie served as concrete proof of credibility in this turbulent arena. Several amīrs ascended to the palace at the head of their new coalition and removed Khayrbak. Claiming a just succession as his sole motive, Qāytbāy denied any interest in the throne himself and had already departed Cairo. But the Īnālīya would no longer accept Timurbughā, whose ties bound him to their hated rivals among the Khushqadamīya. They compelled Qāytbāy to accept the autocracy upon his return, which he reluctantly agreed to do on condition that Timurbughā be allowed to retire honorably.

Qāytbāy thus came to the sultanate by the most circuitous of routes. He spent his first day arranging for an audience of reconciliation with his predecessor, claiming that he would discuss no future policies until justice had been done his khushdāsh. This remarkable act, a harbinger of future behavior, was received with amazement by the officers and soldiers who had backed him. His wishes were obeyed, but on the day of his enthronement no one could have predicted the outcome of his accession. That an individual well into his fifties would survive to rule a vast state for twenty-eight years with his faculties intact was anticipated by no one. But even the most fractious of amīrs welcomed an end to the succession crises that had begun with Khushqadam's death. Thus, Timurbughā was allowed to depart Cairo with the rank of royal retiree, a gesture usually reserved for deposed sons of former rulers who posed no practical threat and could therefore be retained as harmless symbols of royal continuity.[14] Ibn Iyās remarked that Timurbughā's term lasted two months less two days, in other words, one day shorter than the briefest of all reigns during the Mamlūk period, the tenure

lists marriages arranged to stabilize royal successions; C. F. Petry, "Class Solidarity vs. Gender Gain: Women as Custodians of Property in Later Medieval Egypt," in *Women in Middle Eastern History: Shifting Boundaries in Sex and Gender*, ed. N. Keddie and B. Baron (New Haven 1991) 122–142.

14 *'Uqūd*, f. 221, l. 7.

of his ill-fated predecessor, Yilbāy! And what did the future portend? Could Qāytbāy seal his grip on authority? Was he willing to do so? No one could predict the consequences of these extraordinary events, but all acclaimed the probity of the man who now held the sultanate. What was the background to his character?

The Cursus Honorum of a Mamlūk Officer

Qāytbāy was born in the Circassian districts of the Caucasus sometime between 818/1416 and 821/1418.[15] Since no contemporary sources mention any details on his life as an adolescent before his arrival in Egypt in 839/1435–1436, we must presume that none were known. Senior amīrs who formed the ruling oligarchy of the later Mamlūk period rarely dictated their memoirs to personal secretaries, in contrast with several of their predecessors during the Baḥrī period.[16] We therefore can only recover those aspects of Qāytbāy's early life that influenced his selection as a Mamlūk slave recruit (*julb*). The precedent for purchasing youths from Central Asia for service as palace guards or line troops in Muslim armies dates

[15] Al-Sakhāwī (*Ḍaw'* 4, 201, no. 697) states that his birth occurred during the early years of the twenties. But Ibn Iyās (*Badā'i'* 3, 324, l. 16) claims that he was almost 84 at his death on 27 Dhū'l-Qa'da 901/8 August 1496. See *'Uqūd*, f. 221b, l. 14.

[16] For example, the early career of al-Ẓāhir Baybars al-Bunduqdārī, founder of the Mamlūk system of administration. His activities preceding his service on behalf of the Ayyūbid Sultan Najm al-Dīn Ayyūb are discussed in detail by his biographers, Ibn Shaddād and Ibn 'Abd al-Ẓāhir. See P. M. Holt, "Three Biographies of al-Ẓāhir Baybars," in *Medieval Historical Writing in the Christian and Islamic Worlds*, ed. D. O. Morgan (London, SOAS, 1982) 19–29; Irwin, *Middle East*, 26–36; A. Khowaiter, *Baibars the First* (London 1978) 3–8; Thorau, *Lion*, 27–32; S. F. Sadeque, *Baybars the First of Egypt* (Dacca 1956).

back to the late Umayyad period (ca. 730–750 C.E.).[17] The nomadic societies, renowned for their military prowess, that evolved among Turkish-speaking inhabitants of the steppes from the classical Islamic era are well known. Scholars have amply traced the expansion of Turkish dominion into Iran during the Saljuq period (429–552/1037–1157) and after.[18]

The traits sought among adolescent males whom a Muslim sovereign trained to police his capital, bolster his authority, and defend his frontiers have excited the interest of contemporary observers, who often entered into client relationships with these slave-soldiers, and modern historians fascinated by the concept of all-powerful militarists who initiated their careers as a monarch's chattel.[19] These qualities—aggressiveness, intelligence, physical agility—remained constant throughout the long history of military slavery in the central Islamic lands, no matter where these men originated.

17 Ayalon, "Aspects of the Mamlūk Phenomenon: A. The Importance of the Mamlūk Institution," 196–225; D. Sourdel, "Ghūlām," *EI*² 2, 1079–1085; C. E. Bosworth, *The Ghaznavids* (Edinburgh 1963) 98–106; id., "Recruitment, Muster and Review in Medieval Islamic Armies," in *War, Technology and Society in the Middle East*, ed. V. J. Parry and M. E. Yapp (London 1975) 59–77; Patricia Crone, *Slaves on Horses* (Cambridge 1980); P. G. Forand, "The Relationship of the Slave and the Client to the Master or Patron in Medieval Islam," *IJMES* 2 (1971) 59–66; Irwin, *Middle East*, 1–23; Daniel Pipes, *Slave Soldiers of Islam: The Genesis of a Military System* (New Haven 1981).

18 W. Barthold, *Turkestan down to the Mongol Invasions*, 3d ed. (London 1968); C. E. Bosworth, *The Medieval History of Iran, Afghanistan and Central Asia* (London 1977); id., "The Political and Dynastic History of the Iranian World (A.D. 1000–1217)," in *The Cambridge History of Iran* 5, 1–202; A. K. S. Lambton, *Continuity and Change in Medieval Persia* (Albany 1987); id., *Landlord and Peasant in Persia* (London 1953); V. Minorsky, *Medieval Iran and its Neighbors* (London 1982); D. O. Morgan, *Medieval Persia, 1040–1797* (New York 1988); B. Spuler, *Iran in frühislamischen Zeit* (Wiesbaden 1952).

19 A. ʿAbd al-Rāziq, "Al-mamālīk wa-mafhūm al-usrah ladayhim," *Majallat kullīyat al-ʿathār* 2 (Cairo, Cairo University, 1977) 188–207; David Ayalon, "L'esclavage du Mamlouk," *Oriental Notes and Studies* 1 (Jerusalem, Jerusalem Oriental Society, 1951); id., "Preliminary Remarks on the Mamluk Military Institution," 44–58; id., "Mamlūkīyat, A First Attempt to Evaluate the Mamlūk Military System," *Jerusalem Studies in Arabic and Islam* 2 (1980) 321–349.

Historians have often commented upon the bellicose characteristics glorified in Turkish nomadic cultures as especially prized by Muslim rulers. While these traits were luridly described by writers of late antiquity in the West who dreaded the invasions of Huns and Avars, or by Chinese annalists who noted how Mandarin administrators kept the Great Wall in good repair to thwart the Hsiung-Nu, they were not unique to the steppes.[20]

By the High Middle Ages, Muslim regimes had acquired military slaves from a wide variety of sources.[21] Mamlūks from the Caucasus did not appear frequently in Egypt or Syria until the late fourteenth century. But once Sultan Barqūq (784–801/1382–1399) had cemented his position, he deliberately purchased the majority of his recruits from his homeland. All of his successors followed suit to the end of the independent Mamlūk regime in Cairo.[22]

Circassia is not a nomadic region in the sense of an area of sweeping grasslands supporting pastoralists. It is a mountainous zone sustaining both agriculturalists and transhumants. Its populations had been esteemed for centuries by Islamic aristocracies for their beauty and longevity. Several dynasties acquired a Circassian physiognomy, such as grey or blue eyes, fair hair, and light complexions, because so many heirs

[20] On the invasions of the Huns, Avars, and other Central Asian peoples into Europe in Late Antiquity, see H. Gwatkin and J. Whitney, eds., *The Cambridge Medieval History*, 2d ed. (Cambridge 1964) 1, 215–217, 328–366, 660–665 (bibliography); J. Strayer, ed., *Dictionary of the Middle Ages* (New York 1983) 2, 12–13; 6, 352–354. On the Hsiung-Nu, see Denis Twitchett and Michael Loewe, eds., *The Cambridge History of China* (Cambridge 1986) 1, 383–405.

[21] Ayalon, "Aspects: The Importance of the Mamlūk Institution," 196–209; id., "Aspects: Ayyūbids, Kurds and Turks," 1–32; id., "The European Asiatic Steppe: A Major Reservoir for the Islamic World," in *Transactions of the Twenty-fifth Congress of Orientalists* (Moscow 1963) 47–52; J. Bacharach, "African Military Slaves in the Medieval Middle East: The Cases of Iraq (869–955) and Egypt (868–1171)," *IJMES* 13 (1981) 471–495.

[22] D. Ayalon, "Burdjīya," *EI*^{2} 1, 1324–1325; id., "The Circassians in the Mamlūk Kingdom," *JAOS* 69 (1949) 135–147; G. Wiet, "Barḳūḳ," *EI*^{2} 1, 1050–1051.

were descended from Circassian concubines.[23] Yet these districts also acquired a reputation for fierce resistance to interference by foreign conquerors. Although suzerainty theoretically alternated between several Iranian, Tatar, and Anatolian regimes throughout the Middle Period, direct control was imposed only by Russian Czars in the nineteenth century.[24] The populations of Circassia never converted to Islam en masse. Their adherence to indigenous cults and consequent reluctance to adopt any form of monotheism rendered them suitable for recruitment as slave-soldiers, who could not be bought or captured from among Jewish, Christian, or Muslim peoples. Circassian adolescents, despite their reputation for comeliness, amply demonstrated their receptivity to training in military arts and proved themselves fully equal to the pugnacity of their Turkish or Mongol counterparts.

Merchants sent from Cairo regularly traveled to Circassia and the Black Sea steppes during the fourteenth and fifteenth centuries to purchase youths for their royal patrons. They transferred them to Cairo via the Bosphorus and Dardanelles, having paid the Byzantine Emperor for their transit rights at rates set by longstanding treaties.[25] Local villagers,

[23] Robert H. Hewsen, "Circassians," in *The Modern Encyclopedia of Russian and Soviet History*, ed. J. L. Wieczynski (Gulf Breeze, Florida, 1976) 7, 134.

[24] W. E. D. Allen and P. Muratoff, *Caucasian Battlefields: A History of the Wars on the Turco-Caucasian Border, 1828–1921* (Cambridge 1953); John F. Baddeley, *The Russian Conquest of the Caucasus* (London 1908, repr. 1969); Hewsen, "Circassians," 131–133; Firuz Kazemzadeh, "Russian Penetration of the Caucasus," in *Russian Imperialism from Ivan the Great to the Revolution*, ed. T. Hunczak (New Brunswick 1974) 239–263.

[25] M. Canard, "Le royaume d'Arménie-Cilicie et les Mamlouks jusqu'au traité de 1285," *Revue des Etudes Arméniennes* 4 (1967) 217–259; id., "Une lettre du Sultan Nāṣir Ḥassan à Jean VI Cantacuzène (750/1349)," *Annales de l'Institut d'Études Orientales d'Alger* 3 (1939) 27–52; id., "Un traité entre Byzance et l'Égypte au XIIIe siècle et les relations diplomatiques de Michel VIII Paléologue avec les sultans mamlūks Baibars et Qalā'ūn," in *Mélanges Gaudefroy-Demombynes* (Cairo 1934–1945) 197–224; id., "Le traité de 1281 entre Michel Paléologue et le Sultan Qalā'ūn," *Byzantion* 10 (1935) 669–680; F. Dölger, "Der Vertrag des Sultan Qalā'ūns von Ägypten mit dem Kaiser

while resolutely opposed to foreign domination, freely offered the best and brightest of their children for sale because of the prices they commanded, the influence they might one day wield in the capital of an empire, and the consequent beneficence they might bestow on their relatives back home. The youths who were purchased thus exhibited the quick wits and athletic agility that enabled them to cope with a radically new environment. It is in the context of these qualities that we may reconstruct Qāytbāy's personality as a young man.

When Qāytbāy arrived in Cairo, he was already past twenty.[26] The merchant who bought him, Maḥmūd ibn Rustam, was seeking adept horsemen who would excel in archery and lance-casting. Qāytbāy displayed unusual talent in both. Reading back from the traits that distinguished him in later life, we can envision a man who was tall rather than massive and remarkable for his stamina. Throughout his sixties and seventies, Qāytbāy enjoyed rigorous outings in which he often outpaced men decades younger. Upon his manumission, Qāytbāy was appointed an instructor in lance-casting and impressed his contemporaries as a horseman who could direct his mount effortlessly. Although such abilities stem from innate aptitudes and keen vision, they require years of practice to perfect. Qāytbāy's gifts certainly caught the eyes of Cairo's most influential militarists. Immediately upon his arrival, he was recommended to the reigning sultan, al-Ashraf Barsbāy (825–841/1422–1437), for purchase as a palace guard. The

Michael VIII Palaiologos," in *Serta Monacensia Franz Babinger*, ed. H. J. Kissling (Leiden 1952) 60–79; A. S. Ehrenkreutz, "Strategic Implications of the Slave Trade between Genoa and Mamlūk Egypt in the Second Half of the Thirteenth Century," in *The Islamic Middle East, 700–1900*, ed. A. L. Udovitch (Princeton 1981) 335–345; P. M. Holt, "Qalāwūn's Treaty with Genoa in 1290," *Der Islam* 57 (1980) 101–108; id., "The Treaties of the Early Mamlūk Sultans with the Frankish States," *BSOAS* 43 (1980) 67–76; J. Wansbrough, "The Safe-Conduct in Muslim Chancery Practice," *BSOAS* 34 (1971) 20–35.

[26] *Ḍaw'* 6, 201, no. 697, l. 5; *'Uqūd*, f. 221b, l. 17; *Rawḍ*, f. 170b, l. 21.

latter readily agreed that Qāytbāy would be an adornment to his staff.

The junior recruit was assigned to the Ṭāzīya barracks just before Barsbāy's death. He was claimed by Jaqmaq, who retained him as a khāṣṣakī and, upon his manumission, promoted him to the office of third executive secretary (*dawādār thālith*). Following Jaqmaq's decease and Īnāl's succession, Qāytbāy was interrogated for his loyalty. Found to have no record of treachery, he was advanced to the rank of amīr of ten. Īnāl's successor, Khushqadam, promoted Qāytbāy to an amīrship of forty and granted him the superintendancy of royal provisions (*shādd al-shurabkhānāh*). Soon thereafter, Qāytbāy received the ultimate rank of an officer's career, the commandership of a thousand Mamlūks (*taqaddimat alf*), and thereby entered the ruling oligarchy. Sultan Yilbāy appointed Qāytbāy to the captaincy of the royal guard (*ra's nawbat al-nuwwāb*) in place of his comrade and future intimate, Azbak min Ṭuṭukh, who had been dispatched to assume the governorship of Damascus. Yilbāy's successor, Timurbughā, so trusted Qāytbāy that he placed him in the marshalship upon his succession.

This skeletal outline attests to Qāytbāy's competence as an officer, his capacity to remain clear of conspiracies, and his patience. The succession of offices may superficially suggest an uninterrupted, if not meteoric, rise to the zenith of the Mamlūk elite, but we must not ignore the time involved. Qāytbāy served nine sultans before his own accession, over a span of thirty-three years. The chronicles are replete with information on scores of royal subordinates, but Qāytbāy is noticeably absent from their comments on distinctive service or political intrigue.

Qāytbāy's biographers adhered to a tradition upheld for most of the later Mamlūk sultans when they addressed achievements of his reign and largely omitted his prior career. Yet Qāytbāy's lack of visibility in the day-to-day accounts of the period between 839 and 872 implies more than benign neglect. Qāytbāy was not a major actor in the turbulent politics of court and barracks throughout these years. From the respect he earned, we can speculate that he performed his duties well and, more significantly, he did so reliably. Qāytbāy developed a reputation for quiet competence and honesty. He was the sort of officer whom his peers trusted because he coveted neither their own positions nor their prospects. Assuming that Qāytbāy lacked ambition would be naive in light of the strife built into the Mamluk promotional system. And as later behavior starkly underscored, Qāytbāy was fully capable of detecting duplicity and meting out reprisals for it. But there is no record in his preenthronement days that he personally involved himself in the rivalries that ensnared so many of his colleagues. Ibn Iyās noted that not once was Qāytbāy arrested, imprisoned, or exiled during these decades, an extraordinary accomplishment in light of the gnawing fear of revolt all sultans lived with on a daily basis.[27]

Qāytbāy seems to have inspired confidence in his associates that he was the ideal khushdāsh. Authoritative but not overbearing, ambitious yet not megalomaniac, Qāytbāy rose to high office as a consequence of the loyalty and steadiness he exuded. He was the true team player who remained an outsider. Never in this long preaccession phase did he emerge as either a powerful contender or a major partner, except possibly in his relationship with Timurbughā. Had the latter managed to secure his position, he might have relied on Qāytbāy as his effective coruler, just as Qāytbāy would later depend on Yashbak min Mahdī. But prior to Timurbughā's enthronement, we encounter no references to such a relationship. If Qāytbāy identified with any factions throughout his years as an officer, they remain unknown.

One may speculate that a cursus honorum of this sort, free from either marked distinction or marring blemishes,

[27] *Badā'i'* 3, 325, l. 7.

qualified Qāytbāy to succeed after two failed attempts at political consolidation. Qāytbāy seems to have made few bitter enemies. On the one hand, he was something of an unknown quantity to the fiercely competitive Mamlūk factions who identified with both previous sultans and the protective officers who looked after their interests. On the other, he was an individual who could be believed because he stood above the greed that drove so many of his peers. Qāytbāy's succession of offices therefore does not differ appreciably from the pattern held by Yilbāy or Timurbughā. That he succeeded where they failed must be because of these more elusive qualities that so few of his peers exhibited. Such traits acquire enhanced significance if we consider Qāytbāy's personal life.

Qāytbāy was renowned throughout his reign as a defender of Islam, a patron of scholars, and a symbol of piety. His sincerity of belief is so consistently elaborated upon by chroniclers that we may accept their judgment at face value. The salience of piety so early in this sultan's career is noteworthy. Qāytbāy came to the throne as a self-educated person genuinely committed to religious observance. His fascination with judicial proceedings, alternately appreciated and resented by judges, attests to his familiarity with the Sharī'a and his belief that a ruler's sworn oath to uphold it meant more than mere enforcement of cases subordinates had decided. The historian 'Abd al-Bāsiṭ al-Malaṭī noted that Qāytbāy acquired proficiency in Arabic early in his military training.[28] He memorized sections of the Koran and proudly recited them during religious festivals. After Qāytbāy had amassed a substantial fortune and bought his own residence in Cairo, in all probability he invited prominent 'ulamā' and revered figures to his home for prayer sessions. He may well have engaged these persons to tutor him in religious subjects. Precisely how Qāytbāy gained a measure of proficiency in formal learning is a matter for speculation, but his acumen

28 *Rawḍ*, f. 170b, l. 25.

as supreme arbiter following his enthronement attests to the knowledge he had acquired.

Qāytbāy's family life and fiscal planning are more readily discernible from surviving documentation. He was, from all accounts, a vigorous man and yet he seems to have remained remarkably chaste by the standards of his age. Although association with concubines represented a fully acceptible outlet for members of the ruling elite, Qāytbāy partook minimally of their company. He married only once in his life, at an undetermined age before his enthronement, establishing a union that lasted to his death.[29] His wife was Fāṭima bint ʻAlī ibn Khaṣṣbak, the daughter of a respected *walad nās* (descended from Mamlūks) family that traced its origin back to a grand amīr in the service of Sultan al-Nāṣir Muḥammad ibn Qalā'ūn (709–741/1309–1340).[30] Fāṭima was designated by her father as executrix of his own patrimony while her brother, Muḥammad, was still living.[31] Many female members of the Mamlūk caste enjoyed fiscal control over their familial holdings, and Fāṭima exhibited an aptitude for managing assets early in her life. Since she died in 909/1504 at the age of sixty[32] we may assume that she was some three decades Qāytbāy's junior and was almost certainly a child when the two were betrothed.

29 *Rawḍ*, f. 171, l. 2. ʻAbd al-Bāsiṭ mentions that Qāytbāy married Fāṭima after his promotion to the amīrship of ten in 862/1458 during Īnāl's reign.

30 Fāṭima descended from Sayf al-Dīn Khāṣṣbak al-Nāṣirī (d. 743/1334), a prominent amīr during the reign of al-Nāṣir Muḥammad (d. 741/1340) See Ibn Taghrī-Birdī, *Al-manhal al-ṣāfī wa'l-mustawfī ba'd al-wāfī*, ms. Cairo, Dar al-Kutub, Ta'rīkh 1113; G. Wiet, "Les biographies du Manhal Ṣāfī," *Mémoires de l'Institut d'Égypte* 19 (1932) no. 944, 139.

31 Fāṭima appeared in several pious endowment (waqf) deeds appropriated by Sultan al-Ghawrī as supervisor for her two siblings, al-Nāṣir Muḥammad and al-Masūna ʻA'isha. She therefore served as her father's executor, even though there was a surviving son. See Cairo: Wizārat al-Awqāf, Daftarkhānah: Ḥujja 104 jadīd (Muḥammad Amīn, *Catalogue des documents d'archives du Caire de 239/853 à 922/1516* [Cairo, IFAO, 1981] 147, no. 450).

32 *Badā'i'* 4, 64, l. 6.

Nonetheless, Fāṭima may have induced Qāytbāy to initiate the process of developing a personal estate he owned outright, distinct from military fiefs (*iqṭā'*s) parceled out solely on a usufruct basis to officers by the crown in return for service. Indeed, the princess (*khawand*) Fāṭima may have administered its proceeds, freeing her husband to address his formal duties. Because archival records of property acquisition before the Ottoman conquest, aside from charitable trusts, have largely disappeared, we cannot trace the growth of Qāytbāy's and Fāṭima's estate. But we do know that he was buying land as early as 855/1451.[33] This isolated purchase should be interpreted as only a minute aspect of a much larger process of real estate accumulation. Yet it confirms Qāytbāy's status as a property holder while still an amīr. Given the lavish grants to charity that constituted such a hallmark of Qāytbāy's reign, one may assume that he and his wife had built up a substantial fortune well before 872.

We are thus left with the impression of an individual who was not only authoritative, resolute, and trustworthy, but prudent as well. Qāytbāy's concern over money would loom large in his reign, especially when he confronted the prospect of bankruptcy. Whether his extraordinary expenditures on the military and scholastic establishments may be regarded as profligacy must await analysis of the Mamlūk state's fiscal resources and the demands ranged against them. Here suffice it to note that Qāytbāy, in partnership with his spouse of many years, held a large amount of personal property when he came to the throne. He could therefore depend less on unsavory measures to ensure his solvency than his eventual successor, Qānṣūh al-Ghawrī.

33 Dār al-Wathā'iq al-Qawmīya, Maḥkama Shar'īya, Maḥfaẓa 18, Ḥujja 111, dated 19 Dhū'l-Qa'da 855/13 December 1451. See Amīn, *Catalogue*, 24, no. 116; 159, no. 475.

Enthronement: Studied Reluctance?

The events surrounding Qāytbāy's accession were fully in keeping with his enigmatic disdain for self-aggrandizement. Not all observers were convinced of his sincerity, believing that his hesitation was staged by his closest associates. Immediately after he warned the Īnālīya of their deteriorating status, Qāytbāy requested permission from Sultan Timurbughā to inspect his camel corps.[34] He thus arranged to be away from the capital when the struggle erupted between factions loyal to Khayrbak al-Khushqadamī and the Īnālīya. Clashes broke out on Friday the third of Rajab/28 January after noon prayer and continued over the next two days. When Qāytbāy returned on Sunday the fifth, Khayrbak had been apprehended and Timurbughā confined to his house. The recruits of the Ẓāhirīya Khushqadamīya acknowledged the coup removing their leader, Khayrbak, but still barred the staircases leading to the Citadel palace and mosque. They denied Qāytbāy and his lieutenant, Yashbak min Mahdī, ascent until their own safety was ensured.[35] Qāytbāy insisted that he had returned solely to discharge his duty as atābak and demanded to confirm Timurbughā's well-being. Yashbak then took the initiative to nominate Qāytbāy for the sultanate. Qāytbāy demurred and proceeded to the stables to await safe-conduct up to the palace. The deliberations dragged on through the afternoon and evening of the fifth, complicated by wrangling over the Khushqadamīya's guarantees in return for their acquiescence in Timurbughā's deposition and acceptance of Qāytbāy. The latter remained at the

[34] *Rawḍ*, f. 165b, l. 33.
[35] *Rawḍ*, ff. 166, l. 4–11; 166b, l. 8.

stables vehemently remonstrating with Yashbak and other colleagues over his future.[36]

Contemporary historians reacted to Qāytbāy's obstinacy with a mixture of admiration and skepticism. Modern commentators have been less kind, interpreting Qāytbāy's hesitation as a charade rigged to persuade hostile Mamlūk factions that he alone remained an honest broker who accepted the autocracy only to stave off disaster.[37] The venerable chronicler Yūsuf ibn Taghrī-Birdī, a firsthand observer of these events, tended to contradict 'Abd al-Bāsiṭ. Ibn Taghrī-Birdī knew Qāytbāy personally and initially questioned his leadership potential in the face of so much adversity. 'Abd al-Bāsiṭ stressed how Qāytbāy wept and cast off his turban when Yashbak pressed him to accept the sultanate for the realm's stability. Ibn Taghrī-Birdī reacted wryly to this histrionic performance, suspecting that Yashbak had set it up well in advance of the power contest.[38] There is little reason to doubt Yashbak's own motives, for he received a position of second in command immediately upon Qāytbāy's enthronement. But Qāytbāy's behavior may not be so readily dismissed as play-acting. Since he refused to discuss his misgivings publicly, we are reduced to conjecture about his personal feelings. Yet Qāytbāy's respect for Timurbughā was genuine, even after the latter was put aside. Yashbak may well have persuaded Qāytbāy to accept the sultanate for reasons of state security, but he could not downplay the chicanery involved. This certainly mattered to Qāytbāy, who prided his own clean record. There is no reason to disregard Qāytbāy's show of emotion as a sham, even if he had participated in the plot to overthrow Khayrbak.

The aloof stance Qāytbāy had maintained so resolutely for years suggests that his resistance to a convenience draft was something more than token. If Qāytbāy accepted his

36 *Rawḍ*, ff. 168b, l. 17; 169b, l. 3.

37 E. Ashtor, "Ḳā'it Bāy," *EI*² 2, 462; Wiet, *Egypte*, 589.

38 *Ḥawādith* 4, 617, l. 19.

acclamation, he would assume a throne usurped from an individual to whom he had sworn fealty. Nonetheless, he ultimately submitted to pressure and accepted his nomination. The question of his conflicting impulses will probably evade resolution in the absence of personal memoirs. But those who posit Qāytbāy's connivance in a prerehearsed plot have yet to account for his abstinence from earlier conspiracy. Qāytbāy might well have preferred a secondary position in a new regime or corulership with the chosen monarch—compelled to share authority with a new coterie of officers. Such a role was patently more secure and suited to renegotiating a relationship with yet another claimant if a new succession crisis developed. We have seen that Qāytbāy's private fortune precluded any inducement to accept the sultanate for personal gain. Perhaps Qāytbāy ultimately succumbed to the call of duty, yielding to his comrade's pleas that he shoulder the burden of supreme power for the regime's survival.

Whatever his motives, Qāytbāy agreed to mount the throne on the following morning, Monday the sixth of Rajab 872/31 January 1468. He refused to allow any ceremonials until he had personally received a brevet of abdication from Timurbughā, witnessed by four notaries (*shuhūd*), attesting the latter's resignation of his own free will.[39] Once again, on-site observers disagreed over Timurbughā's readiness to part with his office. ʿAbd al-Bāsiṭ described the delegation of notaries led into Timurbughā's presence by Yashbak min Mahdī. He states that the sultan remained seated until he learned of Qāytbāy's unanimous endorsement, whereupon he retired to the Baḥra hall adjacent to the harem and doffed the royal sword and headgear. The amīr Timrāz al-Shamsī, a key accomplice in the deposition, took custody of these emblems of authority, pending Qāytbāy's arrival. Then, the notaries requested Timurbughā's testament

[39] *Rawḍ*, f. 170, l. 7; *Ḥawādith* 4, 617, l. 19; Ibn al-Ḥimṣī, *Ḥawādith al-zamān wa-wafayāt al-shuyūkh wa'l-aqrān*, ms. Feizullah 1438, f. 52, l. 5.

of abdication. He allegedly agreed to step down without coercion. The shuhūd proceeded to the Caliph and the four qāḍīs, who were waiting outside. The judges summarily confirmed Timurbughā's freewill act. Only then was the oath of obedience to his successor valid.[40] Ibn Taghrī-Birdī questioned whether the witnesses actually received an uncoerced abdication from Timurbughā, since he refused to speak until everyone else left the Baḥra Hall and he could address them alone. Ibn Taghrī-Birdī regarded 'Abd al-Bāsiṭ's version as dubious, since Timurbughā could not be sure of his future once Qāytbāy was ensconced. And he bluntly stated that both the witnessses and qāḍīs acted in the face of a *fait accompli*.[41]

Yet, willing or not, Timurbughā had forsworn his own claim to the throne fully in keeping with legal procedure. The instrument of abdication and brevet of succession were conveyed to Qāytbāy, who now agreed to ascend to the Citadel for the enthronement ceremony. In the presence of the Caliph and the chief justices, he was girded with the royal sword. He accepted oaths of obedience (*bay'a*) from them before he would permit the grand amīrs who had engineered his coup to kiss the floor and profess their loyalty. Qāytbāy thus became the forty-first Mamlūk sultan of Egypt and Syria, the fifteenth Circassian, and the tenth to rise from slavery to assume the office.[42] He proceeded to the balcony of the Dihlīz Gallery to accept the acclamation of hosts gathered below.

Qāytbāy then confirmed the retirement of his former sovereign, who would be granted a private audience the next day to ascertain where he would reside as honored emeritus rather than exiled rival.[43] Qāytbāy received Timurbughā on the morning of Wednesday the seventh/1 February, a peer greeting an old friend and confidant. When Timurbughā was

40 *Rawḍ*, f. 170, l. 19.
41 *Ḥawādith* 4, 618, ll. 2–3.
42 *Rawḍ*, f. 170b, l. 1.
43 *Rawḍ*, f. 174b, l. 3.

ushered in, Qāytbāy rose to embrace him. The new sultan then compelled his predecessor to sit next to him on the royal dais, despite Timurbughā's protestation because of his subordinate rank. Qāytbāy than reiterated that his elevation was not of his own choosing. *He* was the victim of coercion, while Timurbughā could leave the cares of office freely with no loss of respect. Whatever Timurbughā's inner reaction to this display of magnanimity, he adopted a mien of dignified concurrence and replied, "You and I are like one person, but God chose you to resolve this affair."[44] Qāytbāy then admitted the new marshal, Jānibak Qulaqsīz, as well as Yashbak min Mahdī, soon to be appointed executive secretary (*dawādār*), Timur the Chamberlain (*ḥājib*), and several other officers. Qāytbāy announced that Timurbughā would journey to Damietta on the Mediterranean coast as a private subject until he himself had chosen his final dwelling. No confiscation of his property or personal effects would be permitted, nor were his intimate retainers to be denied him. Timurbughā departed from Cairo that evening, presumably to bivouac in al-Maṭarīya north of Cairo before proceeding to the port. A noteworthy event had thus taken place: the orderly transition of authority, legally sanctioned, and devoid of brutality. Qāytbāy sought to inaugurate his reign under positive auspices. Although Timurbughā was soon to repudiate his abdication, Qāytbāy could begin the consolidation of his position absolved from any taint of usurpation. Qāytbāy's actions during these tense days signaled more than his personal renunciation of coup tactics. They not only terminated the crisis following Khushqadam's death, but heralded an era of renewed law and order—which this sultan would pledge himself to uphold.

44 *Rawḍ*, f. 174b, l. 16.

Consolidation: Decisiveness after Equivocation

Qāytbāy's penchant for high-minded dealings extended only to his royal peer. On the day of his enthronement he moved to nullify the threat of revolt that had toppled Timurbughā. He ordered the imprisonment of Timurbughā's dawādār, Khayrbak, pending his permanent exile.[45] Qāytbāy then summoned the previous amīr of council and confiscated all his assets—claiming these had been garnered illegally since Khushqadam's days.[46] By this act Qāytbāy could lay his hands on a substantial sum of money for accession bonuses to the officers and troops who had endorsed his accession. On the tenth of Rajab/4 February, Qāytbāy packed Khayrbak off to Alexandria. Unlike Timurbughā, this would-be usurper, dubbed by chroniclers the "Sultan of One Night," was grossly humiliated. Qāytbāy seized all his possessions, and ordered that he remain in solitary confinement until his death. He was sent out in the middle of the night chained to a horse.[47] Ibn Iyās applauded Khayrbak's exile, seeing it as heralding the fall of the Khushqadamīya amīrs, whom he regarded as an oppressive element running rampant since their patron's death.

Qāytbāy recognized the dissolution of hostile factions as his first priority. Over the next several weeks, the new sultan

45 *Rawḍ*, f. 174, l. 14.

46 *Badā'i'* 4, 57, l. 9. Al-'Aynī fled to Medina from Mecca to escape the rebellion of the Bedouin chieftain al-Jāzānī. Sultan al-Ghawrī ordered him brought back to Cairo for further mulcting, but the officer charged with his arrest found him dead. "Thus did God spare him oppression a second time, now at al-Ghawrī's hands."

47 *Rawḍ*, f. 176b, l. 11; *Badā'i'* 3, 7, l. 18.

purged the military elite of several hundred officers.[48] Although the Khushqadamīya suffered the most reprisals, all amīrs suspected of loyalty to previous rulers or senior officials lived in fear of exile. Even the Īnālīya, who had supported Qāytbāy, could not rest assured of promotion or recompense. Qāytbāy heeded reports of trusted spies charged with uncovering plots or even suspicious statements. When he learned that the amīr Qānṣūh al-Khasīf al-Īnālī, who had lent indispensable aid to his accession, had boasted, "Without me, Qāytbāy would never have won the sultanate," the sultan sent his erstwhile ally off to prison in Damietta and subsequently Mecca. "His loose tongue proved his undoing, bringing the sultan's wrath down on him."[49]

Qāytbāy effectively neutralized resistance by dissolving coteries of officers actively or potentially hostile to his position. Although his tactics may seem drastic, they were indicative of his shrewd grasp of reality. Throughout the Burjī era, sultans were plagued by the threat of revolt or deposition by officers whose first allegiance abided with their deceased sponsor. Long-term stability required a clean slate prior to the creation of a reliable network of officers appointed from men who had risen with the new autocrat and whose fortunes were now tied to his. Qāytbāy's policy of exile was consistent with his image as a just sovereign. Few even of his most unrepentent opponents received death sentences. We shall dwell subsequently on the procedure of confiscation. Qāytbāy regarded the assets of anyone with previous service in government as state property, now sequestered by the central treasury to buy the fealty of a new ruling apparatus. He also displayed the courage and mercy that would become

48 *Ḥawādith* 4, 618, l. 5; *Rawḍ*, f. 174, l. 18: sultan exiles several amīrs suspected of opposition to Syria (Aleppo and Jerusalem); ibid., l. 27: their attempts to foment revolt from Syria quelled; *Ḥawādith* 4, 627, l. 6; *Badā'i'* 3, 10, l. 24: three hundred Khushqadamī Mamlūks despatched to garrison duty in Upper Egypt and Nubia.

49 *Badā'i'* 3, 329, l. 6; *Rawḍ*, f. 175b, l. 28.

legendary in later years. Three days after his enthronement, Qāytbāy heeded advice from his colleagues, who warned him that his vendetta should not extend down to line troops recruited by Khushqadam. They argued that the loyalty of these young soldiers was still malleable. Qāytbāy forthwith ordered their restoration to duty and salary, gambling that generous cooption would supplant lingering resentment.[50]

But Qāytbāy would brook no personal insults. A month after his accession, he ordered several Mamlūks flogged who used abusive language to his face when they received their riding camels.[51] Ibn Taghrī-Birdī noted that the sultan "emitted thunder and lightning." He flew into calculated rages at the least show of resistance, thereby inspiring respect from both troopers and commoners. Ibn Taghrī-Birdī found Qāytbāy's behavior tyrannical in these tense days when he tightened his grip on the reins of power. But he admitted that no one dared cross Qāytbāy, who compelled obedience when his predecessors had failed. At the same time, the new ruler showed disdain for idle rumors of rebellion. On the fourteenth of Sha'bān/9 March, Qāytbāy left the Citadel and rode about the square (*maydān*) below with minimal escort to underscore his fearlessness.[52] In coming years, Qāytbāy would regularly plan excursions solely for recreation, but this act of bravado made a decisive impact on the masses, who had not beheld their monarch riding in public unguarded since Khushqadam's early days. In less than two months, Qāytbāy had scattered his opposition, potential and real, without resorting to mass executions or torture. And he forgave impetuous young recruits their initial mutiny on grounds of their inexperience and his own magnanimity. However calculated these ploys may have been, they distinguished Qāytbāy

[50] *Ḥawādith* 4, 618, l. 17.

[51] *Ḥawādith* 4, 624, l. 17; *Rawḍ*, f. 178b, l. 15. Ibn Taghrī-Birdī was critical of Qāytbāy for his excesses. But because of his own death in 873, he could not have predicted that the sultan would survive for twenty-eight years.

[52] *Ḥawādith* 4, 626, l. 3; *Rawḍ*, f. 179, l. 15; *Badā'i'* 3, 10, l. 1.

as something more than a grasping dictator. He now confronted the challenge of building up an effective coterie of associates who would implement his authority.

Qāytbāy's closest colleagues probably agreed before the coup how they would divide the most prestigious executive offices regardless of whether he or Timurbughā held the sultanate. Once Qāytbāy had entrenched himself, he fulfilled these a priori pledges to his followers, provided their loyalty was unswerving. The offices critical to maintaining discipline among the troops and preserving order in Cairo were: the marshal (*atābak*), the executive secretary (*dawādār*), captain of the guard (*ra's al-nawba*), the council officer (*amīr majlis*), minister of war (*amīr silāḥ*), prefect of police (*wālī al-shurṭa*), the grand chamberlain (*ḥājib al-ḥujjāb*), and majordomo (*ustādār*). Qāytbāy appointed amīrs who had been exiled in previous reigns because they were supported by restive factions as a counterbalance to plotters in his coup.[53] He thus aimed to create a ruling council from both trusted followers and individuals abused by his predecessors. He avoided replicating an extant coalition, preferring to promote competition between participants in the succession crisis and men who were absent from Cairo when it had erupted. The latter had every reason to show their gratitude for release from exile by rendering exemplary service. But they bore no love for the parvenus who had risen with Qāytbāy in the preceding months. Qāytbāy realized that such rivalry assured a

[53] *Ḥawādith* 4, 619, l. 10; 620, l. 3; *Inbā'*, 2, l. 3; *'Uqūd*, f. 222, l. 18; *Badā'i'* 3, 5, l. 1; 6, l. 16. These offices were filled as follows: The atābak: Jānibak Qulaqsīz; the dawādār: Yashbak min Mahdī; the amīr silāḥ: Bardibak Ḥajīn; the amīr majlis: Qurqumās al-Julb upon his return from Damietta. Ibn Iyās states that he had previously served as amīr silāḥ and thus accepted a demotion (see also *Rawḍ*, f. 203b, l. 8). The second dawādār: Qānbirdī al-Ibrāhīmī al-Īnālī; the wālī: Qānibāy al-Ḥasanī al-Īnālī. Qarajā al-Ṭawīl al-Īnālī and Timrāz al-Shamsī were both promoted to the rank of muqaddam. The amīr akhūr: Jānibak al-Faqīh; the Ra's Nawba: Nāniq al-Ẓāhirī Jaqmaq; the ḥajib: Timur (retained); the tājir al-Mamālīk: Tānibak Qara al-Īnālī; the shādd al-shurabkhānah: Qānṣūh al-Khasīf al-Aḥmadī. Several of these individuals were replaced within a year. By 873, Qāytbāy's cabinet had stabilized.

degree of dynamic tension indispensable to his own centrality as dispenser of favors. Only he could intervene to stave off a clash between these ruthless officers, any one of whom might attempt to seize the sultanate himself if he remained unchecked. Indeed, not all these individuals survived their appointments by a year. Some were transferred to provincial governorships in Syria, thereby removing them from the inner circle; others died on the first campaign against the Dhū'l-Qādrid rebel, Sūwār.[54]

But two figures emerged during this formative period who would share the highest level of subordinate authority in the regime. They functioned as Qāytbāy's alter egos until the end of their careers. One ultimately pursued his own hegemonic ambitions by attempting to conquer a neighboring territory. The second was content with serving his liege lord as supreme field commander for almost three decades. These two men, each respected for his abilities, were polar opposites. Neither relished the other's company, yet each tolerated the other because his sovereign so willed. Qāytbāy recognized their competence early and relied on them to implement most of the critical policies during the initial and medial periods of his reign. He also bolstered his own power as the mediator between two powerful officers who competed for his attention. These men held the executive secretaryship and grand marshalship respectively.

The man whose appointment to the dawādārīya was a foregone conclusion, Yashbak min Mahdī, had first earned notoriety during Jaqmaq's reign as a garrison commander in Upper Egypt.[55] Yashbak exhibited bravery and cruelty in equal measures throughout his provincial service. He dealt with marauding Bedouins so ferociously that his reputation for savage reprisals became legendary even by that age's

[54] For example, the atābak Jānibak was captured by Sūwār and held for ransom, much to Qāytbāy's secret satisfaction. The ra's nawba, Nāniq, perished in the same campaign. See *Inbā'*, 2, l. 3.

[55] *Ḍaw'* 10, 272, no. 1077; *Badā'i'* 3, 173, l. 6.

standards of violence. He succeeded with such aplomb in compelling their submission that he attracted the sultan's notice back in Cairo. Yashbak advanced rapidly up the military hierarchy in Jaqmaq's last years and during his successors' reigns. But his ambition and irascibility won him many enemies and few allies. He was exiled just when promotion to the highest rank seemed within his grasp. Yet his capacity to crush resistance from both external rebels and internal foes always necessitated his restoration to office. Until he became Qāytbāy's associate during Khushqadam's reign, however, no one took him into his confidence. Exactly how Qāytbāy and Yashbak became such comrades eluded even their biographers. We may surmise that the two senior amīrs, both seasoned in the art of political survival, recognized qualities mutually alien and yet requisite to effective rule. Ever the just arbiter of Sharīʿa, Qāytbāy would often stand aloof from draconian means of implementing his policies. Events might well require such measures, and Yashbak never lost a moment's sleep over their employment. Yashbak became the hated enforcer of his sovereign's will, translating summary commands into brutal deeds.

Qāytbāy rewarded Yashbak with the dawādārīya during the first formal consistory following his enthronement.[56] The executive secretary was traditionally his sovereign's closest military counselor, sharing the monarch's ear with his civilian counterpart, the confidential secretary (*kātib al-sirr*), who presided over the imperial chancery. Qāytbāy thus formally established Yashbak as his intimate adviser. Over the following years Yashbak accumulated a host of other offices, military and bureaucratic.[57] He delegated their administration to adroit but shady subordinates who depended totally

[56] *Rawḍ*, f. 175, ll. 21, 26.

[57] At various times Yashbak held the marshalship and vizierate: *Badāʾiʿ* 3, 26, l. 16; *Inbāʾ*, 23, l. 10, which makes first reference to the rise of Qāsim Shughayta as acting wazīr, one of Yashbak's least scrupulous agents (see also *Rawḍ*, f. 205b, l.11); the majordomoship (*ustādārīya*): *Ḥawādith* 4, 702, l. 9;

on him for their advancement. Yashbak would come to dominate the imperial bureaucracy (*al-dīwān al-sharīf*), subjecting it to a veritable reign of terror when the sultan required emergency infusions of cash to fund his expeditions or to neutralize rebellion. Although he wielded authority second only to the sultan's, Yashbak did not attract—nor did he seek—any other close confidants. He incessantly badgered his clients with abuse and exactions. None of his military peers trusted him—with good reason since none could rest assured of his respect for their own bailiwicks.

But to Qāytbāy, the pious gentleman, Yashbak showed a different face. The two spent a great deal of time together. When Yashbak fell gravely ill in 873/1469, the sultan broke royal tradition to visit the dāwadār at home, attending his khusdāsh until the fever crested.[58] Upon Yashbak's recovery, Qāytbāy proclaimed a day of celebration in Cairo, an extraordinary tribute to the esteem in which he held his ruthless dawādār.[59] In Muḥarram of 874/August 1469, Qāytbāy approved Yashbak's betrothal to Fāṭima, daughter of the former sultan al-Mu'ayyad Aḥmad ibn Īnāl, thereby tying a former slave of unknown parentage to a descendant of royalty.[60] When this union produced a son the following year, Qāytbāy rejoiced as if the infant were his.[61] He honored Yashbak with a magnificent reception, and approved the child's name, Manṣūr, normally reserved for princes. Qāytbāy emphasized the continuity of monarchic authority in his reign by uniting his dreaded adjutant with the scion of a deceased ruler when he received Yashbak and al-Mu'ayyad Aḥmad as equals during this ceremony. Earlier that year Yashbak had been accused before the sultan of neglecting his formal duties in

---

Inbā', 56, l. 9; *Badā'i'* 3, 28, l. 23; and the ministership of war (*umra silāḥ*): ibid., 149, l. 11.

58 *Inbā'*, 67, l. 7; *Rawḍ*, f. 219, l. 21; *Badā'i'* 3, 31, l. 7.

59 *Ḥawādith* 4, 706, l. 3.

60 *Inbā'*, 123, l. 8; *Rawḍ*, f. 247, l. 5; *Badā'i'* 3, 38, l. 3.

61 *Inbā'*, 283, l. 9; *Badā'i'* 3, 60, l. 12.

Cairo while allowing his subordinate, Ibn Gharīb the wazīr, to collect huge sums from the provinces illegally. The sultan confronted Yashbak with a secret report that he had withheld some two hundred fifty thousand dīnārs (gold coins) in taxes from Upper Egypt.[62] Yashbak did not deny the report, but instead munificently bestowed the funds upon his sovereign as a gift from one peer to another. Yashbak implied that he answered to no one else in the realm save the sultan, and would continue fattening his purse unless the latter expressly forbade him. Qāytbāy then reprimanded Ibn Gharīb with a symbolic dismissal, but refused to chastize Yashbak, who had brazenly sanctioned the wazīr's actions. This immunity from personal reprisal on Qāytbāy's part was to last until Yashbak's demise. Why Qāytbāy so valued Yashbak's service that he placed him above the law is examined below. Here, we note that the dawādār emerged as the most feared member of Qāytbāy's inner circle. He would retain his unrivaled status until his ill-fated expedition to northern Iraq thirteen years later.

Qāytbāy's other close colleague did not assume the marshalship until Ṣafar of 873/August–September 1468, when its incumbent, Jānibak Qulaqsīz, fell into the hands of Shāh Sūwār. Azbak min Ṭuṭukh was purchased by a royal merchant from Circassia around 840/1436–1437.[63] Entering the service of Sultan Barsbāy as a recruit, he was transferred to the corps of Sultan Jaqmaq in 842/1438. While the young man showed signs of future promise as an officer, he did poorly in his formal studies. One of his instructors noted that "he understood not a word of Arabic!" Nonetheless, Azbak persevered in his religious training and sought to compensate for his scholastic mediocrity by cultivating the favor of eminent 'ulamā'—thus initiating a penchant for the company of literati that would last to the end of his life. Jaqmaq

62 *Inbā'*, 186, l. 10.
63 *Ḍaw'* 2, 270, no. 844.

promoted Azbak to the rank of amīr of ten in 852/1448–1449 and granted him a captaincy of the guard. Azbak married a daughter of the respected jurist and dīwān official Nāṣir al-Dīn ibn al-Bārizī,[64] thereby cementing his ties with the civilian elite. When Jaqmaq died, his son promoted Azbak to an amīrship of forty and bestowed the directorship of treasuries (*khāzindārīya*) on him. But following al-Manṣūr's deposition in 857/1453, Sultan Īnāl arrested Azbak for suspected treason and exiled him first to Alexandria and then Ṣafad in northern Palestine. Īnāl ultimately rescinded this harsh sentence and released Azbak on condition that he retire to Jerusalem. Al-Sakhāwī met him there, and was impressed with his character and learned circle of associates.[65]

Īnāl permitted Azbak to return in 861/1457 at the intercession of his wife, who wielded some influence at court. Azbak developed a close relationship with the sultan's son, who arranged for his restoration to the amīrship. He joined the elite circle of muqaddamīn just before Īnāl's death. His successor, Khushqadam, immediately arrested Azbak, and once again he found himself isolated in Alexandria. It is only at this juncture that al-Sakhāwī mentioned his relationship to Qāytbāy. Since Qāytbāy vouched for Azbak's character, we can assume that the two had nurtured a close association over the years, but details of their friendship remain unknown. In any case, Khushqadam relented and restored Azbak to the muqaddamīn in 868/1463–1464. The sultan appointed Azbak grand chamberlain and then supreme captain of the guard. Azbak married Khushqadam's second daughter (his first wife died in 867), having earned his liege lord's confidence as an aide. Upon Khushqadam's demise, Sultan Yilbāy sent Azbak to assume the viceroyship of Damascus. It was from this office that Qāytbāy recalled him to take over the atābakīya from Jānibak Qulaqsīz.

64 *Ḍaw'* 9, 137, no. 350; Petry, *Civilian Elite*, 207–208.
65 See *Ḍaw'* 2, 270, line 28.

Qāytbāy seems from the beginning to have been dissatisfied with Jānibak's conduct in office, possibly suspecting him of coveting the sultanate. He placed him in command of the first expedition he organized to check the ambitions of Shāh Sūwār in southeastern Anatolia, as much to cool his ardor as to exploit his military ability. When Jānibak was captured and held for ransom, Qāytbāy summoned Azbak to Cairo.[66] Ibn Taghrī-Birdī penned a lengthy analysis of this appointment, since the sultan consulted him about the legality of replacing an officer who was still alive. Azbak publicly refused the post out of deference to Jānibak, but in fact both he and Qāytbāy could scarcely conceal their pleasure over Jānibak's misfortune. Despite Azbak's courteous demurral, Qāytbāy invested him as marshal in a festive reception. Ibn Taghrī-Birdī and Ibn Iyās noted how scholars from all the madhhabs (legal schools) hastened to congratulate the new atābak. He was to enhance his reputation as a patron of learning and charity throughout his long tenure in office.

Azbak's relationship with Qāytbāy seems to have been less intimate than Yashbak's, although the sultan and marshal exhibited similar personalities. Neither displayed Yashbak's impetuosity or disregard for the criticism of discomfited associates. Azbak amassed an enormous fortune, although apparently by legal means. He acquired no reputation as a ruthless oppressor, but rather posed as a champion of popular rights. Qāytbāy placed his atābak in supreme command of his armies primarily because he enjoyed the esteem of all Mamlūk factions, in contrast with Yashbak, who was beloved by none. Yet Qāytbāy would often assign Yashbak responsibility for an expedition when he faced a particularly dangerous adversary abroad. Azbak, on the other hand, took charge of most long-range military planning. It was he who organized the major campaigns against the Ottomans, who were

66 *Ḥawādith* 4, 676, l. 10; *Rawḍ*, f. 203, ll. 14, 21; *'Uqūd*, f. 227b, l. 18; *Badā'i'* 3, 20, l. 20.

harassing the sultan's frontiers in southern Anatolia during the late 880s and early 890s. Yashbak was the meteoric war leader whose ferocity intimidated everyone against whom he marched; Azbak remained the cautious strategist who advised the sultan to stand by time-tested principles of preserving the status quo in foreign affairs—hold the line in the face of aggression but undertake no risky expansion. Qāytbāy valued Azbak above all for his common sense. He became the anchor of Qāytbāy's administration, stepping in repeatedly to calm obstreperous troopers when they felt their prerogatives had been slighted. Yet Azbak was quite prepared to abuse their rights if these cost too much money, and he was not above ordering summary executions or exile if soldiers got out of hand.

Azbak coveted no other major office. Unlike his restive colleague, he stood resolutely aloof from the machinations of fiscal bureaucrats. Qāytbāy appointed him supervisor of the Manṣūri Hospital, a traditional sinecure for the atābak,[67] but he accepted no inordinate compensation for this office. Nonetheless, Azbak received the largest income from military fiefs of any officer in the realm after the sultan. He invested widely in a host of commercial enterprises and administered the estates of his former and current wives. He presided over an enormous household, and by the late 870s was searching for a new setting fit for his heightened circumstances, finally selecting a site by a dry lake near the Lūq district, west of the old city. He already maintained a camel stable there, and now began to plan the transformation of the entire zone.[68] He dug a channel from the Nāṣirī canal to refill the lake, then constructed a palace, mosque, academy, library, Ṣūfī hospice, and several belvederes around its shores. Shaded promenades linked these buildings, widely acclaimed for their splendor, and a vast park planted with gardens and orchards

[67] *Ḥawādith* 4, 677, l. 10.

[68] *Badā'i'* 3, 116, l. 8; 196, l. 7 (on fireworks displays); 267, l. 8 (on public reception by the lake shore).

was opened to the public. Indeed, Azbak intended the whole complex to serve the popular interest. He encouraged wealthy notables to build their homes around the lake and paid for annual fireworks displays to which thousands of commoners were invited. The complex was known as the Azbakīya and survives today as Cairo's central park. It became a landmark of the capital, and Ibn Iyās considered it one of Egypt's wonders—rivaling even the Pyramids.[69]

Azbak thus counterbalanced Yashbak, who amassed copious riches by draconian methods and spent them enhancing his own position along with his sovereign's. Qāytbāy relied on Yashbak as his hatchet man expected to perform brutal tasks the sultan wished to avoid; Azbak stood as Qāytbāy's pillar of military rectitude. Venerated by the army, Azbak guaranteed its loyalty to the sultan through the vagaries of cash shortfalls and devastating defeats for twenty-seven years. That the two proud men cordially loathed each other suited Qāytbāy's own design well. Each realized that the autocrat alone prevented their latent rivalry from erupting into a civil war that might dash both their fortunes.

By Dhū'l-Qa'da of 872/May–June 1468, Qāytbāy could look upon the consolidation of his authority with some measure of confidence that his reign rested on secure foundations. His military network was taking shape, and capable civilian clients were extending their control over the fiscal dīwāns. But on Wednesday the twenty-fourth/15 June, Qāytbāy received disturbing news from Alexandria. His "brother ruler," Timurbughā, who had parted from him in amicability and peace, had escaped and was seeking asylum in Syria.[70] Ibn Taghrī-Birdī and 'Abd al-Bāsiṭ described Qāytbāy's stunned

69 Ibn Iyās devoted a large section of his treatise on Egypt's marvels, *Nuzhat al-umam fī'l-'ajā'ib wa'l-ḥikam*, ms. Aya Sofya 3500, f. 246, l. 2, to a detailed description of the Azbakīya. Since the work remains unedited, few have read its eloquent descriptions of soirées in the belvederes, mystic rituals in the hospice, or dialogues between nightingales and evening flowers in its gardens.

70 *Badā'i'* 3, 15, l. 4.

reaction. His composure "dissolved in an instant" and he visibly trembled over the prospect of revolt once the Khushqadamīya factions learned of this development. Timurbughā had been aided in his escape by several Bedouin shaykhs whose tribes had been severely pounded by Yashbak. He was accompanied by amīrs whom the sultan had also exiled. They had allegedly arranged for Timurbughā to be received by the viceroy of Aleppo, who was exploiting the bruised egos of amīrs recovering from their recent defeat by Shāh Sūwār in Anatolia.[71] Timurbughā had been encouraged to assume command of a combined Bedouin and Mamlūk army and march on Cairo to reclaim the throne. Qāytbāy dispatched an amīr just back from Aleppo with news of the setback in Asia Minor to return immediately and ascertain the extent of hostility against him there. But this unfortunate man was caught by Bedouin partisans of Timurbughā and stripped of his clothes, purse, and the sultan's secret missives.[72] Qāytbāy then placed Yashbak in charge of capturing Timurbughā and crushing the Bedouin who had plotted his escape. But the governor of Ghazza, gate to Palestine, succeeded in apprehending the fugitive before Yashbak arrived. Reports differed as to how Timurbughā was taken into custody. Some alleged that his Bedouin guard resisted, others that he yielded without a fight. In any case, he was taken on the first of Dhū'l-Ḥijja/22 June and conveyed back to the Delta for delivery to Yashbak in Bilbays.[73] The dawādār brought Timurbughā to Alexandria to await Qāytbāy's decision about his future. The sultan pondered his response, weighing how much residual opposition to his own coup endured at home and abroad.

On the seventh/28 June, while mulling over the situation, Qāytbāy received a letter from Timurbughā explaining his behavior. The sultan asked Ibn Taghrī-Birdī to attend

71 *Ḥawādith* 4, 637, l. 23; *Rawḍ*, f. 184b, l. 15.

72 *Ḥawādith* 4, 638, l. 11.

73 *Ḥawādith* 4, 643, l. 15; *Rawḍ*, f. 185b l. 16.

him while he studied it, and initially requested him to read it aloud, in deference to the historian's superior erudition.[74] Ibn Taghrī-Birdī refused, stating that only an equal should read a prince's private thoughts. Qāytbāy then ordered the hall cleared except for the historian and read the letter to him. Its contents reveal the delicate balance between collegiality and despotism inherent in the Mamlūk power structure. Timurbughā referred to himself as the sultan's Mamlūk, that is, his possession, but also noted that he did not fear "the royal knowledge of what God had empowered" (his attempt at flight). He claimed he had been misinformed about his lord's intentions following his arrival in Alexandria. When he was told that Qāytbāy planned to treat him as a prisoner, he had fled—but only with the goal of retiring in Mecca as a pious recluse. "Now the Mamlūk placed himself under the sultan's justice and mercy. For this was indeed a time of clemency and beneficence. He who had previously received the sultan's kindness now beseeched his renewed favor." On the margin, Timurbughā recalled their old friendship, which should not be lightly abandoned. Qāytbāy reflected long on this missive and finally decided to restore Timurbughā to his position as a respected retiree, though he was more closely watched and access to him by other amīrs was restricted. While the affair had clearly shaken Qāytbāy, he did not resort to cruelty in the aftermath of Timurbughā's escape. He continued to enlarge his network of civil associates, thereby seeking to broaden his influence beyond the military elite. The specter of rebellion from within the military could not be eradicated completely, but the sultan's support from other significant sectors of society could be augmented.

Qāytbāy inherited a bureaucratic apparatus that had undergone considerable modification in the preceding century. Its evolution reflected a steady shift away from the regime's reliance on taxes and other traditional generators of revenue

[74] *Ḥawādith* 4, 648, l. 22; *Rawḍ*, f. 186, l. 28.

to more clandestine sources. This phenomenon was clearly demonstrated by the decline of the vizierate in both function and prestige, and the emergence of two fiscal supervisors: the controller of a special bureau (*nāẓir al-mufrad*) and controller of a privy fund (*nāẓir al-khāṣṣ*).[75] The wazīr, or prime minister, once served the monarch as chief fiscal officer, responsible for monitoring the flow of revenues to the central treasury. But as the percentage of the regime's annual cash receipts from taxes, tariffs, and tolls diminished, the wazīr became more of an outright procurer charged with manipulating budgets of various bureaus to squeeze maximum yields. As the office declined in esteem, its incumbents tended to be men from humble backgrounds below the scholarly class. By contrast, the fiscal supervisors were charged with overseeing all revenue-generating ministries to rationalize their collection procedures and monitor attempts at underreporting assets. The privy fund and special bureau reflected the sultanate's early effort to create its own private fisc: a network of revenue-monitoring departments directly under the monarch's thumb, thus devoid of intermediaries who might siphon off funds before they reached his coffers. Individuals appointed to these two offices came from the most senior ranks of the 'ulamā' and had often served in the courts or dīwāns with distinction. Wazīrs, on the other hand, became increasingly the pawns of powerful amīrs who recommended them for their adroitness with little regard for their scruples. Sultans and their aides often pitted wazīrs and nāẓirs against each other, challenging them to provide yields higher than their competitors in return for rewards or promotions and threatening them with arrest if they came up with less.

Qāytbāy's reign saw no deviation from this pattern. The sultan accepted Yashbak's choice, and confirmed one of the

[75] Petry, *Civilian Elite*, 205, 212–220; Popper, *Egypt and Syria under the Circassian Sultans*, 96.

latter's clients, Qāsim Shughayta, as wazīr in Sha'bān of 872/ February–March 1468.[76] This man, destined for intermittent dismissal and recall throughout Qāytbāy's reign, was the son of a lowly miller (*ṭaḥḥān*) who ground grain in the cemetery (*qarāfa*) district. Born in 833/1429–1430, Qāsim became a baker who sold bread at the Qarāfa Gate. He entered the service of al-Bibāwī, chief cook at the Citadel barracks and became a money changer (*ṣayrafī*) under him. When al-Bibāwī received the vizierate, he relied on Qāsim as his closest assistant. Upon al-Bibāwī's execution by Sultan Khushqadam, Qāsim succeeded to the office. He administered it for a brief interlude without any interference, since his overseer, the nāẓir of the royal household, had been removed. But he then lost out in a confrontation with the nāẓir once this official was reinstalled. When Yashbak requested the vizierate from Qāytbāy, he immediately opted for Qāsim as his deputy. Qāsim's subsequent ploys figured heavily in schemes the sultan's bureaucrats concocted to garner sums needed for his military adventures.

The other dīwān officials who manipulated the regime's finances were: the supervisor of the army department (*nāẓir al-jaysh*), responsible for assigning military fiefs (*iqṭā*'s) to recently promoted officers and guaranteeing, in theory, that none were alienated; the controller of the fiscal bureaus (*nāẓir al-dawla*), charged with their coordination; the majordomo (*ustādār*), who served as senior regulator of the royal court; the agent of the state treasury (*wakīl bayt al-māl*); the secretary of the Mamlūks (*kātib al-mamālīk*), who dispensed salaries and bonuses to the troops; the market inspector (*muḥtasib*), responsible for regulating commercial practices and assuring (again in theory) standard weights, measures, and rates of currency exchange; the supervisor of religious minority taxes (*nāẓir al-jawālī*); and the supervisor of pious endowments (*nāẓir al-awqāf*). In 872 and 873,

76 *Ḍaw'* 6, 179, no. 609; *Rawḍ*, f. 179, l. 30; *Ḥawādith* 4, 651, l. 5.

Qāytbāy chose his dīwān officers from a mélange of holdovers from Khushqadam's reign and newcomers recommended by Yashbak.[77] The former were retained because of their track record of successful procurement, the latter because of their promise. But Qāytbāy regarded one office, the most prestigious of all, as sacrosanct for as long as its incumbent lived.

The confidential secretary (*kātib al-sirr*), who presided over the imperial chancery (*dīwān al-inshā'*), remained the preserve of Zayn al-Dīn Abū Bakr ibn Muzhir al-Anṣārī al-Dimashqī al-Shāfi'ī.[78] Born into a prominent scholastic family from Damascus in 831/1427–1428, Ibn Muzhir excelled in the religious sciences. But unlike many of his contemporaries, he entered the bureaucracy early rather than working his way up the academic or judicial ladders. He held controllerships over the royal stables, minority taxes in both Egypt and Syria, the hospice (*khānqāh*) of Sa'īd al-Su'adā', the state treasury, and the army department in rapid succession, serving "superbly in each" with no hint of corruption. Sultan Khushqadam made Ibn Muzhir his confidential secretary in Dhū'l-Qa'da of 866/July–August 1462, and he occupied the post until his death twenty-seven years later. The kātib al-sirr directed a bureau that combined the functions of diplomacy, intelligence, and archives. No civilian enjoyed

77 *Inbā'*, 4, l. 11: controller of the military bureau (*nāẓir al-jaysh*): Kamāl al-Dīn ibn Kātib Jakam; wazīr: Shams al-Dīn Muḥammad al-Ahnāsī, soon replaced by Qāsim Shughayta; majordomo (*ustādār*): Sharaf al-Dīn Mūsā ibn Kātib Gharīb, replaced by Yashbak; controller of the privy fund (*nāẓir al-khāṣṣ*): Tāj al-Dīn 'Abd-Allah ibn al-Maqsī; agent of the treasury (*wakīl bayt al-māl*): Sharaf al-Dīn al-Tatā'ī al-Anṣārī; deputy confidential secretary (*nā'ib kātib al-sirr*): Nūr al-Dīn al-Anbābī; *Inba'*, 8, l. 10: secretary of Mamlūks (*kātib al-mamālīk*): 'Abd al-Karī ibn Jallūd, a youth who succeeded his father, but competent; ibid., 41, l. 15; *Badā'i'* 3, 25, l. 2: market inspector (*muḥtasib*): Yashbak al-Jamālī, succeeding Qānṣūh al-Khasīf. Held office for almost a decade. *Ḥawādith* 4, 735, l. 14; *Inbā'*, 120, l. 1; *Rawḍ*, f. 246, l. 17; *Badā'i'* 3, 37, l. 16: controller of minority taxes (*nāẓir al-jawālī*): Shihāb al-Dīn Aḥmad ibn Kātib Jakam, brother of the nāẓir al-jaysh, replaced eighteen months later by his rival, Zayn al-Dīn Abū Bakr ibn 'Abd al-Bāsiṭ. The sources are silent on the supervisor of charitable trusts (*nāẓir al-awqāf*) until 889/1484.

78 *Ḍaw'* 11, 88, no. 233; *'Uqūd*, f. 234, l. 18; *Badā'i'* 3, 255, l. 1.

closer access to the autocrat than he, who often served as his sultan's moral conscience. There can be no doubt of Qāytbāy's admiration for Ibn Muzhir. Confirmed in his office right after Qāytbāy's accession, Ibn Muzhir presided over the sultan's civilian cabinet as an incorruptible grey eminence, in stark contrast with most minions placed in charge of the fiscal ministries. Never accused of any improper act during his tenure, Ibn Muzhir interacted closely with countless officials who were. He intervened on behalf of several more than once, his aid suggesting his familiarity with the ad hoc system of embezzlement that undergirded the state's finances.[79] But Ibn Muzhir himself was untainted, his reputation without blemish. Qāytbāy welcomed him into his personal circle of companions, the sole civilian to rub shoulders with Yashbak min Mahdī or Azbak min Ṭuṭukh as a peer with no fear of reprisal.[80] He eventually became the only 'ālim who could personally dissuade Qāytbāy from implementing a policy the monarch considered useful, and thus commanded a degree of authority unique for a member of his class.

Ibn Muzhir became the leading representative of a host of prominent jurist-scholars whom Qāytbāy cultivated as an aristocracy of literati that dominated Cairo's cultural life. These individuals collectively countered the influence of Qāytbāy's senior military colleagues. They jealously maintained their prerogative of judicial and scholarly autonomy

[79] For example, the case of Sharaf al-Dīn al-Fayyūmī, a monster of corruption whom Ibn Muzhir staunchly defended despite his crimes of embezzlement. A loyal client of the chancellor, al-Fayyūmī was arrested on the tenth of Ramaḍān 876/21 February 1472 and flogged to compel his divulgence of hidden assets. Ibn Muzhir acknowledged al-Fayyūmī's guilt with reluctance. Apparently, al-Fayyūmī performed services his patron avoided because of his status. See *Inbā'*, 407, l. 15.

[80] Examples of Qāytbāy's respect for Ibn Muzhir: *Inbā'*, 45, l. 18: sultan hosted by chancellor at Birkat al-Ḥabsh; ibid., 208, l. 7: sultan attends Ibn Muzhir while latter is ill; ibid., 287, l. 19: sultan visits Ibn Muzhir's home, unprecedented for civilian; *Badā'i'* 3, 93, l. 1: sultan blesses chancellor, invoking God's baraka for him as treasure of the realm. His obituary: *'Uqūd*, f. 234, l. 18; *Badā'i'* 3, 255, l. 1: eminent poets compose eulogies.

in the face of repeated efforts by militarists to encroach upon it. Qāytbāy made its preservation a prime objective of his career, thereby ensuring a high level of personal rapport with the 'ulamā'. Such a tie goes far to explain not only the widespread esteem for Qāytbāy among them, but his capacity to extract money in dire straits as well. A certain degree of resignation on the part of revenue producers in such situations to the demands of so august a ruler may elucidate the enormous sums Qāytbāy could tap—in comparison with Qānṣūh al-Ghawrī whose methods were more draconian.[81] Ibn Taghrī-Birdī, commenting on events of 872, mused over a year of unprecedented turmoil.[82] Not since Timur Lenk invaded Syria in 803/1401 had the Mamlūk state endured such tribulation, and all of it generated from within. Four sultans had reigned during the year, and many observers had despaired of any prospect for restored stability. Yet in less than six months, Qāytbāy had made remarkable progress not only in building a reliable bureaucracy but in renewing public confidence as well. The sultan could turn his attention to foreign issues with his house in order.

The Rebellion of Shāh Sūwār: Provincial Insurrection

Issues abroad were pressing, and Qāytbāy was soon obliged to deal with them. The most trying of Qāytbāy's foreign opponents, Shāh Sūwār ibn Dhū'l-Qādr, had deposed his brother and renounced his ties of vassalage to the Egyptian sultanate. Shāh Sūwār belonged to a Turkmān dynasty that had entrenched itself in the region of Little Armenia (Ilbistīn) in far

[81] Qāytbāy's capacity to raise these sums is all the more remarkable, if the economy is considered. Prices on grains, foodstuffs, and commodities inflated throughout 872 and 873.

[82] *Ḥawādith* 4, 651, l. 16.

eastern Anatolia during the mid-eighth/fourteenth century.[83] Extending their rule over a strategically important buffer between the northern march of the Mamlūk Empire, the beylik of Qaramān, and the Ottoman sultanate to the west, the Dhū'l-Qādrids played on their neighbors' rivalries for their own advantage. Through most of their history to 872 they nominally accepted Mamlūk suzerainty, but were always poised to take advantage of any succession crisis to reassert their autonomy. When Shāh Sūwār drove his more compliant brother, Shāh Budāq, into exile, he revoked his sibling's allegiance to Sultan Khushqadam. The Egyptian monarch was planning an expedition to crush this insolent vassal when he expired.[84] After Qāytbāy had quelled the threats against his accession, he resurrected his predecessor's aborted campaign. He exploited the urgency of this provincial revolt to rally troops from rival factions behind a common cause, and ordered preliminary reviews of squadrons within two weeks of his enthronement.[85]

An expedition set out from Cairo on Monday the twelfth of Sha'bān/7 March. In command was the atābak, Jānibak Qulaqsīz, who had reluctantly accepted responsibility for this venture coming so soon after his appointment. He may have suspected the sultan begrudged his ambition in view of his prominent role in the coup and was seeking to get him out of the way.[86] The host reached Aleppo without incident some two months later and drove Shāh Sūwār's supporters from the city of 'Ayntāb soon thereafter.[87] But

83 J. Mordtmann and L. Menage, "Dhū'l-Ḳādr," *EI*² 2, 239.

84 *'Uqūd*, f. 223b, l. 7.

85 *Ḥawādith* 4, 619, l. 24; *Rawḍ*, f. 175b, l. 16; *Badā'i'* 3, 7, l. 4. On troop review: *Ḥawādith* 4, 621, l. 11, 15; *Rawḍ*, f. 177, l. 30. On expedition bonus: *Badā'i'* 3, 8, l. 18.

86 On departure of first expedition: *Ḥawādith* 4, 635, l. 8; *Rawḍ*, f. 178b, l. 29; *Badā'i'* 3, 9, l. 18. On extra bonus to commanders sent secretly to al-Raydānīya: *Rawḍ*, f. 179, l. 22.

87 On arrival at Aleppo: *Rawḍ*, f. 180b, l. 27. On reoccupation of 'Ayntāb: *Ḥawādith* 4, 629, l. 21; 630, l. 10; *Rawḍ*, f. 181, l. 24.

the governor of Damascus, Azbak min Ṭuṭukh, who would soon replace Jānibak, dispatched a missive to Cairo warning that the resistance at 'Ayntāb had been fierce and victory had been compromised by pleas for aid from the bey of Qaramān, whom the Ottomans were harassing in collusion with Sūwār. The sultan should not anticipate a clean sweep of the region.[88]

The nā'ib's warnings proved disturbingly accurate. For several weeks no further reports reached Cairo. Then, on the twenty-third of Dhū'l-Qa'da/14 June, an amīr from Damascus arrived with a message of disaster. Shāh Sūwār had reoccupied 'Ayntāb, then lured the Egyptian army into ambush after waylaying its scouts—a tactic he would employ again. Although the numerically superior Mamlūk force verged on triumph three times, the Dhū'l-Qādrids turned the tide on the fourth engagement, inflicting a crushing defeat. Jānibak was only the most prominent of the officers captured and held for ransom. Several amīrs were executed by Sūwār personally when they offered insults to his face. All baggage, equipment and horses were seized as booty. Azbak led the tattered remnants of the army back to Aleppo, where he faced the dismal duty of reporting his escape and explaining the rout.[89]

Upon receiving this report, Qāytbāy and the entire court were paralyzed by shock. An upstart chieftain of no international standing had defeated a large expedition sent by the great power of the central Muslim world. Although led by seasoned officers with proven tactical experience, the Egyptian army had been drawn into hostile terrain where it could not break the enemy in one encounter. Ibn Taghrī-Birdī claimed that the sultan feared for his reputation, sullied so soon after his accession. He had lost the services of numerous amīrs who had abetted his rise to the sultanate.[90] Qāytbāy pondered his

88 *Ḥawādith* 4, 630, l. 21; *Rawḍ*, f. 181b, l. 10.

89 On the defeat: *Ḥawādith* 4, 633, l. 9, 21; *Rawḍ*, f. 182, l. 3, 15; *Badā'i'* 3, 12, l. 8; 13, l. 12.

90 *Ḥawādith* 4, 634, l. 14.

response for a week before he received a second report from Azbak in Aleppo, who warned him against tarrying. All of Aleppo Province lay open to invasion. Its garrison, now seriously undermanned, could not possibly hold off Sūwār should he choose to advance south. The sultan's dominions were threatened; a rigorous counterattack was necessary.[91] Galvanized by Azbak's missive, Qāytbāy called upon all ranks of the military to meet the challenge with courage and resolve. A defiant posture, but the sultan was profoundly shaken by the defeat and uncertain how to finance a second expedition so soon after the first. The dawādār Yashbak offered to pay bonus money for the commanding officers out of his own purse, and convened civil notables to extract the soldiers' salaries.[92] Hasty preparations for a second campaign were complicated by the arrival of deputies returning to Cairo bound by oaths sworn to Sūwār that they would collect ransoms pledged him by the captured officers. Jānibak alone had promised thirty-four thousand dīnārs. One of the amīrs, Yashbak Qamar, brought with him a detailed report of the battle that dismayed the sultan with its revelations of incompetence and defective intelligence gathering. The Egyptian army had ridden into ambush "as if setting out for a hunt,"[93] while Sūwār had planned meticulously, believing that his only chance for victory lay in stealth. Qāytbāy admonished the commanders of the second contingent to deal with Sūwār as if he were their equal.

As the dawādār and other fiscal agents scraped together the money to fund a second expedition, Qāytbāy considered taking the field himself. Ibn Taghrī-Birdī advised him against such a drastic step, since by so doing he would seem to make Sūwār his equal.[94] Qāytbāy's military aides agreed; the risk to the sultan's person was too great and the realm could

91 *Ḥawādith* 4, 641, l. 6.
92 *Rawḍ*, f. 185, l. 17; *Badā'i'* 3, 15, l. 18.
93 *Ḥawādith* 4, 646, l. 10.
94 *Ḥawādith* 4, 679, l. 7; *Inbā'*, 18, l. 4.

not suffer another succession crisis. Qāytbāy concurred and decided to dispatch two separate contingents. The first would set out as soon as feasible to show the sultanate's readiness to check Sūwār's marauding. It would number only five hundred Mamlūks. But because of alarm among the troops over the defeat, Qāytbāy had to call several reviews before he could muster enough participants.[95] So devastating were the first expedition's losses that the sultan summoned Mamlūks who had served former monarchs and were now retired. Many no longer retained their arms or horses and had to expropriate weapons and mounts. Such ad hoc preparations gave the populace little encouragement. They observed the reviews with misgivings, wondering whether the funds squeezed from them would serve any positive purpose.

In the midst of these harrowing events, the sultan received even more disturbing news. A proclamation sent by Sūwār to the inhabitants (*ra'īya*) of Syria had been intercepted in Aleppo and forwarded to Cairo.[96] Even Sūwār's salutation exuded audacity since he dared use titles reserved for kings. This rebel clearly posed as the sultan's peer, who now challenged his authority over Syria. Sūwār addressed himself to "merchants, caravaneers, cultivators, plowmen, buyers, and sellers in the realms of Damascus, Aleppo, and Ṭarābulus who desire peace and security." Those wishing to enhance their own welfare would be well advised to shift their allegiance to the lord of Ilbistīn, who offered both. Those so willing would receive the prince's blessing and protection for themselves and all their property. Prior to the defeat, Qāytbāy and his colleagues would have dismissed such a missive as the ravings of a lunatic. But now they interpreted it as a menace and pressed the troops to quicken their preparations. Even so, the first contingent could not set out before the sixth of Rabī' II 873/24 October 1468. The officer in

95 *Ḥawādith* 4, 682, l. 4; *Inbā'*, 22, l. 13; 23, l. 3; 26, l. 3; *Rawḍ*, f. 205b, l. 1; *Badā'i'* 3, 21, l. 11.

96 *Ḥawādith* 4, 686, l. 7; *Inbā'*, 30, l. 7; *Rawḍ*, f. 207, l. 19.

charge, Azdamur al-Ibrāhīmī, proceeded directly to Siryāqūs without the customary rendezvous at al-Raydānīya.[97] Leading a small relief force, he could move rapidly toward Aleppo. The urgency of his mission became starkly apparent with the arrival of reports spelling out yet another disaster. Sūwār had captured the fortress of Darandā at the headwaters of the Euphrates,[98] executed its governor, and seized his assets. Even more unsettling was the complicity of its populace, who had betrayed the sultan's lieutenant in return for Sūwār's promises of autonomy. Less than a year from Qāytbāy's accession, Mamlūk authority over southeastern Anatolia was unraveling.

Qāytbāy spent the following two months selecting troops for the large expedition. Since he intended it to be of a size sufficient to crush Sūwār once and for all, he had to deal sternly with his soldiers' demands for inordinate bonuses.[99] Qāytbāy acted as an unyielding war leader, heeding no plea of indisposition at home and accepting no offer of truce from abroad. When Sūwār dared send an emissary requesting a parley, Qāytbāy refused to receive him, proclaiming that no upstart rebel warranted a king's hospitality.[100] Qāytbāy ordered all the Sulṭānī Mamlūks to present themselves, their mounts, and their weapons for inspection on pain of court martial and deprival of iqṭā'. He would tolerate no relief from duty unless a fief-holder provided a substitute or the sum of one hundred dīnārs. Non-landed stipendiaries were permitted to buy their way out for twenty dīnārs. Senior officers, Qāytbāy's collaborators, were summoned to these councils and compelled to take charge of a cavalry unit or risk demotion. The recently appointed council officer, Qurqumās al-Julb, confronted the sultan over his own designation on the grounds that his assistance in Qāytbāy's succession should

97 *Ḥawādith* 4, 687, l. 12; *Inbā'*, 31, l. 10; *Rawḍ*, f. 208b, l. 8.
98 *Ḥawādith* 4, 695, l. 6; *Inbā'*, 44, l. 1; *Rawḍ*, f. 211b, l. 28.
99 *Ḥawādith* 4, 696, l. 19; *Inbā'*, 46, l. 13; *Rawḍ*, f. 212b, l. 8.
100 *Ḥawādith* 4, 697, l. 5; *Inbā'*, 47, l. 3; *Rawḍ*, f. 212b, l. 21.

waive expeditionary service.[101] The two engaged in a heated argument that terminated abruptly when Qurqumās stormed out of the Citadel, closeted himself in his own palace, and intimated revolt. Qāytbāy did not relent and ignored any rumor of insurrection. He recalled his new atābak, Azbak, from a Delta inspection tour to raise emergency revenues and ordered him to lead the expedition. Insulted by his sovereign's lack of grace in pressing him prior to any bonus payment, Azbak refused. Ever correct, he threw no tantrum but retired to his house to await the sultan's decision.[102] As rumors of impending rebellion mounted, Azbak knew that Qāytbāy would seek a rapprochment since his skills as a mediator were too valuable to jeopardize by quarreling over an emolument. Eventually, Qāytbāy dispatched the historian Ibn Taghrī-Birdī to "reason" with Azbak.[103] The sultan agreed to pay Azbak his bonus (which presumably the latter's rival, Yashbak, would have to supply), and Azbak magnanimously accepted command. Qurqumās was also reconciled after similar negotiations.

Since the sultan hoped to see the expedition off by early Sha'bān 873/February 1469, preparations were stepped up. Reports reached Cairo of famine and dissension within Sūwār's army, and Qāytbāy hoped to profit from his enemy's discomfiture. During the month of Rajab/January–February, a fiscal agent was sent off to Syria with a purse of one hundred thousand dīnārs to hire archers, footsoldiers, and Turkmān scouts who would escort the main cavalry units into Anatolia.[104] Distribution of baggage, mounts, and draft animals proceeded at such a rushed pace that ominous incidents occurred. On the twenty-fourth of Rajab/17 February,

101 *Rawḍ*, f. 214, l. 12; *Badā'i'* 3, 27, l. 9.

102 *Ḥawādith* 4, 699, l. 3; *Inbā'*, 50, l. 16; *Rawḍ*, f. 214b, l. 9.

103 *Ḥawādith* 4, 702, l. 3; *Rawḍ*, f. 216b, l. 30. Ibn Taghrī-Birdī acted as a senior counselor, a worthy member of the Mamlūk elite, when he reminded Azbak of duty, honor, and possibly his own future.

104 *Inbā'*, 54, l. 7; 55, l. 8; *Rawḍ*, ff. 215b, l. 17; 216, l. 4; *Ḥawādith* 4, 701, l. 21.

when a herd of camels was driven into the Rumayla Square for division among the Sulṭānī Mamlūks, the beasts panicked, stampeded wildly, and jammed into one of the entry gates.[105] More than two hundred of the costly animals died, an evil portent in the eyes of the populace, who worried over the regime's capacity to score a victory after such incompetence. Nonetheless, the expedition was ready to depart by the first week of Sha'bān, and the sultan witnessed its formal procession out of Cairo toward al-Raydānīya on the ninth.[106] Qāytbāy scheduled a private strategy meeting with Azbak at the bivouac before he set out for Syria.

The expedition made rapid progress for its size, reaching Aleppo within the month and forging ahead into Sūwār's territory. Sūwār fell back before this intimidating force and allowed it to fire fields and plunder local villages without resistance. His behavior heartened Azbak and Qurqumās, who hoped to force the rebel into a stand. This he did in early Dhū'l-Qa'da, to his regret. The Egyptian army routed Sūwār's cavalry and captured his brother Mughulbāy, who died soon after from his wounds.[107] His head was sent back to Cairo for public display at the Bāb Zuwayla. Azbak and Qurqumās gave Sūwār no respite but hounded him as he fled toward the Ottoman frontier. Qāytbāy received reports of these developments with delight and ordered the city decorated for a victory celebration. But his hopes were dashed once again. On the twenty-third of Dhū'l-Ḥijja/4 July, a dromedary courier arrived with news of an extraordinary setback.[108] Sūwār had retreated into a narrow gorge riddled with defiles and culs-de-sac. When the Egyptian army arrived, its officers disagreed over whether to enter in pursuit.

105 *Ḥawādith* 4, 701, l. 11; *Inbā'*, 54, l. 13; *Rawḍ*, f. 215b, l. 21; *Badā'i'* 3, 28, l. 2.

106 *Ḥawādith* 4, 702, l. 22; *Inbā'*, 57, l. 4; *Rawḍ*, f. 218, l. 11; *Badā'i'* 3, 29, l. 8.

107 *Inbā'*, 70, l. 4; *Rawḍ*, f. 221b, l. 8; *Badā'i'* 3, 32, l. 21

108 *Ḥawādith* 4, 714, l. 13; *Inbā'*, 77, l. 9; *Rawḍ*, f. 223b, l. 28; *'Uqūd*, f. 224b, l. 4; *Badā'i'* 3, 34, l. 16.

Given their fatigue, several amīrs urged a return to Aleppo, while Qurqumās admonished the army to seize this chance of bringing Sūwār to bay and crushing his rebellion decisively. Azbak reluctantly sided with his recommendation. But since discord persisted, the army divided; one contingent headed back to Aleppo, the other under Qurqumās and Azbak entered the gorge. Sūwār's troops, familiar with the terrain, were lying in wait. They rolled boulders down on the Egyptians, hamstrung camels to prevent their escape, then cut the troops down as they plunged into the defiles. Qurqumās died fighting, but Azbak escaped and overtook the retreating wing.[109] Critically weakened, the Egyptian host was harried as it withdrew and arrived in Aleppo severely mauled. Once they entered the city, discipline broke down completely. Encountering derision from the populace, both officers and soldiers began to depart for Cairo furtively without the sultan's permission. When the latter's emissary arrived in Aleppo with funds to pay four months of their salary, he was reviled

109 Azbak dispatched a letter to Yashbak upon his return to Aleppo, which al-Ṣayrafī claimed to have seen. Its contents, as he reports them, merit recounting since Azbak dodged the issue of responsibility for the debacle, and made no mention of Qurqumās when the rash decision was taken. "We had arrived at the town of Mar'ash, where victory was granted us against the accursed enemy. We followed his tracks, razed his fortress (*qaṣr*), burned his villages, chopped down trees, and plundered his stores we found in underground granaries. We discovered that the enemy had constructed narrow passageways he blocked with stones. I dismounted myself to carry them off on my back. We occupied several fortresses (*qilā'*), and appointed governors over them. We reinstalled the son of Dhū'l-Qādr [Budāq] in Sūwār's place. This occurred after I proceeded to the mountain named al-Karakī. Because of hunger, deprivation, and short supplies, we turned back. The sultan had already requested his royal army to return. They set out from Darb Sīs [a fort in Armenia]. I had admonished the army not to proceed via the narrow gulch, but they did not agree with me. When we reached al-Durband, the Turkmān accompanying Sūwār accosted us. An uncounted number of them were killed. But the affair ended [badly] when they slashed the tendons of camels and mules, thus preventing any Mamlūk from egress. Upon our return, we proclaimed the son of Dhū'l-Qādr ruler of the enemy's territory. We placed him under the supervision of Aleppo's governor. He resides there now, where desolation and famine reign." *Inbā'*, 120, l. 5.

and pelted with stones as he remonstrated with the troopers and ordered them to stand fast. Victory thus eluded Qāytbāy a second time. Although Sūwār suffered critical losses, he had not been captured. The sultan's reputation as commander in chief was now tarnished throughout the central Islamic lands.

The new year began with the disquieting prospect of outfitting yet another campaign. But in the midst of these dismal preparations, the sultan's staff received refreshing news. His governor of Malaṭya had driven off Sūwār's army from the town and defeated him in the field.[110] Qāytbāy gratefully dispatched five thousand dīnārs to this nā'ib, admonishing him to keep up the pressure on Sūwār until a new expedition left Cairo. The capital itself was rife with rumors ranging from rebellion smoldering within Sūwār's ranks to his accidental death by a stray arrow.[111] Although none were proved, a reliable message from Azbak's own hand arrived from Aleppo with the welcome report that Ibn Ramaḍān, chieftain of Sūwār's Turkmān rivals, had stormed the fortress of Sīs and wrested it from the Dhū'l-Qādrids.[112] The tide seemed finally to be turning in Qāytbāy's favor.

Sūwār now weighed the liabilities of confronting Qāytbāy's dogged resolve. He waived the ransom he had imposed on the captured officers—withheld by Qāytbāy as a show of contempt—and released them in Jumādā I/November–December, on condition that they approach their master about the possibility of a truce. Jānibak Qulaqsīz journeyed back from Aleppo, while Azbak remained behind with remnants of the third expedition. Qāytbāy received his former atābak with full honors, but demoted him to the post of arms minister (*amīr silāḥ*).[113] Although speculation fluttered briefly over Jānibak's reaction to his lower status, he accepted

110 *Inbā'*, 129, l. 14; 135, l. 6; *Rawḍ*, f. 247, l. 26; *Badā'i'* 3, 38, l. 13.
111 *Inbā'*, 138, l. 11; *Rawḍ*, f. 247b, l. 6.
112 *Inbā'*, 146, l. 8; 150, l. 6; *Rawḍ*, f. 248, l. 18; *Badā'i'* 3, 41, l. 4.
113 *Inbā'*, 151, l. 3; 159, l. 10; *Rawḍ*, ff. 248, l. 31; 249, l. 7, 23–29; *Badā'i'* 3, 41, l. 11.

his reduced position without protest. The sultan flatly rejected Sūwār's offer of a truce, but did not close the door on any future proposal. He sent word to Aleppo that Azbak should return, with no worry over responsibility for the ambush. Azbak arrived on the fifth of Ramaḍān/9 March and crossed the city in formal procession. In tow were Sūwār's brothers Budāq, who renewed his fealty as the sultan's vassal, and Yaḥyā Kāwir, who received a jail sentence for professing loyalty to the rebel.[114] Qāytbāy extended a hero's welcome to his trusted lieutenant, and no mention was made of his dubious performance. The sultan gave thanks to the All High for the atābak's safe return, emphasizing his inestimable service.

Some three weeks later, an emissary from Sūwār ascended to the Citadel.[115] Qāytbāy did not snub him this time, but listened carefully to his master's terms. Considering how precarious Sūwār's domestic situation had become, these were startlingly presumptuous. The sultan was to bestow on Sūwār amīrship over all Turkmān in southeastern Anatolia. He was also to grant his vassal the rank of commander of one thousand in Aleppo Province. In return, Sūwār pledged to restore 'Aynṭāb to the sultan's governor. Qāytbāy rejected the terms, but engaged the emissary in lengthy discussions over his master's intentions. The latter departed without a robe of honor or any gifts to be conveyed back to Ilbistīn.

Qāytbāy sent a relief contingent off to Aleppo in Muḥarram of 875/June–July 1470 to reinforce its garrison.[116] He had quarreled with its commander, Īnāl al-Ashqar, who had presumptuously demanded the viceroyship of Damascus as a reward for his service. Qāytbāy brusquely informed him that the compensation he had requested outweighed his merits and, in any case, such a favor had best await the outcome of his engagement with the enemy. Despite his domestic problems, Sūwār had managed to counter his Turkmān rival,

114 *Inbā'*, 162, l. 10; *Rawḍ*, f. 250, l. 30; *Badā'i'* 3, 43, l. 22.
115 *Inbā'*, 163, l. 13; *Rawḍ*, f. 250b, l. 19; *Badā'i'* 3, 44, l. 10.
116 *Inbā'*, 192, l. 7, 17; 199, l. 6, 15; *Badā'i'* 3, 52, l. 6.

Ibn Ramaḍān, and was reported to be advancing toward Aleppo. Qāytbāy refused to react with alarm, but spent the next several months planning the next expedition—which he placed under his redoubtable adjutant, Yashbak. The sultan allowed his khushdāsh a free hand in extorting funds and equipment from the populace of Cairo. Al-Ṣayrafī claims that Yashbak spent a thousand dīnārs per day on his own baggage and Mamlūk division (*ṭulb*), which numbered four hundred men.[117] Yashbak was ready to ride by the fourth of Shawwāl/26 March, and staged a lavish procession of departure in order to impress both the locals and foreign ambassadors.[118] He took with him a huge treasury and supply of ceremonial robes to reward agents in Syria and Anatolia. The various units convened at al-Raydānīya on the tenth.[119] Some two thousand elite cavalrymen were poised to depart. Qāytbāy spent the night conferring with the bāsh al-ʿaskar (commander of the army) and his subordinates over past mistakes. When Yashbak bade his liege lord and comrade farewell at dawn the following day, he radiated such confidence that his men cheered him as the Almighty's sword on Earth.

Yashbak did not press his troops to hasten toward Aleppo, but proceeded at leisure during the first two months of 875/May–June. His host thus reached the war zone in prime condition. Īnāl al-Ashqar, sent previously to ensure the city's

117 *Inbāʾ*, 260, l. 3.

118 *Inbāʾ*, 268, l. 22. Al-Ṣayrafī provides insights to the symbolism surrounding the departure of an expedition. The dawadar's tent preceded him to al-Raydānīya, where he would bivouac before setting out for Palestine. Surrounding the tent were Yashbak's mobile magazines and stables to house the two hundred horses and one hundred dromedaries with their golden trappings that made up his personal train. A separate shrine tent sheltered sacred Korans, holy relics, and Ṣūfī prayer leaders taken to bless the venture. Al-Ṣayrafī claimed that the uniforms worn by Yashbak's Mamlūks outshone those of his sovereign's purchased Mamlūks. Yashbak seemed to embody the imperial office itself as he rode forth from the city. Yet none suspected him of disloyalty to the sultan, who wholeheartedly endorsed the spectacle.

119 *Inbāʾ*, 271, l. ; 272, l. 16; *Badāʾiʿ* 3, 59, l. 9.

safety, set out with the dawādār for Ilbistīn. The two worked well together on campaign, Īnāl eagerly leading forays to flush Sūwār out of hiding while Yashbak saved the main contingent for siege operations and the big confrontation when it should occur. The strategy worked brilliantly. During the early months of 876/July–August, Qāytbāy and his two closest advisers remaining in Cairo, Azbak the marshal and Ibn Muzhir the chancellor, received a series of reports describing Sūwār's successive defeats and the liberation of all the fortresses he had seized.[120] There were setbacks. Sūwār captured the governor of Malaṭya while the latter was pursuing him after a raid.[121] For his previous humiliation, Sūwār exacted a terrible vengeance on Qāytbāy's faithful defender of his northern march. He impaled the governor on a tree and left him suspended there until he expired. This disheartening event could not dampen the populace's rejoicing at the news of Yashbak's successes as these missives arrived in the capital. Qāytbāy would order Ibn Muzhir to read them to him in private before having them announced to the troops and masses. Al-Ṣayrafī recounted, with some dismay, that wild celebrations erupted spontaneously in the city, the people indulging in drunken orgies, women casting aside their veils, and couples engaging in illicit pleasures with no regard for decorum.[122]

The decisive battle occurred at the end of Jumādā I/November 1471. Unable to sustain the allegiance of his troops if he continued dodging his enemy, Sūwār decided to confront Yashbak at the Jayḥūn River.[123] The dāwadār sent a detailed description of the engagement in which he frankly acknowledged Sūwār's tactical skills. Sūwār hurled insults across the

120 On the fall of 'Ayntāb: *Inbā'*, 324, l. 20; *Badā'i'* 3, 62, l. 16; on Ṭarsūs and Adana: *Inbā'*, 328, l. 5; *Badā'i'* 3, 63, l. 4; on Sīs (recaptured from Ibn Ramaḍān the preceding year): *Inbā'*, 332, l. 3.

121 *Inbā'*, 323, l. 11; *Badā'i'* 3, 62, l. 6.

122 *Inbā'*, 319, l. 8.

123 *Inbā'*, 362, l. 9; 367, l. 1; *Badā'i'* 3, 65, l. 20.

stream, hoping to lure hot-blooded officers across. Several amīrs almost succumbed to the ruse, but Yashbak maintained iron discipline over his host. He deployed them in units under orders to divide Sūwār's fractious Turkmān squadrons, which his scouts had reported as squabbling and impoverished. Several of Sūwār's bands turned against him and came over to the dawādār. Sūwār was himself partially incapacitated by a leg fractured in a hunting accident the preceding month. When he beheld the rout of his army, Sūwār sought refuge in the fortress of Zamanṭū with his family. But his wife, who had remained in the baggage train, was separated and could not catch up before Yashbak overtook her.[124]

A stalemate ensued over the next several months. Desperate as his circumstances appeared, Sūwār held out for a negotiated settlement. His audacity amazed even such a hardened warrior as Yashbak, who informed his sovereign that Sūwār offered surrender only if he were granted a full pardon, restored to his vassal status, and retained in his ancestral territories.[125] Yashbak dismissed these demands and dispatched requests home for more money to shore up his troops' morale. Although Sūwār finally gave up the keys to the citadel at Darandā, the choicest prize of his rebellion, Yashbak demanded his submission to the sultan's justice. The end finally came by deceit. Worrying over mounting impatience among his officers, Yashbak managed to lure Sūwār out with a pledge of safe-conduct. One of Sūwār's brothers, who had been discussing a compromise, conveyed the dawādār's sworn promise to his sibling.[126] Sūwār hesitated a full month before he accepted his enemy's word of honor. When he came down, however, he was separated from his bodyguard and taken prisoner. Several of Yashbak's colleagues who had participated in the delicate bargaining reacted with outrage over their sullied virtue. Ever

124 *Inbā'*, 377, l. 7.
125 *Inbā'*, 419, l. 1; *Badā'i'* 3, 69, l. 19.
126 *Inbā'*, 439, l. 20; *Badā'i'* 3, 72, l. 23.

the pragmatist, Yashbak dismissed their denunciations with a retort that Sūwār had damned himself when he betrayed his sultan. He could expect nothing more than a traitor's fate.

During Ṣafar and Rabīʿ I of 877/July–August 1473, Yashbak proceeded back to Egypt with his prisoner. Elaborate preparations were ordered for the miscreant's trial.[127] A special committee of jurists was appointed to draft fatwās condemning Sūwār for his crimes against the integrity of the Dār al-Islām. Yashbak arrived at al-Raydānīya on the seventeenth of Rabīʿ I/22 August, where he received the deputy majordomo, several other amīrs, and the four chief justices prior to entering the city. The next day, Yashbak traversed Cairo and ascended to the Citadel.[128] Those officers who still resented his ruse refused to ride in the procession, but Yashbak had been granted a savior's triumph by his khushdāsh. Sūwār preceded his captor, clad in a simple black frock, shackled with an iron collar, and mounted on a horse. Some twenty of his relatives were paraded behind in the prefect's custody, all dressed in white. Qāytbāy had ordered the streets magnificently decorated with silk banners. Male and female cantors were stationed along the Bayn al-Qaṣrayn and Darb al-Aḥmar from the Bāb al-Naṣr to the Rumayla Square, lauding the dawādār's God-given victory. Cymbalists, drummers, and fifers performed at the various stages of steps leading up to the Palace.

The sultan awaited his comrade and the prisoner in the Audience Hall. When Yashbak presented Sūwār, Qāytbāy demanded no prostration but simply rebuked him while he stood. Sūwār remained silent, impressing the assembled court with his stoic resignation. After the fatwās condemning him were read out, he was conveyed to the Bāb Zuwayla. Sūwār now donned a simple white gown, while his brothers were

127 *ʿUqūd*, f. 225, l. 2; *Badāʾiʿ* 3, 75, l. 8, 22.
128 *Badāʾiʿ* 3, 76, l. 6.

stripped nude and seated backwards on camels. As they proceeded down the street, couriers shouted, "Thus are punished those who plot against the sultan!" The procession reached the southern gate, where hooks were strung on chains for the gibbeting of Sūwār and his siblings. None of the rebels requested recitation of the Fātiḥa or any other Koranic verses for salvation of their souls. Yet one of Sūwār's brothers, Salmān, so moved the throng with his youth and fine looks that they pleaded with the dawādār for clemency. Yashbak relented, desiring to show himself merciful, and commuted Salmān's sentence to incarceration. All the remaining prisoners were led to the Lake of Dogs where they were drawn and quartered. Sūwār and his brothers were left hanging from the Bāb Zuwayla in public view for a day and a night before they were taken down and washed for burial.

Thus was Qāytbāy delivered of his redoubtable foe. Ibn Iyās reflected that the affair, lasting five years, had cost the sultan dear in men and money. His prestige had been besmirched before fellow rulers, and even peasants dared cast insults against their overlords because of Sūwār's victories. Ibn Iyās, indeed, expressed admiration for Sūwār's ability and courage in the face of adversity. He met his end with pride, having gained unprecedented success against the sultanate of Egypt. Qāytbāy had paid a fabulous treasure to subdue this man. The anonymous author of the *Ta'rīkh Qāytbāy*, tallying up the arduous campaigns, found their costs to total more than a million dīnārs, exclusive of ancillary expenses.[129] But Qāytbāy had never faltered from his determination to maintain the cohesion of his realm. He would spare no expense or military effort to defeat any opponent who challenged his authority. The lesson was not lost on his neighbors. For more than a decade, no foreign enemy contested Mamlūk suzerainty in southwest Asia.

129 *Ta'rīkh Qāytbāy*, f. 6.

The Medial Years: Facade of Grandeur

While savoring his triumph, Qāytbāy had to replenish the loss of so many trusted colleagues. He magnanimously welcomed back several officers whom he or his adjutants had exiled during his consolidation in the early 870s.[130] But the sultan had no intention of permitting any factions to conceal their conspiracies against him in the aura of good feelings following Sūwār's execution. Conferring with Yashbak, Qāytbāy began systematically whittling down the last significant group of officers whose loyalties were bound to a previous autocrat: the Īnālīya. Despite their crucial support of his coup and their bravery during the Sūwār episode, Qāytbāy and Yashbak wished to diffuse every remnant of the previous military order, leaving the sultan's own purchased Mamlūks with a monopoly over all ranks of the ruling elite. Following Yashbak's directives, Qāytbāy allowed his wrath to fall on several respected members of the Īnālīya, concocting a number of dubious charges. Sultan and khushdāsh moved cautiously to avoid antagonizing the whole faction with blatantly false accusations at once, since such a ploy would invite a full-scale revolt. But over the next several years, Qāytbāy prosecuted enough charges of treachery to rid himself of every Īnālī officer who posed a potential threat.[131] Some were made objects of humiliation. In Rajab of 879/November–December 1474, the sultan arrested one Shādbak Abāza al-Īnālī on

130 For example, the former atābak Jurbāsh Kurt, who had been imprisoned in Damietta, and the former dawādār Yashbak Faqīh al-Mu'ayyad . The sultan personally received both officers from the previous reign (Khushqadam's), extended full pardons, and allowed them to retire with all their assets restored. *Badā'i'* 3, 69, l. 3, 71, l. 10.

131 *Badā'i'* 3, 99, l. 5; 100, l. 17; 144, l. 17; 152, l. 8; 188, l. 5.

charges of plotting against the dawādār. He ordered the amīr clad in a servant's smock and put him on the auction block in the Khān al-Khalīlī as a common slave. Because his original deed of ownership was traced back to Sultan Jaqmaq's son al-Manṣūr, Qāytbāy refused to remit whatever price Shādbak might draw, but sent the bill to al-Manṣūr, who had to redeem his former Mamlūk. Not even the atābak Azbak could persuade the sultan to relent from such disgraceful behavior to a member of his own caste. But upon Shādbak's arrival in Damietta, where al-Manṣūr lived in retirement, the prince manumitted him—an act of clemency a powerless figurehead could afford. Shādbak was allowed to live as an out-of-service amīr in Damascus. Qāytbāy thus cleverly balanced benevolence against severity to deter those who might challenge his prerogatives.

These draconian measures, necessary as they might be, were overshadowed by the sultan's majesty and piety. His status as the greatest Muslim monarch of Sunnī Islam might be disputed by the Ottoman ruler, but was not actively contested for more than a decade. Qāytbāy became the paragon of royal serenity. He now made routine his inspection trips and recreational outings that projected his presence vividly before the commons. Even before Sūwār's execution, the sultan's primacy was widely acknowledged by foreign potentates. In Jumādā II of 876/November–December 1471, the sultan of India (*al-Hind*), Ghayth al-Dīn, sent an ambassador requesting formal authorization (*taqlīd*) from the 'Abbāsid Caliph for his assumption of power.[132] The ambassador, on behalf of his master, recognized Qāytbāy as his suzerain, who in turn sanctioned the Caliph's confirmation of Ghayth al-Dīn's accession.

Qāytbāy relished opportunities to escape the Citadel's confines and, being in excellent health, he spent time away on trips ranging from brief pleasure jaunts to extended sojourns.

[132] *Rawḍ*, 362, l. 14; *Badā'i'* 3, 65, l. 16.

He first abandoned the security of his palace, an impregnable fortress, to show his disdain for rumors of revolt.[133] Deliberately travelling with minimal escort, Qāytbāy demonstrated confidence over his subordinates' loyalty. During the uneasy first months after his enthronement, Qāytbāy took a calculated risk, since several of his predecessors had met their deaths at the hands of rivals while on excursion. But as his reputation soared in the aftermath of Sūwār's defeat, he increased the frequency of his outings, clearly enjoying these occasions as an escape from the tensions of office.[134] Yet the threat of rebellion never disappeared. In Ṣafar of 884/April–May 1479, at the height of his powers, Qāytbāy departed for the town of Sunayt after publicly scorning reports of revolt by Īnālī Mamlūks outraged at the exile of one of their most esteemed officers.[135] Apparently, the strategy adopted by Qāytbāy and Yashbak to diminish their influence had not gone unnoticed, but the sultan's tactic served its purpose. No incident erupted in his absence. Nonetheless, prudence marked all of Qāytbāy's actions and placed certain limits on his movements. In Dhū'l-Qa'da of 876/April–May 1472, he canceled an extended trip upon the advice of his marshal, who warned him his absence would, at this particular time, invite local rioting in the capital.[136] The sultan delayed his departure until a more propitious date.

Despite such admonitions, Qāytbāy found enticements of the hunt or sojourn at a belvedere too alluring to forego.

133 *Rawḍ*, f. 214, l. 26. The sultan spent a day banqueting at the Za'farān Canal immediately after his argument with Qurqumās over the latter's obligatory service in the Sūwār expedition. The sultan ignored rumors of revolt, riding back and forth with minimal guard.

134 *Inbā'*, 242, l. 3. Al-Ṣayrafī was enormously impressed with Qāytbāy's courage during recreational outings. He described his private walks while sojourning at the Pyramids in Rajab of 875/December 1470-January 1471 as unparalleled in history: a monarch so serene that he had nothing to fear. Since no assassination attempts were reported, one must assume that al-Ṣayrafī's praise was credible.

135 *Badā'i'* 3, 152, l. 9.

136 *Inbā'*, 429, l. 11.

From 875 to the end of the 880s, when infirmities of age began to creep up on him, the sultan set out from the Citadel for recreation at least once a month. He often accepted an invitation to reside at a colleague's country residence by the Nile shore or overlooking a scenic vista. The dawādār and the atābak vied for the sultan's visits, each attempting to outdo the other's lavish receptions.[137] These affairs culminated in huge banquets involving the roasting of lambs, chickens, and geese by the hundreds and consumption of sweets or fresh fruit by the bushel. The cost of such a soirée might exceed a thousand dīnārs, but no host sought to curb expenses when entertaining his royal guest. The pyramids, banners waving from their summits, were favored as a site for mock battles and troopers parading their festive garb. Gifted singers were engaged to serenade the monarch and his courtiers while they reveled through the evening. Ibn Iyās observed that, when Qāytbāy accepted Azbak's invitation to grace the inaugural ceremonies for his splendid pavilions surrounding the lake he had made, the sultan also sojourned at Yashbak's lodge in al-Maṭarīya. He consistently divided his time equally between these two haughty aides, never playing favorites.

Qāytbāy's longest trips were aimed at widening his knowledge of regional conditions in the provinces or abroad. He inspected every building project he endowed and the state of public works throughout his realm. These tours, although carefully planned, were often undertaken in secrecy with no fanfare of departure in order to avoid restiveness over the monarch's absence. Receptions celebrated only the sultan's return and formal entry into Cairo. The earliest of Qāytbāy's progressions was scheduled for the Fayyūm in Rajab of 875/December 1470. Subsequently, to the year 891/1486, Qāytbāy made several trips to this oasis, the Delta districts, the coastal ports, and the Syrian provinces.[138] Clearly driven

137 *Inbā'*, 212, l. 12; 213, l. 18; *Badā'i'* 3, 53, l. 12; 55, l. 13.

138 *Inbā'*, 241, l. 8; 242, l. 13; *Badā'i'* 3, 405, l. 8 (on the Fayyūm in 875); *Inbā'*, 419, l. 21 (sultan in Awsīm to inspect public works); 473, l. 20 (sultan

by wanderlust, the sultan delighted in observing local customs and harvesting techniques. Ever alert to the fickle loyalties of Bedouin tribes inhabiting the fringes of the Nile valley, Qāytbāy took advantage of these trips to honor powerful shaykhs with symbolic but prestigious titles.[139] Al-Ṣayrafī described the sultan's behavior, which was high spirited throughout his travels. While riding from Būlāq to Awsīm in Shawwāl of 876/March 1472, Qāytbāy was spotted by local peasants who rushed up to welcome him.[140] Waving back his bodyguard, Qāytbāy allowed the villagers to crowd around his horse and clutch at his garments, touching the royal person. None were beaten or driven off as he made his way to the river landing at Sakhtūr. Al-Ṣayrafī remarked that Qāytbāy savored this kind of experience, eagerly cementing personal bonds between himself and the masses, who were so often exploited but otherwise ignored.

Qāytbāy's trips to the Mediterranean ports and Syria required more advance preparation. The sultan's visit to Alexandria in Rabīʿ I of 882/June–July 1477, depicted in detail by Ibn Iyās (see note 138), involved his official entry into the city prior to his examination of the harbor tower and guard chains. Qāytbāy was received by the governor, Qajmās al-Isḥāqī, and the former sultan al-Mu'ayyad Aḥmad

---

inspects new fountain and cistern in al-Qurayn [Delta]); 474 (sultan observes dyke maintenance in Delta); *Badā'iʿ* 3, 108, l. 14 (Rabīʿ II 880/August 1475: sultan plans, then cancels Syrian trip); 111, l. 13 (Jumādā II/October: sultan proceeds to Damietta to see netting of Būr fish); 112, l. 11 (Rajab/November: sultan departs to inspect holy shrines and his charities in Jerusalem); 115, l. 11 (Dhū'l-Qaʿda/February–March: sultan visits the Fayyūm to tour model plantation of amīr noted for agrarian innovation); 130, l. 10 (Rabīʿ I 882/July 1477: sultan visits Alexandria); 134, l. 16 (Jumādā I/August–September: sultan departs for extended trip through Syria, reaches Euphrates). See also: *ʿUqūd*, f. 227b, l. 16; Ibn al-Ḥimṣī, *Ḥawādith*, f. 18b, l. 5; Ibn al-Jīʿān, *Al-qawl al-mustaẓraf fī safar mawlānā al-malik al-Ashraf*, French transl. H. Devonshire, *IFAO Bulletin* 20 (1922) 2–40; *Badā'iʿ* 3, 143, l. 1 (Dhū'l-Qaʿda 882/February 1478: sultan inspects royal horse herds in al-Jīza); 224, l. 13 (Muḥarram 891/January 1486: sultan examines river levees in Sharqīya).

139 *Inbā'*, 405, l. 8.

140 *Inbā'*, 419, l. 21.

ibn Īnāl, who bore himself as "one king welcoming another." Qāytbāy then led a procession through the gates, followed by his troops all heavily armed (to impress resident European merchants who, presumably, would report the sultan's military might to their governments). The atābak, Azbak, carried the royal parasol and bird over his head. The troops rode in tight columns, while some 250 riderless horses bore the royal saddles encrusted with gold, silver, and crystal. The sultan's fifers and trumpeters sounded march cadences as the procession wound its way toward the harbor square. Ibn Iyās recorded a near-disaster during the spectacle. When Frankish merchants cast gold pieces before the sultan's mount, a mob rushed forward to gather them up, almost unseating their sovereign. The commander of the guard wielded his staff liberally to beat them back. Such an incident reveals the proximity of the ruling elite to the commons during public spectacles. Threatened as they might be by their own peers, they gave little thought to tighter security against assassination attempts from other sectors of society.

Upon conclusion of his Alexandria tour, Qāytbāy departed without notice for Ghazza and the Syrian provinces. He was accompanied by only forty of his bodyguards (*khawāṣ*), a few junior officers, and several civil officials, including the kātib al-sirr, Ibn Muzhir, and his assistant, Zayn al-Dīn ibn al-Jīʿān. The latter kept a detailed log of the journey, which was remarkable for its pace and the variety of sites visited.[141] The Syrian chronicler Ibn al-Ḥimṣī noted that Qāytbāy had been informed in advance of several cases of corruption among the judiciary of Damascus. He heard testimony against them before proceeding on to Aleppo.[142] Ibn al-Ḥimṣī was amazed at the sultan's strict discipline over his soldiers during the progression, allowing no spoliation of any village or orchard. Ibn Iyās waxed effusive on the public's

141 See Ibn al-Jīʿān's *Al-qawl al-mustaẓraf* (supra n. 138).
142 Ibn al-Ḥimṣī, *Ḥawādith*, f. 64, l. 1.

acclamation of their ruler when they learned of his adventure at such an advanced age. Several poets composed odes commending Qāytbāy's inquisitiveness and stamina; Ibn Iyās recorded in full verses by Badr al-Dīn al-Zaytūnī, which he deemed the most eloquent.[143] All these excursions, whether for pleasure, linkage, or inspection, reinforced the sultan's image as a fearless lord who took a personal interest in the state of his dominions and his subjects' welfare. Contemporary observers dwelt on them as proof of their monarch's exceptional courage and humaneness.

Noteworthy as these excursions were in historians' eyes, they merely embellished the sultan's stance as supreme legal arbiter over his subjects. Qāytbāy shared a keen interest in judicial proceedings from his early days as an amīr, and as monarch rigorously indulged his penchant for hearing appeals cases or petitions. Several of Qāytbāy's predecessors had taken their appellate (*maẓālim*) duties seriously, whereas others found them tedious and delegated their authority to subordinates. Qāytbāy cherished his legal functions. During the medial years, he would intervene in numerous appeals, whether trivial or weighty, enhancing his reputation as a paragon of justice in a regime riddled with corruption. While strategic motives behind this commitment can be assumed, no objective observer could deny the sincerity of Qāytbāy's convictions. The sultan saw himself as a devout believer, obligated to deliver rulings consonant with principles of Sharī'a. That he trusted his own knowledge of jurisprudence testifies to the self-confidence that had become so basic to his style as ruler.

Qāytbāy sponsored charitable projects in Cairo and elsewhere that overawed his generation with their splendor. The list of monuments, service institutions, and commercial facilities he commissioned is remarkable, especially if one weighs their enormous cost against both the fiscal crisis of the times

143 *'Uqūd* f. 228b, l. 6.

and other obligations competing for funds. Qāytbāy's first dated project was a fountain (*sabīl*) he endowed in the Taḥt al-Rab' district of Cairo in Sha'bān of 874/February–March 1470.[144] Over the next quarter-century, despite repeated demands on his treasury, Qāytbāy patronized construction of mosques, colleges, mystic hospices (*khānqāhs*), orphanages, libraries, and caravansarys in the capital, the Delta, Jerusalem, Mecca, and Medina. He repaired several shrines, including the Mosque of Ibn Ṭūlūn, the Citadel Mosque erected by al-Nāṣir Muḥammad, the Prophet's Sanctuary at Medina, the Ḥaram complex in Mecca, and the Umāyyad Mosque in Damascus.[145]

True to his desire to inspect every work he commissioned, Qāytbāy visited his projects in Cairo and its environs regularly. These visitations illustrate the piety that is so indelible a characteristic of the sultan's legacy. For example, when Qāytbāy rode forth from the Citadel on the seventeenth of Rajab 876/30 December 1471 to examine one of his fountains, he led prayers there and at the madrasa of 'Alam al-Dīn ibn al-Jī'ān, which the public attended.[146] Al-Ṣayrafī dwelt reverently on how the sultan served as imām, guiding worshippers through their devotional postures. When he departed the madrasa precinct, the masses crowded around his horse, as enraptured as the peasants during his rural excursions, wishing him a long and prosperous reign.

Qāytbāy's charitable donations (*awqāf*) were commensurate with his building programs. One in particular exemplifies Qāytbāy's vision of social welfare on a grand scale. On the eleventh of Rabī' I 877/16 August 1472, the sultan assembled the court in celebration of the Prophet's birthday.[147] Traditional ceremonies, such as recitation of the entire Koran or

144 *Rawḍ*, f. 249b, l. 22; *Badā'i'* 3, 43, l. 2.
145 See Amy W. Newhall, "The Patronage of the Mamlūk Sultan Qā'it Bāy, 872–901/1468–1496" (diss. Harvard University 1987).
146 *Inbā'*, 387, l. 10
147 *Inbā'*, 478, l. 18; *Badā'i'* 3, 164, l. 21 (provides date eight years later).

reading of al-Bukhārī's *Ṣaḥīḥ*, were observed in the festival tent set up in the Palace courtyard. Upon their completion, Qāytbāy received Ibn Muzhir, who led a procession of bearers carrying six basins filled with gold and rubies. Their contents were valued at sixty thousand dīnārs. When the sultan accepted the chancellor's accounting of this sum, Ibn Muzhir delivered an eloquent oration in which he proclaimed the monarch's shame over the poverty of so many worthy believers marginally eking out their existence in the holy shrines of Medina, the Prophet's burial place. When the sultan had performed his own Ḥajj rites several months earlier, he had witnessed their sorry plight and resolved to amend it. This grant, drawn from his own coffers, was therefore to be invested in prime Delta land. Its monthly yield would alleviate the privation of indigent Muslims living in Medina. Qāytbāy charged Yashbak the dawādār and the war minister Jānibak with investing equal shares of the money. But Yashbak refused responsibility, wishing to avoid any conflict of interest. Qāytbāy then enjoined the treasurer (*khāzindār*) to purchase the Delta estates and arrange for their placement in trust. Power of attorney was vested in the Ḥanafī chief justice, Muḥibb al-Dīn ibn al-Shiḥna, whom Qāytbāy admonished to preserve the trust once it had been deeded. Substitution of any properties so acquired could occur only in strict accordance with legal procedure.

Al-Ṣayrafī, who attended the ceremony, extolled his sovereign's beneficence—but at the same time told how the sultan provided for his own family members out of the trust's proceeds. He claimed that no royal precursor could match Qāytbāy's solicitude for the indigent faithful. Although the regime often manipulated charitable trusts for less benevolent purposes, donations of such magnitude won Qāytbāy universal praise as a devout Muslim, who equated the comfort of humble believers with his own. Certainly, Qāytbāy predicted the popularity he gained by such massive gifts. Yet political acumen and generous impulse are not mutually exclusive, and the sultan's pious motives are no less impressive for their practicality.

If acts such as these are weighed along with Qāytbāy's courage, his disdain for factional squabbles, and penchant for inspecting public works, we see the maturation of a distinctive ruling style during these medial years. Qāytbāy faced no serious challenge to his authority until well into the 890s, when his natural vigor ebbed. His illustrious status overcame popular anxiety and intracaste connivance even in the aftermath of accidents. The sultan suffered two leg fractures during his reign, the first in Muḥarram of 876/June 1471.[148] An autocrat's serious injury often occasioned a palace coup by his enemies, but the loyalty Qāytbāy inspired among the military elite manifested itself in spontaneous demonstrations of grief over his condition. Even when indisposed, the sultan kept his grip on the government, and his appearance at a palace window sufficed to preserve order. In these medial years, Qāytbāy departed from the capital on the Ḥajj or foreign trips confident that trusted lieutenants would maintain his regime until he returned. Few counterparts in any phase of the Mamlūk era enjoyed equivalent freedom of movement. In the mid-880s, Qāytbāy's ruling apparatus was badly shaken by the reckless ambition of his confidant Yashbak min Mahdī, but he reconsolidated his ruling oligarchy and retained his undisputed authority.

In the aftermath of his triumph over Sūwār, Yashbak found himself in an untenable situation. Driven by an unassuageable lust for power, he could never hope to realize his dream so long as Qāytbāy lived. Unswervingly loyal to his khushdāsh, Yashbak had to remain content with being effective second in command so long as he resided in Egypt. Despite his unprecedented amalgamation of offices, Yashbak chafed over his dilemma throughout the 880s. Also, his plots against his rivals seem to have caught up with him, and he

148 *Inbā'*, 320, l. 20; 322, l. 5; *Badā'i'* 3, 61, l. 14.

now lived in fear of assassination whenever he left the confines of his palace.[149] The Julbān recruits were rumored to have sworn his murder since they were convinced he had planned the execution of several of their most respected officers. Always willing to spare Qāytbāy any censure for these acts, the recruits focused their hatred on Yashbak and resolved to get rid of him when the opportunity arose.

Yashbak thus was highly receptive to any encouragement he might receive about a foreign adventure, and fate ensnared him in her web when, in Rabīʿ I of 885/May–June 1480, he entertained a visiting delegation from the court of Uzun Ḥasan's son, Yaʿqūb, ruler of the White Sheep (Aqquyunlū) principality in Iraq and western Iran. Yashbak was informed of Yaʿqūb's tenuous position following his father's death. Many of Uzun Ḥasan's senior officers loathed his heir and were casting about for some dashing figure on whom they might fix their loyalty. When one of the emissaries told Yashbak, "If you attack them [the officers], they will not resist and all the Kingdom of Iraq will be yours," the dawādār became obsessed with the prospect of conquering the principality. Apparently, Qāytbāy found the idea attractive. The sultan would be relieved of mounting tensions over Yashbak's presence. If Yashbak succeeded, his liege lord would gain in having an intimate as an ally ruling a strategically important territory that at present menaced his suzerainty in Syria. Both Qāytbāy and Yashbak had every reason to assume a positive outcome to such an enterprise in light of Yashbak's record as a field commander, which inspired fear and respect throughout Southwest Asia. Accordingly, Qāytbāy assented to Yashbak's proposal, but insisted that he select his troops from among the disaffected Īnālīya, whom the dawādār had previously abused. The sultan hoped to rid himself of these potential rebels and compelled Yashbak to reconcile with them. Such a ploy made more sense than might seem likely

149 *Badāʾiʿ* 3, 166, l. 6.

at first glance. While the Īnālīya officers bitterly resented their fall from grace after their patron died some seventeen years earlier, they held no implacable grudge against Yashbak. Were he to offer them the chance for superior status in a new regime, they would forgive his previous oppression.

Yashbak may have set his sights on new horizons ripe for plunder, but he took precautions before abandoning Cairo to his opponents. He harbored intense suspicions about one rival, Azdamur al-Ṭawīl, whom he had convinced Qāytbāy to exile in Asyūṭ several years earlier. Astrologers had informed Yashbak that a person named Azdamur would murder him, and he presumed that this was the implicated man. When Yashbak bivouacked at al-Raydānīya before riding east to Ghazza, he sent word to his khushdāsh stating, "I shall not depart from here until I have seen the head of Azdamur al-Ṭawīl with my own eyes."[150] The sultan dispatched the police chief of Qūṣ to the prefect of Asyūṭ with an execution order, to be carried out upon its verification. When Yashbak was shown the severed head of his enemy, he prepared to ride with his worries allayed. But Ibn Iyās wryly observed that the dawādār had mistaken this Azdamur for his true nemesis of the same name. Having caused one head to be sundered from its shoulders unjustly, he would soon lose his own.

Yashbak set out the next month with an expeditionary force of five hundred Mamlūks, but none of the fanfare that had heralded his previous departure to subdue Sūwār.[151] He was accompanied by the chamberlain, Barsbāy Qarā, and Tānibak, one of the muqaddamīn without office—each hoping to share the spoils of conquest. Yashbak chose as an expedient excuse the rebellion of Sayf, Bedouin chief of the Āl Faḍl tribe, who was marauding throughout northern Syria. Upon learning of Yashbak's pursuit, Sayf fled from the vicinity of

[150] *Badā'i'* 3, 167, l. 14.
[151] *Badā'i'* 3, 167, l. 10. In his abbreviated version, *'Uqūd al-jumān fī waqā'i' al-azmān*, Ibn Iyās moves the date back one year to 886. But both al-Ṣayrafī and Ibn al-Ḥimṣī corroborate the departure as in *Badā'i'*.

Ḥamā toward Aleppo. When Yashbak arrived in Damascus some time during Rajab/September–October, he convinced its viceroy, Qānṣūh al-Yaḥyāwī, to join his venture and contribute several thousand more cavalry.[152] Fearing that Sayf would alert Ya'qūb to their impending invasion, Yashbak pressed on immediately to Aleppo and then hastened toward the Euphrates, the frontier between the Mamlūk and Aqquyunlū Empires. After receiving reports from his scouts that Sayf had taken refuge in the fortress of al-Ruhā (Urfa), east of the river, Yashbak besieged it.

The prefect of the town was one Bāyandhūr, a vassal of Ya'qūb.[153] Yashbak so intimidated Bāyandhūr that the latter offered to turn Sayf over and raise a cash indemnity if Yashbak would lift the siege and depart.[154] Yashbak contemptuously rejected Bāyandhūr's terms, since he intended to use the fortress as a base of operations against Mardīn, Ya'qūb's capital. On Sunday, the sixteenth of Ramaḍān/19 November 1480, Yashbak hurled his men against the walls in an all-out assault, but Bāyandhūr issued forth and routed the Mamlūks. Yashbak was captured, along with the chamberlain and the governors of Damascus, Aleppo, and Ṭarābulus, while many soldiers died on the battlefield. Such disorder ensued among the Egyptians and Syrians that their horses bolted, dragging their masters's bodies behind them. Ibn Iyās lamented that Yashbak exercised none of the caution that had marked his confrontation with Sūwār. Rather, he risked his forces in one engagement and suffered casualties worse than those suffered during the Dhū'l-Qādrid campaign.

Bāyandhūr, savoring his stunning triumph over such a famous adversary, paraded Yashbak through the streets of al-Ruhā before locking him up in the citadel dungeon. But his flush of victory soon gave way to fear that this redoubtable prisoner might find accomplices within his own household.

152 *Badā'i'* 3, 169, l. 18.
153 Rendered Bak Yandur by Ibn al-Ḥimṣī, *Ḥawādith*, f. 85, l. 12.
154 *Badā'i'* 3, 170, l. 19; *'Uqūd*, f. 213b, l. 19.

The prefect secretly sent a black slave to Yashbak's cell by night three days after his capture to cut off his head. Equipped only with a dagger, the slave failed several times before achieving his objective, causing his victim terrible suffering. At daybreak, Yashbak's mutilated body was cast out nude into the street, where it lay for hours until a groom covered it with straw. It was finally reclaimed and embalmed by one of Yashbak's secretaries whom Bāyandhūr had released. According to rumors circulating in the aftermath of this grisly affair, Yashbak asked the slave his name when he appeared at his cell door. When he replied, "Azdamur," Yashbak knew his hour had come. Ibn Iyās observed that at least the soul of Azdamur al-Ṭawīl was revenged against Yashbak's perfidy.

Bāyandhūr sent Yashbak's head off to his master in Mardīn, who rejoiced over such a humiliating defeat of the sultan's henchman and ordered the head displayed on a lance throughout his kingdom. Prizing it as a trophy, Ya'qūb refused to send it back with the body for burial in Cairo. Soon, however, he would regret his barbaric treatment of a fellow believer's remains and dread the wrath of his powerful neighbor. In Ṣafar of 886/April 1481, Ya'qūb approached Qāytbāy humbly via emissaries, claiming that his vassal had acted improperly by ordering Yashbak's execution without prior consultation.[155] He submitted himself as Qāytbāy's loyal Mamlūk in Mardīn and agreed to yield all surviving prisoners along with Yashbak's head in return for a truce. But in the aftermath of Yashbak's murder in Ramaḍān, Ya'qūb accepted Bāyandhūr's captives with all their baggage and valuables.

When Qāytbāy and the court learned of Yashbak's end, they were incredulous. The hero of Ilbistīn had seemed an invincible campaigner whom none could vanquish. Qāytbāy sent Azbak to Aleppo to verify the report and resolve all

155 *Inbā'*, 514, l. 17; *Badā'i'* 3, 180, l. 19.

the speculation that had erupted in Cairo over whether the dawādār was alive or dead. Qāytbāy contemplated going himself since he regarded Syria as ripe for invasion.[156] He refused to have any of Yashbak's blazons removed from his palace gate, and all his staff were to remain at their posts until their patron's death was confirmed. In Dhū'l-Qa'da/December 1481–January 1482, Azbak wrote from Aleppo that Yashbak had indeed suffered defeat and death. His body, minus its head, had been released for conveyance back to Cairo. Upon its arrival, some questions over authenticity were raised, but Yashbak's secretary bore a brevet from Azbak stating that he was to show the sultan birthmarks known only to Yashbak's intimates. When these were examined, Yashbak's death was publicly acknowledged and he was interred in his mausoleum. Only then would Qāytbāy assume custodianship over Yashbak's vast estates and properties or approve replacements for his numerous offices.

Qāytbāy had lost his composure when he was informed of Yashbak's debacle. Al-Ṣayrafī asserted that Bāyandhūr had allegedly sent a message to Qāytbāy disavowing any responsibility for these disquieting events.[157] He insisted that Yashbak had initiated hostilities that no one in Iraq had sought and had rejected attempts at a negotiated settlement. He thus brought down destruction on himself. The courier, upon hearing of the sultan's despair, feared to deliver his letter in person and prevailed upon the atābak to read it for him. Supposedly, Qāytbāy tore it up after he received its contents. But he soon regained his dignity. Once Qāytbāy was persuaded of Yashbak's fate, he accepted the loss of his closest companion and redistributed his offices. A vital prop had fallen but the regime would go on. Azbak had ascertained that Ya'qūb, after an abortive move against Malaṭya, did intend to recognize the status quo. No Aqquyunlū sorties

156 *Badā'i'* 3, 174, l. 21.
157 *Inbā'*, 494, l. 7.

across the Euphrates were anticipated. Yashbak's officers who so wished were welcomed into Ya'qūb's retinue, but the sultan need fear no further hostilities.[158]

As for Yashbak, he died as he had lived, playing for high stakes and scorning to tread the safe path of an adjutant. Since conspiracy for the throne of Egypt was impossible while Qāytbāy lived, Yashbak opted for seizure of another—and paid the ultimate price for failure. But did contemporaries interpret his actions as folly? Not necessarily. Ibn Iyās considered the dawādār an individual endowed with sovereign qualities that fortune denied him any opportunity to employ.[159] Should one who refused a vice-monarch's status receive pity for his frustrated attempt to supplant a rival prince? God's compassion was reserved, after all, for the meek of this world, and few would list humility among Yashbak's cardinal virtues.

The Ottoman Campaigns: Containment of a Peer

Relations between Cairo and Istanbul had been correct, if not cordial, through the early and medial years of Qāytbāy's reign. While hindsight has tempted modern historians to depict Ottoman hegemony over the central Islamic lands as inevitable, events during the eighth and ninth decades of the fifteenth century suggest a mutual recognition of stasis. For his part, Qāytbāy never endorsed aggression. He took action solely to guard against rebellion or the threat of invasion. The attitude of the Ottoman sultanate, although more complex, was not disposed toward confrontation with a kindred power until late in the century. Still, the steady drive of Ottoman power to the east made friction a certainty.

158 *Inbā'*, 506, l. 18.
159 *Badā'i'* 3, 173, l. 6.

The earliest reference to Ottoman affairs during Qāytbāy's tenure, provided by Ibn Taghrī-Birdī, portended future developments. The historian mentioned that, in Dhū'l-Ḥijja of 872/June–July 1468, Aḥmad ibn Ramaḍān, prince of the Qaramān beylik in southeastern Anatolia, had repelled an expedition sent by Mehmet II, the illustrious conqueror of Constantinople.[160] While contemporary writers in Egypt differed over why the Ottomans failed to defeat the Qaramānids, they concurred about Qāytbāy's alarm over their designs. The Qaramān beylik alone survived among the principalities restored to their rulers by Timur Lenk, the invader from Central Asia, in the early part of the century.[161] The bey of Qaramān, well aware of both his tenuous position and his valued status to the Cairo government as a buffer, sent the new sultan messengers reminding him of his strategic importance.[162] Qāytbāy, new to his office and unwilling to provoke hostilities, received the ambassador warmly but made no binding promises. He had reason to exercise caution and hoped for domestic discord to defuse the situation. Several months earlier, Qāytbāy had received reports of dissension within the Ottoman ruling hierarchy over the Qaramān episode.[163] Enraged at the sorry performance of his crack Janissary units against a lowly provincial whose forces practiced outmoded techniques, Mehmet had arrested his wazīr, Maḥmūd Pasha, whom he accused of faulty planning. Allegedly, the Ottoman expedition had been focused on

160 *Ḥawādith* 4, 650, l. 19, 23. These events were repeated by 'Abd al-Bāsiṭ, who qualified some of Ibn Taghrī-Birdī's details on the defeat. See *Rawḍ*, f. 186b, l. 31.

161 After Timur defeated Yilderim Bāyazīd, he posed as liberator of fellow Muslims from imperialism and restored the beyliks absorbed into Ottoman domains over the preceding century. Within the next few decades, however, all save the Qaramān had been gathered back into the Ottoman fold. See Beatrice Forbes Manz, *The Rise and Rule of Tamerlane* (Cambridge 1989) 73; John E. Woods, *The Aqquyunlu: Clan, Confederation, Empire* (Minneapolis 1976) 52.

162 *Inbā'*, 162, l. 21; *Rawḍ*, f. 250b, l. 7.

163 *Ḥawādith* 4, 684, l. 14; *Inbā'*, 27, l. 11.

other adversaries further east (presumably the Aqquyunlū), and had not intended to confront the Qaramānids at this moment. Maḥmūd Pasha had advised his master that Ibn Ramaḍān posed no threat. But the Qaramānid had fallen upon the Ottoman army and thrashed it. Mehmet vented his spleen on his hapless prime minister, whose worthy career was abruptly terminated. When Qāytbāy received this news, he could expect that events elsewhere would prolong the status quo. The Ottoman ruler was, after all, preoccupied with problems of global scale. Ibn Taghrī-Birdī mused that 872 was replete with international upheavals. The Ottomans engaged in costly battles against the Europeans, several of which ended inconclusively. They took many casualties and yet failed to defeat the Christians.[164] Qāytbāy therefore adopted a posture of fraternal support for his Ottoman peer against the infidel, while privately rejoicing in his frustration over the stalemate that prevailed. But although this stalemate endured more than a decade, it could not last forever.

As the 870s passed, the two empires maintained a facade of mutual respect symbolized by periodic exchange of ambassadors.[165] When Mehmet died in 886/1481, he was succeeded by his introspective son Bāyazīd, who was more disposed to resolving differences by diplomacy than force of arms. No disputes marred relations between Istanbul and Cairo through the early 880s, an era of tranquility in foreign

164 *Ḥawādith* 4, 652, l. 11.

165 *Inbā'*, 341, l. 10 (21 Rabī' I 876/7 September 1471: Ottomans present Qāytbāy with European pirates captured off Damietta); 407, l. 13; 411, l. 13; *Badā'i'* 3, 69, l. 11 (1 Ramaḍān 876/11 February 1472: Ottoman ambassador arrives on way to Ḥajj, presents gifts of pelts and slaves); *Inbā'*, 445, l. 16 (Dhū'l-Ḥijja 876/May 1472: return of the Shaykh 'Alā' al-Dīn al-Ḥiṣnī in disgrace from mission to Ottoman court); *Badā'i'* 3, 90, l. 14, 91, l. 17 (Ṣafar 878/June–July 1473: sultan designates ambassador to Ottoman court, dies en route); 94, l. 2 (Dhū'l-Qa'da 878/March–April 1474: sultan charges Yashbak al-Jamālī with ascertaining the new sultan's disposition and foreign policy); 99, l. 16 (Jumādā I 879/September 1475: Yashbak returns).

affairs from Cairo's view. Only one issue rippled the smooth waters of this medial period, a dilemma presenting Qāytbāy with no attractive option for a response. In Jumādā II of 886/July–August 1481, Bāyazīd's estranged brother Jem arrived at the Mamlūk frontier and asked permission to present himself before the sultan in person.[166] As a prince of the House of 'Uthmān, Jem ranked as a royal colleague whom Qāytbāy could not refuse a hearing, according to imperial protocol. Throughout Islamic history, rival courts had often offered sanctuary to brothers who had fallen out with their siblings who gained absolute authority, and Qāytbāy could find no excuse for turning Jem away without losing face. He thus reluctantly instructed his governor of Aleppo to admit the Ottoman prince, with his mother and children in tow, and send him on to Egypt under a modest escort. If Jem requested only a transient's safe-conduct, his brother in Istanbul could not fault the sultan of Egypt for extending one Muslim's hospitality to another. Jem reached al-Khānqāh, north of Cairo, in Sha'bān/September–October.[167] The sultan's audiencer conducted him to the Citadel via the Cemetery route, thereby avoiding excessive public notice. Qāytbāy received his royal guest in the central courtyard rather than the throne room, and remained seated when Jem was introduced. Ibn Iyās remarked on this deliberate slight, speculating that the sultan was more concerned with placating Bāyazīd by avoiding an equal's greeting than with emphasizing the superiority of his own status. Qāytbāy draped the Ottoman prince with a sable robe of honor and granted him freedom of the city. No discussion of Jem's grievances was reported.

Over the next several months, Jem remained in Cairo as the sultan's guest. Although elaborately entertained at banquets and military reviews, he received no pledges of support

166 *Badā'i'* 3, 183, l. 6, *'Uqūd*, f. 231, l. 16.
167 *Badā'i'* 3, 185, l. 5.

for his proposed supplanting of his brother. When the pilgrimage caravans departed for the Ḥijāz in Shawwāl/November–December, Jem went along to fulfill his religious obligation and, possibly, to allay his boredom.[168] Qāytbāy bestowed on him a generous sum of money to distribute among the needy in Mecca and Medina but refused to involve himself in any revolutionary scheme. When Jem returned to Cairo in Muḥarram of 887/February–March 1482, he asked the sultan's leave to confront his brother.[169] Qāytbāy convened his senior amīrs to debate the consequences of such a move. They interrogated Jem at length as to how he expected to realize his objective, and the atābak rebuked him when he explained his designs. Whether Azbak did so because of their defective planning or their high risk is unclear, but his misgivings reflected Qāytbāy's own unease. Regardless of Jem's success or failure, his actions could not but arouse Bāyazīd's suspicions about Egypt's neutrality. Ultimately, Qāytbāy allowed Jem to depart, although with no armed contingent from the Mamlūk sultanate. In hindsight, Ibn Iyās found this decision unwise since it ensured Bāyazīd's rancor, and other chroniclers attributed subsequent hostilities and their devastating consequences to this affair. Five months later, Qāytbāy received word of Jem's defeat by his brother's troops. Yet the elusive prince seemed blessed with nine lives, for he escaped capture, accepted European custody, took ship, and found sanctuary in France and later the Vatican.[170] Stripped of money and supplies, Jem was destined to play the role of a pawn held by Christian powers as a hostage to encourage the Ottoman sultan's non-belligerence. Qāytbāy might have been expected to relish his rival's discomfiture, but in fact he feared that blame for the affair would be laid at his door.

His unease over the future was well founded. Little more than a year later, in Muḥarram of 889/January–February

168 *Badā'i'* 3, 190, l. 2.

169 *Badā'i'* 3, 192, l. 3; Ibn al-Ḥimṣī, *Ḥawādith*, f. 95b, l. 13.

170 *Badā'i'* 3, 195, l. 16; 196, l. 3.

1484, Qāytbāy learned that Bāyazīd had offered Sūwār's brother 'Alī Dawlāt his "protection," a thinly veiled threat of invasion were the Dhū'l-Qādrid to refuse submission.[171] Ibn Iyās considered this development a signal of renewed hostilities, the termination of a truce that Qāytbāy had hoped to prolong indefinitely. He sent off the armaments minister, Timrāz al-Shamsī, who had conducted such brilliant reconnaisance missions against Sūwār years ago, to Aleppo with a contingent of Mamlūks. Qāytbāy charged Timrāz with ascertaining the situation in southeastern Anatolia and reinforcing the Aleppo garrison. Timrāz's reports confirmed the sultan's worst fears. The Ottomans were indeed undermining Cairo's influence over the lords of the marches, who found their position increasingly delicate. Qāytbāy nonetheless took no aggressive action immediately, but hesitated until year's end before sending another emissary to Istanbul. He chose Jānibak Ḥabīb, a skilled interlocutor who had conducted positive negotiations with the Aqquyunlū ruler Ya'qūb over the release of prisoners.[172] The sultan entrusted Jānibak with gifts worth some ten thousand dīnārs to sweeten his case for both sides keeping the peace. He also had ordered the Caliph to draw up a formal confirmation of the Ottoman ruler's legal authority over the former Byzantine realm (al-Rūm) and any territories he might wrest from the Christians. This document enlisted many passages from the Koran, Prophetic traditions (*ḥadīth*), and treatises by revered scholars of the past that emphasized the mutual advantage to be gained by arbitrated settlement of disputes. Jānibak was instructed to dwell on such precedents at length.

The ambassador departed on his mission forthwith. For several months no news reached Cairo either of his deliberations in Istanbul or of the actions of Ottoman forces in southeastern Anatolia. Then, in Jumādā I of 890/May–June

171 *Badā'i'* 3, 205, l. 21 ('Alī Dawlāt is rendered 'Alā' al-Dawla in other sources).

172 *Badā'i'* 3, 213, l. 12; 215, l. 4; *'Uqūd*, f. 233, l. 16.

1485, the governor of Aleppo dispatched couriers with dismal tidings. An Ottoman contingent had seized the Mamlūk frontier stronghold of al-Kūlāk and was pressing on toward Sīs, Tarṣūṣ, and Adana.[173] The governor appealed to Qāytbāy for an expeditionary force capable of confronting the Ottomans before they marched south toward Syria, and urged the sultan to take the field himself to show his righteous anger at such wanton aggression. Qāytbāy elected to remain in Cairo, but ordered the muster of a large contingent under the atābak's command.[174] Preparations for the expedition caused widespread hardship in the capital, since its restive participants resented being dispatched to face such a formidable adversary and the seizure of many of their supply animals and provisions without compensation. So many mules were stolen from grain mills that flour became short in supply, according to Ibn Iyās. Despite such inauspicious events, the contingent departed for Aleppo and the northern border. Ibn al-Ḥimṣī reported that the Mamlūk troops almost crossed paths with the entourage of Jānibak Ḥabīb returning from his abortive negotiations.[175] When Jānibak presented himself before the sultan in Dhū'l-Qa'da/November, he informed his sovereign that Bāyazīd and his advisers intended to pursue their expansionist policies. His arguments had fallen on deaf ears and his embassy had been shabbily treated in Istanbul. Such breach of protocol indicated Ottoman contempt for the Egyptian sultanate.[176]

Thus the year 890 ended with widespread foreboding in Cairo. The Ottomans had suffered a devastating defeat only once in their history of unparalleled conquest, and that at the hands of the dreaded Timur Lenk, whom none could have resisted. How could the Egyptians hope to prevail? But in Ṣafar of 891/February 1486, extraordinary news arrived from

173 *Badā'i'* 3, 218, l. 17.
174 *Badā'i'* 3, 219, l. 14.
175 Ibn al-Ḥimṣī, *Ḥawādith*, f. 111b, l. 4.
176 *Badā'i'* 3, 221, l. 12.

Aleppo. Azbak's troops had scored a brilliant victory near Adana.[177] The Ottomans allegedly suffered forty thousand casualties and the capture of a highly respected commander, Aḥmad ibn Hirsik. Azbak had confiscated many battalion standards (*sanājik*), which he was taking back to Cairo along with more than two hundred heads of officers fallen in battle to display in his victory procession. Ibn Iyās claimed that Qāytbāy was beside himself with delight over such good fortune and ordered the city decorated for Azbak's homecoming. Drummers struck military cadences in the Citadel when the officer conveying the standards, heads, and prisoners ascended.

Such ecstatic displays proved somewhat premature, however. Less than three months later, Qāytbāy was informed that the Ottomans were reassembling their Anatolian contingents in preparation for further operations.[178] The dogged resolve of this regime, undeterred even by staggering losses, depressed the Egyptian court. Qāytbāy once again considered taking the field himself, partly out of a desire to assess his opponent at first hand. Another muster was hastily prepared, another expeditionary force departed to the Aleppo garrison. But in fact, events did not lead to a confrontation. Bāyazīd opted for an undeclared truce and no further hostilities occurred during the remainder of 891 and all of 892/March 1486–January 1487. Both sides watched each other warily, yet neither broke the stalemate. Not until Jumādā I of 893/April–May 1487 did Cairo receive reports of further unsettling developments. Word then arrived that the Ottomans had reoccupied Adana and the fortress of Ayās.[179]

The sultan and his associates now decided that nothing less than a decisive response would check this menace. The Ottoman aggression contrasted markedly with that of

177 *Badāʾiʿ* 3, 226, ll. 4, 18; 228, l. 2; Ibn al-Ḥimṣī, *Ḥawādith*, f. 113, l. 8.

178 al-Sakhāwī, *Dhayl*, f. 187, l. 27; *Badāʾiʿ* 3, 229, l. 22. The news reached Cairo in Jumādā II 891.

179 *Badāʾiʿ* 3, 250, l. 8; 251, l. 11.

Sūwār, who, for all his tactical genius, could never raise a great power's army but relied on his strategic boldness to lure his opponent into conditions favorable to his style of warfare. The Ottomans, on the other hand, could endure severe losses and still raise vast replacements. Qāytbāy thus planned to send more than a contingent suited for quelling a local upstart. He charged the atābak with gathering an army larger than any host assembled by his predecessors. Ibn Iyās stated that the royal and veteran Mamlūks alone numbered four thousand. Eleven muqaddamīn and sixty officers would preside over them. Bedouin skirmishing bands were conscripted from the Jabal Nāblus to keep the enemy off balance, since the Ottomans' Turkmān auxiliaries could not match the Bedouin's maneuverability. The Egyptian army rode out of Cairo in mid-Jumādā II/late May.[180] No cost had been spared on outfitting these troops. The regiments of Azbak and Qānṣūh Khamsmi'a, an ambitious officer with a turbulent future, cut particularly dashing figures. Qānṣūh was rumored to have lavished no less than eighty thousand dīnārs on arms and uniforms—this at a time when funds for such ventures were raised by forced assessments. Ibn Iyās believed that not even the expeditions Barsbāy raised earlier in the century for his Cypriot invasion could equal this army in size or spendor.

After the host had departed, an uneasy calm settled over Cairo as the court waited for news of its meeting with the Ottomans. The governor of Aleppo reported that an Ottoman fleet had attempted a landing at the coastal fortress of Bāb al-Malik, but that Azbak had driven it off.[181] A storm had wreaked havoc among the enemy's vessels, casting many of them against reefs along the shore. Survivors attempting to

180 *Badā'i'* 3, 252, l. 9. Since Ibn Iyās's descriptions of events during this period were often based on secondhand informants, they do not compare with the detail al-Ṣayrafī often offered. The latter presumably would have recounted the types of weapons, uniforms, and supplies at great length.

181 *Badā'i'* 3, 254, l. 16; 255, l. 19.

crawl to land, their firearms soaked and useless, were easily dispatched. Qāytbāy ordered prayers of thanksgiving offered in mosques across the capital for God's intervention on the side of the Egyptian cause. The major battle had yet to be joined and the All Highest's aid at this juncture was regarded as a positive omen. It proved sound. A missive sent by the atābak himself arrived at the Citadel proclaiming a decisive victory on the eighth day of Ramaḍān/16 August.[182] The engagement occurred near Adana and lasted most of the day. Each side suffered heavy casualties and neither found the other vulnerable to strategic forays. But the Ottomans lost far more men than the Egyptians, and when their chain of command broke down they were routed. Ibn al-Ḥimṣī remarked that Azbak and his fellow commanders had taken stock of their opponents' reliance on artillery and stayed out of range when they fired their cannons off, charging in while attempts were made to reload. Later, Ottoman use of firepower lent a decisive edge to such engagements, but this time a technical advantage could not overwhelm skilled horsemanship.

Upon receipt of this news, the sultan proclaimed a seven-day victory festival. The Citadel drummers struck their cadences for the entire week while the city reveled. Azbak wasted no time savoring his triumph but pursued his enemy to Adana. Most of the surviving Ottoman units had little stomach for defending the town and abandoned it to the Egyptians. But the Adana garrison, fearing reprisal for its earlier capitulation, held out for three months before surrendering—presumably after pardons had been negotiated. Azbak therefore did not return to Cairo with the army for his victory procession until Rabīʿ I of 894/February–March 1489.[183] Enhancing the spectacle were the columns of troops, possibly including some Janissaries who had deserted

182 *Badāʾiʿ* 3, 256, l. 10, 23; Ibn al-Ḥimṣī, *Ḥawādith*, ff. 116b, l. 5; 117b, l. 11.
183 *Badāʾiʿ* 3, 261, l. 7.

the Ottoman army and offered their services to the Egyptian sultanate. Qāytbāy eagerly welcomed them and granted them a special status. They took the title "al-Dīwān al-'Uthmānī" and retained their cohesion until al-Ghawrī's reign. The atābak also handed over several traitorous officials from Aleppo who, anticipating the success of the Ottoman drive south, had provided the enemy with intelligence about the Egyptian army.[184] Qāytbāy, who so often posed as a paragon of Muslim charity, showed no mercy to those who violated their state's cause. He ordered these renegades flayed alive in the Maqshara Prison after they had been paraded nude through the streets. A dreadful penalty for an error in judgment, yet one certain to give future doubters pause before rashly underestimating their sovereign's resolve.

In the aftermath of this defeat, the Ottomans extended peace feelers to Cairo. In Jumādā II of 894/May 1489, Bāyazīd's wazīr, Dā'ūd Pasha, sent an emissary to Qāytbāy inquiring whether he was willing to appoint negotiators to Istanbul.[185] Recalling the discourtesies heaped on Jānibak Ḥabīb, Qāytbāy replied, "If he (the Ottoman ruler) releases my merchants he has detained, and returns the keys of fortresses he has seized, we can write to him about terms for a settlement and dispatch an ambassador to that effect." No further moves toward terminating hostilities occurred that year. Once again, the Ottomans tapped their huge resources to rebuild their armed forces. By the early months of 895/November–December 1489, they were pressing into southeastern Anatolia. Qāytbāy and his marshal resolved on yet another expedition. Azbak set out from Cairo on the twenty-second of Rabī' II/15 March 1490, at the head of some three thousand troopers, many of whom were veterans of previous campaigns.[186] He rested his cavalry at Aleppo and then proceeded into the war zone. The Ottomans

184 *Badā'i'* 3, 265, l. 24.
185 *Badā'i'* 3, 266, l. 9.
186 *Badā'i'* 3, 270, l. 12; al-Sakhāwī, *Dhayl*, f. 202b, l. 29.

had now divided their forces among the local strongholds of Sīs, Darandā, Kūlāk, and Zamanṭū, which over the past two decades had alternately endured Dhū'l-Qādrid, Mamlūk, or Ottoman control and whose residents wished above all for peace. Since no single engagement could decide the region's fate this time, Azbak's force was compelled to split in two contingents: one to besiege Darandā, the other to surround Kūlāk. The Ottomans refused to face the Egyptians directly, so Azbak pursued them deep into central Anatolia, skirmishing around Qaysārīya and leaving a swath of scorched earth behind him.[187] When he finally laid siege to Kuwāra in Dhū'l-Qa'da of 895/September–October 1490, his troops confronted him and refused to proceed any further. Supplies were running low, and fear that their adversaries might be enticing them into a trap was spreading through the ranks. Being a prudent general who hazarded few risks, Azbak complied and began the march home with no decisive resolution.

When Qāytbāy learned that the army was returning without permission, he privately nursed his irritation but made no public display. In 893, Azbak had scored a greater victory against a foreign enemy than he ever had, and Qāytbāy was in no position to challenge his general's decision. Also, the burden of fielding these massively expensive expeditions, which could not produce a definitive settlement, had begun to tell. The sultan's tactics for raising funds had created broad resentment he could no longer ignore. Qāytbāy sent orders requesting Azbak to remain in Aleppo until further notice, but the atābak and his officers defied their sovereign's command and proceeded on to Damascus, arriving at the end of 895. Qāytbāy reacted angrily to Azbak's behavior, but still granted him a victor's reception when he entered Cairo in Muḥarram of 896/November–December

[187] *Badā'i'* 3, 273, l. 3; 274, l. 9; 275, l. 16.

1490.[188] Rising to greet his marshal, he draped a hero's robe over his shoulders. Yet this show of gratitude in the face of an inconclusive venture could not mask mutual resentments. Azbak would lead no future campaigns. And Qāytbāy now received Ottoman truce overtures with a will to conclude the war.

These overtures duly arrived. The Ottoman government was focusing its attention on the deteriorating authority of the Aqquyunlū regime. The Egyptian sultanate had proven its resolve in securing its grip over the march territories in southeastern Anatolia. Accordingly, the first Ottoman emissary to reach Cairo since the 895 campaign arrived at the Citadel in Jumādā II of 896/April–May 1491.[189] Tidings of his intended visit had preceded him in Muḥarram, and Qāytbāy prepared to receive him with full honors. The status of this emissary betokened the importance Bāyazīd attached to his mission. He was the senior qāḍī of Burṣā, Mullā 'Alī ibn Aḥmad al-Jalabī. An expert on judicial procedure, he embodied the Ottoman ruler's desire to negotiate a lasting agreement. He was accompanied by Māmāy min Khudād, Qāytbāy's own representative in Istanbul.

The mullā presented keys of fortresses occupied by the Ottomans to the sultan as earnest of his patron's intent to terminate hostilities and restore the status quo. Qāytbāy threw a lavish reception for the amabassador and invited him to participate in Friday prayer at his private loge in the Citadel Mosque. He turned over to Mullā 'Alī several Ottoman officers captured in previous engagements—including Iskandar ibn Mīkhāl, a Janissary who had been held for years. Qāytbāy granted Iskandar a Mamlūk uniform to replace the tattered outfit he had worn in prison to preserve his dignity on the way home. Al-Sakhāwī noted that, despite cordial appearances, deliberations were heated. The

188 *Badā'i'* 3, 276, l. 15.

189 al-Sakhāwī, *Dhayl*, f. 205, l. 20; Ibn al-Ḥimṣī, *Ḥawādith*, f. 123b, l. 3; *Badā'i'* 3, 281, l. 21.

Ottoman regime was to recognize formally the suzerain status of the Egyptian autocrat, who alone remained the defender of Orthodox Islam. He extended exclusive protection over the Ka'ba shrine in Mecca, the Prophet's sepulcher in Medina, the Dome of the Rock in Jerusalem, the Patriarchal tombs in Hebron (al-Khalīl), and the mausoleums of Imāms al-Layth and al-Shāfi'ī in Cairo. No other Muslim monarch could claim equivalent powers over or benefits to the community of believers. His legitimacy rested on unrivaled qualifications. He and his predecessors had singlehandedly held both European pirates and marauders from Central Asia at bay (a pointed reference to the ignominous defeat suffered by Yilderim Bāyazīd I in 1402 by Timur Lenk). The Egyptian sultan thus served the Umma (Muslim commonwealth) as its guardian, and no other sovereign could dispute his primacy. Neither al-Sakhāwī nor Ibn Iyās dwelt on Mullā 'Alī's rejoinder to these grandiose claims but he did not impede the discussions. The Burṣā qāḍī departed with proposals for a binding treaty.

Soon thereafter, in Rajab, Qāytbāy dispatched to Istanbul another senior officer, Jānbalāṭ min Yashbak, who ten years later would briefly hold the sultanate.[190] His mission focused on settling final differences between the parties, and he bore with him costly gifts for the Ottoman ruler. When he returned, he presented another Ottoman jurist, who brought along the remaining keys to the captured fortresses, proffered in a splendid case wrapped in Burṣā silk. Upon these final discussions, the treaty ending the conflict was signed and sealed. It was to last through the rest of Bāyazīd's and Qāytbāy's reigns. Given the fundamental contrasts in approaches to imperial dominion of the Mamlūk and Ottoman governments, no permanent cooexistence was possible, but for the present peace had been restored. When the Cairo court learned of subsequent Ottoman

190 *Badā'i'* 3, 283, l. 15; *'Uqūd*, f. 236, margin.

operations against the Aqquyunlū in 897/1492, the sultan and his associates were uneasy but took no action.[191] With the curbing of Ottoman aggression into Mamlūk territory, neutrality seemed the best policy: the truce had been too dearly bought to risk. More than a decade later, Qānṣūh al-Ghawrī would find out how dangerous foreign intrigue against the Ottomans could be.

Qāytbāy continued to monitor the Ottoman situation to the end of his life. The grand amīr Māmāy was sent once again to Istanbul in 899/1493–1494 on an embassy that was largely symbolic. So festive an air surrounded his departure that he hosted a soirée in his belvedere overlooking the Raṭlī Lake.[192] Fireworks cast brilliant reflections on its surface, and shadow plays entertained the throng with their irreverent parodies of Ottoman political figures. Singers enthralled guests with lyrics commissioned for the event. The reception lasted for twenty evenings before Māmāy set out. No further complications marred this "era of good feelings." In Ṣafar of 900/November 1494, the court received word that Prince Jem had died, still the Pope's hostage.[193] He had attempted to raise an army of reconquest in France but lost royal favor there when he refused to adopt the Christian faith. Thus was Qāytbāy finally rid of any tie with this enigmatic figure. During Qāytbāy's final months, his last emissary to Istanbul could report that Bāyazīd now opposed armed conflict more resolutely than ever, because his army had weakened and posed no threat to the sultan's domains.[194] Qāytbāy could therefore end his career with deep satisfaction over the modus vivendi he had worked so long to shore up. His effective containment of the most bellicose power in the Muslim world contributed enormously to the prestige he enjoyed as one of the most august rulers of medieval Egypt. None of

191 *Badāʾiʿ* 3, 286, l. 11.
192 *Badāʾiʿ* 3, 299, l. 14.
193 al-Sakhāwī, *Dhayl*, f. 259, l. 28.
194 *Badāʾiʿ* 3, 315, l. 22.

the sordid events accompanying his growing infirmity could detract from his stature, which would be recalled often during disasters that ensued after his death.

Decline, 891–901: Insidious Rivalry

When Qāytbāy entered upon his last decade in office, he had already passed his seventy-third year. Although his health was remarkable, the sultan could no longer maintain his previous schedule of rigorous exercise, arduous excursions, and stringent attention to administrative detail. Nor could he rebound unscathed from accidental injuries he incurred because of his strenuous lifestyle. The Mamlūk system of absolute vertical authority required an individual at its summit whose capacity to check factional rivalry was bolstered by his physical stamina. While this vigor showed its first visible signs of slackening in 891/1486, fissures in Qāytbāy's edifice appeared in the late 880s. In Dhū'l-Qa'da of 887/December 1482–January 1483, the sultan was compelled to issue a proclamation forbidding judges or notaries to license marriages for his Mamlūks unless they could produce written permission from their barracks officers (*aghāt*).[195] Betrothal arrangements for in-service troopers had routinely been banned throughout the Mamlūk period to prevent divided loyalties, but the chroniclers do not refer to such prohibitions earlier in Qāytbāy's reign. Ibn Iyās mentioned this edict in conjunction with the growing surliness of Mamlūk recruits in Cairo, who were now plundering mercantile establishments with mounting audacity. Whether they were so impelled by inadequate stipends or behaved as predators because of diminishing respect for their master remains a complex question. But such unruliness under Qāytbāy first occurred at this time, and Ibn Iyās

195 *Badā'i'* 3, 197, l. 8.

observed that, once commenced, it continued with increasing frequency. Over the following two years, the recruits resumed their penchant for disorderly conduct that had marred the reigns of Qāytbāy's predecessors. Ibn Iyās reported full-scale riots ensuing from the punishment of a soldier who refused a dealer his stated price for a bolt of cloth.[196] These insurrections were focused on both the merchants and the officers responsible for upholding discipline among the ranks. That the Mamlūk recruits (*julbān*) dared mutiny in this barbarous fashion boded ill for the regime's reputation as guardian of public order. Once the Julbān abandoned their restraint, other lawless elements of society quickly followed suit.[197]

The year 891/1486 saw a downturn in Qāytbāy's personal fortunes. He was a man whom fate had blessed with good luck along with keen intelligence, but the powers of evil chance now seemed to rally against him. During the year's early months, several of the sultan's trusted civil officials died, leaving gaps in his bureaucracy difficult to fill with persons of equal reliability.[198] The economy took a turn for the worse as food prices rose sharply because of poor harvests and hoarding, ending a period of prosperity.[199] But calamity occurred as a consequence of the sultan's favorite pastime: horseback riding. Early in Rabīʿ I/March, Qāytbāy was exercising a spirited new mount in the palace courtyard. Attempting to subdue its waywardness, he violently reined the animal in. The horse reared and bucked, throwing his rider off before falling on top of him.[200] The sultan suffered severe bruises and lacerations, but the critical damage was done to his leg. The femur was shattered, the bone jutting out from his thigh. When Qāytbāy lost consciousness from the pain and blood loss, his horrified aides feared he had died

196 Ibn al-Ḥimṣī, *Ḥawādith*, f. 102, l. 5; *Badāʾiʿ* 3, 202, l. 1.
197 *Badāʾiʿ* 3, 219, l. 2; Lapidus, *Muslim Cities*, 153–164.
198 *Badāʾiʿ* 3, 224, l. 4.
199 *Badāʾiʿ* 3, 224, l. 14.
200 *Badāʾiʿ* 3, 227, l. 3; 228, l. 10; 229, l. 3.

on the spot. After he was found to be alive, a bodyguard carried him into the Duhaysha Palace, where the fracture was set by physicians, who could not guarantee his recovery. Alarm spread rapidly through the capital, since a ruler's sudden death precipitated a power struggle. A bad omen had portended the sultan's misfortune. Two days preceding his riding accident, cross-beams below the minaret of the Citadel Mosque from which oil lamps were suspended collapsed. Despite the warnings of soothsayers, the sultan had paid no heed and had gone on with his personal routine. Now he lay comatose as his amīrs and dīwān staff converged to keep vigil and ponder their own futures if he expired.

But such was the cohesion of Qāytbāy's oligarchy that no member of it, civil or military, broke his allegiance while the monarch clung to life. Most recalled the succession crisis before Qāytbāy's enthronement and none could rest assured of his own welfare if insurrection broke out. The sultan's only son remaining to him after the ravages of plague had been born in 887 and therefore could not yet command any loyalty on his own.[201] It was the sultan's chancellor, Ibn Muzhir, who took steps to break the paralysis that gripped the court. Since the sultan still breathed, he ordered edicts to be delivered throughout Egypt and the Syrian provinces assuring regional governors that Qāytbāy was alive with his faculties intact. In Cairo, all troops were confined to their barracks until the outcome of this accident was ascertained. For the next several days Qāytbāy hovered on the brink of death, but his extraordinary constitution intervened yet again to save him. Gangrene did not set in, and he made slow but steady progress. Although the sultan suffered terribly, he insisted on attending court ceremonies while lying prone on a litter. By the next month he could sign decrees with his own hand and

201 *Badāʾiʿ* 3, 197, l. 4. This son was not the product of the sultan's marriage to the khawand Fāṭima. He was born to the sultan's favorite concubine, Aṣalbāy al-Jarkasīya. He became the sultan's sole heir after his older children succumbed to the plague.

receive delegations of his subjects, who assembled to wish him well. Their felicitations, albeit heartfelt, were certainly enhanced by donations they accepted in Qāytbāy's name. A thousand dīnārs were distributed to the poor of Cairo who, in turn, prayed for their lord's speedy recovery.

By the end of Jumādā I/June, some fifty days after his mishap, Qāytbāy had recuperated enough to survey some new horses from a palace window and enter the bath. The next week he presided over Friday prayer in the Citadel Mosque after riding unassisted across the very courtyard where he had been thrown. His wife, the khawand Fāṭima, arranged a ceremony to commemorate the event. All the Harem eunuchs were perfumed with saffron. The princess distributed sashes of gold silk to the spectators, who cheered the sultan's fortitude. Upon his return to the palace, Qāytbāy was serenaded by Cairo's most esteemed singers, who chanted odes composed for the occasion. Fāṭima herself welcomed her husband and cast gold coins over him as he dismounted. His route was demarcated by a huge silk tapestry that ran from the Duhaysha to the Mosque. After prayer the sultan distributed robes of honor to the physicians and barbers who had attended him (and presumably thanked their lucky stars that he had come through whole and well). Cairo was decorated and a week's celebration was permitted. The Caliph and four qāḍīs ascended to the Citadel to offer their congratulations. Qāytbāy then held his first consistory since the injury, seated on the dais of the Justice Hall, hearing appeals and taking petitions. Truly a remarkable convalescence, especially for a man so advanced in years. The populace marveled that their sovereign resumed his riding exercises. Qāytbāy obviously sought to quell any rumor that he was still incapacitated. But the unrest smoldering among his subordinates had not been dispelled.

The Julbān revolted twice again in the latter part of 891. They claimed their monthly stipends, tardy as they were, could not keep abreast of the escalating cost of foodstuffs and fodder. In Shawwāl/October, they sacked the house of Badr al-Dīn ibn Muzhir, the muḥtasib and chancellor's son, asserting that he was profiteering from the price increases.[202] His father prostrated himself before Qāytbāy three times and pleaded with him to release his son from an untenable office. The frequency of these mutinies must be understood in light of the onerous Ottoman campaigns Qāytbāy undertook during the 890s.[203] Together, their inflationary pressure and the heightening of the recruits' status following triumphs on the battlefield combined to stimulate the troops' rebellious instincts.

The sultan and his aging coterie of intimates persevered in the face of this endemic unrest with their show of ceremonials and consistories. In Rajab of 895/May–June 1490, Qāytbāy planned a festival honoring the circumcision of his heir, al-Nāṣir Muḥammad. The prince would undergo the rite with sons of other notables, including the Caliph, the former sultan al-Manṣūr ibn Jaqmaq, and the Ottoman prince Jem.[204] All the capital's markets displayed banners depicting their crafts as the youths proceeded through the city. Ibn Iyās noted that the populace exploited the festival to deport themselves wantonly without fear of reprisal or spoliation. Since the army was away on campaign in Asia Minor, the masses were temporarily free of Mamlūk oppression and

202 *Badā'i'* 3, 233, l. 7.
203 *Badā'i'* 3, 234, l. 20; 235, l. 21 (troop revolts); 236, l. 19 (scarcity of sacrifice animals); 237, l. 20 (bread shortage); 239, l. 17 (salt scarcity); 243, l. 19 (dismissal of Cairo prefect because of uncurbed riots); 245, l. 6 (early distribution of troops' sacrifice animals to preempt revolt); 245, l. 21 (troop revolts); 247, l. 5 (high cost of drinking water); 200, l. 13 (Mamlūks return from Ottoman campaign undisciplined); 261, l. 12 (recruits demand larger bonus); al-Sakhāwī, *Dhayl*, f. 199, l. 27 (dawādār's Mamlūks plot his deposition); *Badā'i'* 3, 273, l. 22 (Anatolian Mamlūks arrested for public wine drinking); 275, l. 22 (Mamlūks returning from Ottoman expedition threaten mutiny); 276, l. 20; al-Sakhāwī, *Dhayl*, f. 205, l. 14 (Julbān demand bonus, sultan threatens abdication); *Badā'i'* 3, 295, l. 11 (Julbān revolt).
204 al-Sakhāwī, *Dhayl*, f. 202, l. 7, 32; *Badā'i'* 3, 271, l. 5, 22; *'Uqūd*, f. 236, l. 8.

could behave with abandon. The sultan accepted gifts worth fifty thousand dīnārs, a sum sorely needed to replenish his coffers. After the prince had been circumcised, he qualified for status as an adult heir even though he was only eight years old. The sultan had built a palace for his son in the Elephant Lake district and bade him take up his residence there to emphasize his fitness to succeed.[205]

Under these circumstances, several new figures rose to prominence in the ruling hierarchy. Of these, the least scrupulous was Qānṣūh min Ṭarābāy, who bore the peculiar sobriquet "Five Hundred" (Khamsmi'a), a Sulṭanī Mamlūk who was first mentioned by Ibn Iyās as amīr of the Ḥajj caravan in 878.[206] This Qānṣūh Khamsmi'a penetrated the monarch's inner circle as an adjutant to Yashbak. Both the dawādār and the sultan noted his bravery, ambition, and self-confidence. Properly tempered, such qualities could prove useful in a loyal retainer. So, favorably impressed with this brash young officer, they advanced him rapidly. In Sha'bān of 884/October–November 1479, one year before Yashbak's disastrous adventure in Iraq, Qānṣūh was promoted to the rank of muqaddam.[207] The same day, Qāytbāy similarly elevated the amīr destined to become Qānṣūh's implacable rival, Aqbirdī min 'Alī Bāy, a junior associate of the sultan. Ever alert to possible conspiracy, Qāytbāy rarely promoted one ambitious officer without countering him by a competitor whom he trusted. How Qānṣūh's career would have developed had his mentor, Yashbak, triumphed at al-Ruhā is moot. After Yashbak's execution, Qānṣūh began to emulate his behavior—with one notable exception. Yashbak's greed was checked by his loyalty to Qāytbāy; Qānṣūh Khamsmi'a regarded no one as his superior.

205 *Badā'i'* 3, 275, l. 1
206 *Badā'i'* 3, 91, l. 22. This individual should not be confused with Qānṣūh al-Ghawrī, whom he briefly preceded as sultan after al-Nāṣir Muḥammad's deposition.
207 *Badā'i'* 3, 158, l. 17.

In the late 880s, Qānṣūh attained the highest levels of the military apparatus. Qāytbāy ultimately appointed him head of the royal stables in Muḥarram of 886/March 1481, an office permitting him residence within the Citadel.[208] The sultan, mindful of this man's vsions of grandeur, deliberately denied him his mentor's office, the dawādārīya. This Qāytbāy reserved for Aqbirdī, who held it to reign's end. Qāytbāy was following his political instincts when he made this decision and these had served him well before. But now, his favoritism of Aqbirdī earned Qānṣūh's undying malice towards the new dawādār and covert resentment of the sultan himself.

Qānṣūh kept his peace for the present, but established binding ties with the sultan's other confidant, Azbak. In 892/May–June 1487, he contracted a marriage with Azbak's daughter.[209] Since Azbak had no surviving son, the daughter, whose maternal grandfather was al-Ẓāhir Jaqmaq, enjoyed the status of his heir and executor of his estates. That the marshal agreed to the betrothal is a measure of the status Qānṣūh had attained by the early 890s. Because of its ostentation, Ibn Iyās described in detail the consummation ceremony following the contract. The bride's trousseau, composed of her own possessions from her parents' house, was transported across Cairo to Qānṣūh's palace by four hundred bearers. Its contents were rumored to be worth two hundred thousand dīnārs. On the nuptial eve Azbak hosted the public to a huge banquet at his lakeside belvedere. Qānṣūh traversed the city in a procession of a sort usually reserved for royalty alone. The muqaddamīn preceded him in full regalia, while the imperial guard carried torches to light his way. A gaudy spectacle, Ibn Iyās observed somewhat wryly—one might have thought that this vain officer already wore the royal turban and sword. But fate intervened to mar Qānṣūh's enjoyment of this grandiose moment. The Julbān recruits

208 *Badāʾiʿ* 3, 179, l. 10.
209 *Badāʾiʿ* 3, 241, l. 5; 242, l. 1.

had also stationed themselves along the parade route. Bearing little love for this man, who placed his own career above the welfare of former barracks mates, they resolved to spoil his evening. When the procession passed by, they snatched torches, seized turbans, and struck several commanders before dashing off into the night. Qāytbāy did nothing to rebuke their scandalous disruption.

By the late 890s, Qānṣūh was firmly entrenched in the ruling circle. Now very close to the aging Azbak, he had openly proclaimed his hostility toward the dawādār, Aqbirdī, whose office Qānṣūh believed should have devolved upon him. An unabashedly arrogant man, Qānṣūh displayed none of the *noblesse oblige* so evident in Qāytbāy or Azbak. When designated to lead the Maḥmal caravan to Mecca in 898/1493, Qānṣūh only grudgingly agreed.[210] Not relishing the prospect of leaving the capital to his rivals, he behaved himself disgracefully. Traveling with a luxurious retinue, Qānṣūh shared none of his supplies if other participants ran short en route. When his own camels died, he physically cast other riders off theirs, leaving them to reach their destination on foot. And tiring of the whole tedious affair, he abandoned many returning pilgrims in the port of Yanbuʿ to reach Cairo on their own by sea. So outraged were the pilgrims whose safety he was charged with that they held aloft black banners of protest when they finally reached the capital. Such behavior won Qānṣūh the uniform antipathy of the military class, civilian elite, and the masses. But such was the authority he now wielded that Qāytbāy or anyone else could do little to reprimand him.

Thus progressed the last decade of the fifteenth century: a rising tide of unrest, troop rebellion, self-serving opportunism. And heaping misery on malaise, the plague erupted once again in mid-897/January–April 1492.[211] Twice

210 *Badāʾiʿ* 3, 296, l. 17; 297, l. 18.
211 al-Sakhāwī, *Dhayl*, f. 217, l. 23; Ibn al-Ḥimṣī, *Ḥawādith*, f. 126b, l. 10; *Badāʾiʿ* 3, 286, l. 5; 289, l. 10; 292, l. 3.

before during Qāytbāy's reign the dreaded scourge had decimated Cairo's population. Especially vulnerable were recent immigrants, including all first-generation Mamlūks, African slaves, and resident foreigners. Epidemics traumatized every sector of the populace, however, who interpreted them as signs of a vengeful God's wrath inflicted on delinquent believers. During Qāytbāy's last years the plague compounded the manifestations of unrest discussed above. Ibn Iyās indulged in a rare discourse on lapsed morality when he laid responsibility for the epidemic squarely on reprehensible acts of the Mamlūk caste.[212] Visions were now commonly received wherein the Prophet warned of God visiting pestilence on Egypt if believers of every station failed to repent and fast ten days. Many heeded such admonitions but to no avail. Ibn Iyās quoted a ḥadīth that warned, "When they give immorality free license, they will find annihilation (*fanā'*)." He cited the great sage of the ninth century Ibn Ḥajar al-'Asqalānī, who had commented on the tradition as follows: "The lesson in this is that death ransoms wantonness. If it goes unpunished, God gives license to the demons (*jinn*) to kill the libertines. And if the indecency was committed furtively, then God authorizes the wraiths to kill them in secret—with no one aware. The chastisement underscores an invariable rule: it embraces both the guilty and the innocent. Divine mercy is, after all, exceptional. Only on Judgment Day are one's [true] intentions justly rewarded."

As the plague raged in Cairo, families high and low lost loved ones. The sultan's daughter titled "Lady of the Circassians" (*Sitt al-Jarākisa*) was stricken in Rajab. Her mother, a royal concubine, died the very same day.[213] As scores of officers succumbed, Qāytbāy and his associates desperately advanced junior men to replace them who normally would have required a decade more of seasoning before promotion

212 *Badā'i'* 3, 286, l. 16.
213 *Badā'i'* 3, 288, l. 9.

to executive office.[214] Ibn Iyās reported that the bureau of inheritances (*dīwān al-mawārīth*), taking stock of total fatalities when the epidemic subsided at the end of Rajab/May 1492, estimated the deceased in Cairo's vicinity at roughly two hundred thousand persons.[215] Allowing for exaggeration, this bout of plague wrought havoc in the capital and its provinces, leaving behind a decimated military and a ravaged populace. Many of Qāytbāy's comrades were carried off this year, shrouding him with loneliness and isolation that would endure to his own death. At decade's end, many rumormongers spread stories of dark omens forecasting the sultan's imminent demise. While Ibn Iyās scoffed at such predictions, their frequency attested to the disquiet of the times.[216]

The year 900/October 1494 thus began ominously for the cohesion of Qāytbāy's government. The endemic quarrels between officers jockeying for advantageous positions in the event of their sovereign's death should not, however, obscure the success of his foreign policy or an upturn in the economy. Throughout the year, the Nile was high, harvests plentiful, food prices low. But the certainty of the sultan's incapacity to rally made infighting inevitable. The sultan himself now exhibited the peevishness of old age. Paranoid over the prospect of revolt from every quarter, he turned against his own son, whom he suspected of serving as a willing tool in the hands of those who sought to supplant him.[217] Muḥammad was turned

214 *Badā'i'* 3, 289, l. 14.

215 *Badā'i'* 3, 288, l. 12 (serial promotions to rank of muqaddam); al-Sakhāwī, *Dhayl*, f. 221, l. 18 (sultan shuffles officers and orders them to observe truce); *Badā'i'* 3, 294, l. 3; 297, l. 16; 302, l. 21 (sultan promotes khāṣṣakīs to rank of amīr of ten for money).

216 For example (*Badā'i'* 3, 303, l. 2), the concurrence of the 'Īd al-Fiṭr in Shawwāl of 899/July 1494 with a Friday, necessitating the preaching of two khuṭbas. The sultan's titles were announced twice in one day, implying that his time remaining was short. Ibn Iyās observed that two simultaneous khuṭbas had occurred five times during Qāytbāy's reign with no negative result. But such were unsettled emotions in these trying times that many people seized on the least excuse to predict impending doom.

217 *Badā'i'* 3, 308, l. 11.

out of the residence his father had built for him and forced to sweep up after the troops in the Citadel Barracks, where he now lived as a common trainee. Not even the marshal Azbak could restore him to Qāytbāy's favor. The sultan also grasped at familial ties, however dubious, because of his personal losses. In Sha'bān/April–May, a man arrived in Cairo who claimed to be Qāytbāy's brother from Circassia.[218] Having resided in Europe for years, this individual, along with his two sons, sought the sultan's patronage. Qāytbāy took all three in, provided that they submit to circumcision. Whether he fully acknowledged the fraternal claim is unclear, but he granted the three a stipend of eighty thousand dīnārs and allowed them to tour the Syrian provinces and holy cities. The sultan had always been disposed to beneficent treatment of those he regarded as peers, but his eager reception of these strangers with suspect credentials convinced many within his entourage that his critical faculties were failing.

Qāytbāy now approached his eighty-third year. No preceding autocrat had ruled to such an age. While he suffered from bouts of dysentery and fever, the lines of dispute over his succession were sharply drawn between Aqbirdī and Qānṣūh. Their clash was prefaced by attempts of the Julbān to assassinate Qānṣūh before he could seize the sultanate. In Shawwāl/June–July, they pillaged his palace near the Bridge of Lions.[219] Only Qānṣūh's unforeseen absence on an impromptu inspection tour of his rural estates during the Nile crest saved his life. When he returned in Dhū'l-Qa'da/August, he was furious over the destruction of his residence and blamed Aqbirdī, who he believed had incited the recruits. On the first of Dhū'l-Ḥijja/23 August, he rallied comrades who supported his candidacy for the sultanate and rode to the atābak's home. Many amīrs of lesser rank joined him there,

218 Ibn al-Ḥimṣī, *Ḥawādith*, f. 155, l. 8; al-Sakhāwī, *Dhayl*, f. 262b, l. 17; *Badā'i'* 3, 308, l. 16.
219 Ibn al-Ḥimṣī, *Ḥawādith*, f. 157, l. 5; al-Sakhāwī, *Dhayl*, f. 60b, l. 1; *Badā'i'* 3, 309, l. 15.

as did a host of Sulṭānī Mamlūks. By midday a veritable army of mutineers had assembled at the Azbakīya with the apparent blessing of the sultan's staunchest colleague from the old guard.[220]

When Qāytbāy learned of the muster, he played the card that had quelled dissension in the past. Relying on his charisma, he descended to the reviewing pavilion at the Chain Gate looking out over the Rumayla Square and took up vigil there. A proclamation was read out requesting all army units to submit to God and their sultan, protector of His religion. All officers and troops still loyal did so at once. When the rebels at the Azbakīya learned that most of the army acknowledged Qāytbāy's authority, many withdrew their support from Qānṣūh, rode over to the Rumayla and begged the sultan's forgiveness. Qānṣūh realized he could never supplant their deep-seated allegiance to Qāytbāy and went into seclusion. But Azbak opted to beseech his old comrade's pardon on the grounds of twenty-seven years as a devoted aide. Washing himself thoroughly and saying a prayer of two prostrations (*rak'as*), he set out in a penitent's white tunic for the Citadel. When he ascended to the courtyard, the Julbān sought to strike him down as a traitor. The dawādār Aqbirdī reviled him for his error in judgment. But Qāytbāy welcomed his confidant. He was granted sanctuary in the Baḥra Hall, where the recruits dared not enter. There he remained for several days while the dawādār flushed out the other rebel leaders. No trace of Qānṣūh Khamsmi'a could be found, and rumors that he still plotted to overthrow Qāytbāy agitated the capital. When Qāytbāy invited Azbak to join him at Friday prayer in the Citadel Mosque, he warned his atābak of the recruits' resolve to murder him whenever the chance arose. Disheartened, Azbak returned to the Baḥra where, after mulling over his lot, he requested permission

220 Ibn al-Ḥimṣī, *Ḥawādith*, f. 158b, l. 4; *Jawāhir*, f. 397, l. 14; *Badā'i'* 3, 310, l. 21; *'Uqūd*, f. 237, l. 18.

to take voluntary exile in Mecca. When Qāytbāy consented on the eighth of Dhū'l-Ḥijja/30 August, Azbak resigned the marshalship and departed Cairo in disguise for the Red Sea port of al-Ṭūr.[221]

Qāytbāy spent his final months attempting to restructure the military hierarchy after the arrest, exile, or flight of so many key officers. Aqbirdī now strutted about as if he were sultan in all but name, although overtly acknowledging the rights of al-Nāṣir Muḥammad. Qāytbāy's insistence on participating in these decisions was remarkable in light of his frailty. He had abandoned all cavalry exercises and rarely made public appearances. But he still clung to life as the weeks came and went. Residual loyalty to so venerable a figure precluded any insult to his face, at least so long as Qānṣūh remained in hiding. But in Shawwāl/June–July, the hidden malcontent, never formally stripped of his post, gambled on the sultan's magnanimity, emerged from concealment, and threw himself on his liege lord's mercy.[222] Receiving him in the Audience Hall, Qāytbāy ordered him to don a tunic of Ba'albakkī cloth, normally used for wrapping corpses, then present himself to the troops. Qāytbāy guessed that they would be swayed by a man who begged their absolution in his own shroud. His instincts proved sound, and as a contrite prodigal Qānṣūh was exonerated. After he kissed the floor before the sultan, Qāytbāy restored him to his former status.

But no one doubted that Qānṣūh intended to settle his score with the dawādār. Nor were his ambitions diminished. In Dhū'l-Qa'da/July–August, Qānṣūh's own recruits stormed Aqbirdī's residence and then announced revolt once again. For the last time, Qāytbāy, who could now barely stand, rode down to the reviewing stand to show himself and call

221 Ibn al-Ḥimṣī, *Ḥawādith*, f. 159, l. 7; al-Sakhāwī, *Dhayl*, f. 278b, l. 5; *Badā'i'* 3, 314, l. 6.
222 *Badā'i'* 3, 321, l. 20.

upon all factions to respect the peace.[223] But this time few heeded his summons. During the late summer months the sultan had slept outside his palace on a porch overlooking the courtyard. When a barracks spy had warned him that some even of his guardians intended to assassinate him with arrows by night and thus clear the way for a younger man in his prime, Qāytbāy realized his days were numbered. Yet he stubbornly maintained his dignity. Fighting a worsening fever, he kept up his vigil at the Rumayla Square with only a few khāṣṣakīs in attendance. The scene, as Ibn Iyās describes it, quite poignantly captures the pathos of such a conclusion to a glorious career. Reverence for the old man remained, but power was slipping away by the hour. Finally, too ill to sit upright any longer, Qāytbāy managed to climb back on his horse and ascend to the Citadel. When informed that Aqbirdī had gone into hiding, he took to his couch and sank into a coma.

Now that the sultan no longer retained control over his senses, the new atābak, Timrāz al-Shamsī, renowned during the Sūwār campaigns, decided that the sultan's heir should be installed until the succession struggle worked itself out in his own favor. On Friday the twenty-fifth/5 August, he ascended to inform Qāytbāy, but the latter gave no sign of cognizance.[224] Timrāz then brought out Muḥammad, a reclusive boy of fourteen, from the barracks and proclaimed him sultan at the Chain Gate. When Qānṣūh Khamsmi'a learned of the atābak's ploy, he rushed to circumvent his bid to be power broker behind the throne. Rallying troops seeking an authority figure now that their patron lay dying, Qānṣūh captured Timrāz and placed him in irons. Over the next twenty-four hours all members of Aqbirdī's faction were hunted down and either executed or exiled. Qānṣūh and his fellow plotters then agreed to recognize al-Nāṣir Muḥammad as sultan and

223 *Badā'i'* 3, 322, l. 6, 17.
224 *Badā'i'* 3, 323, l. 13; *'Uqūd*, f. 239, l. 15.

thereby mitigate at least in part their act of usurpation. On the twenty-sixth/7 August, the Caliph and four qāḍīs formally sanctioned his enthronement. The next day, Qāytbāy expired, mercifully spared any awareness of the sordid events surrounding his son's acclamation. Ibn Iyās stated that the man who had defied the forces of nature so long died a shadow of his former self. Dysentery had prevented him from eating through his final illness and the corpse washers were shaken at his emaciation when the body was brought to them.[225] Qāytbāy's interment in his mausoleum occurred with little fanfare.

So passed one of the more imposing figures of the Muslim Middle Ages. We may be tempted to speculate over what passed through Qāytbāy's mind as he spent his last lucid hours seated in the Chain Gate pavilion. Might he have tasted the bitter gall of failure as he stared about the empty square where he had received the accolades of loyal soldiers and adoring subjects so many times before? Such remorse is only a remote possibility. Qāytbāy died a figure whose infirmity had weakened his capacity to rule, but one who was esteemed for his legion achievements. From his own perspective he had made no mistakes and thus had no cause for regret. Few could match the legacy of this revered monarch. The squabbling that overshadowed his last year emerged as the natural consequence of a political process embedded in the Mamlūk system. As a conservator, Qāytbāy sought to maintain what he inherited. His contemporaries respected him for his rejuvenation of the Mamlūk institution; none regarded him as an innovator bent on restructuring it. During his life Qāytbāy thought of himself an integral member of the military caste, for whom rivalries were never aberrant. A great autocrat, by his personal force, might temporarily neutralize factional infighting, but he would never eliminate it through institutional reform.

225 *Badā'i'* 3, 324, l. 16; *'Uqūd*, f. 239b, l. 14.

It is more likely, as Qāytbāy looked out over the Rumayla this last day of his active reign, that he faced the inevitable with the stoic resolve of a soldier born to strife and the vagaries of power. An emotion far more probable than remorse was the comfort that Qāytbāy found in his Islamic faith. All who knew the sultan were impressed with the depths of his piety. Unflagging religious convictions certainly sustained him as he prepared to face the judgment of his Maker, the only opinion that mattered to a man who had commanded sole authority for so long. And Qāytbāy could assuredly look to that judgment with confidence that he had done his best as a ruler and a believer in the years God allotted him. It is a serenity of this kind that continues to infuse al-Ashraf Qāytbāy's legacy. It stands in marked contrast to the unsavory memories associated with his ultimate successor, Qānṣūh al-Ghawrī.

Chapter Three

Qānṣūh al-Ghawrī
Vilified Innovator

AL-GHAWRĪ'S sultanate ... lasted fifteen years, nine months, twenty-five days, each of which weighed down on the people like a thousand years.

He was a prince who inspired respect, of somber bearing, imposing in processions, pleasing to look upon. Had it not been for his injustices, the frequency of his confiscations against the masses, his insatiable love of riches, he would have been ... one of the better rulers over Egypt.

On his fingers he wore ruby rings, turquoises, emeralds, diamonds, sapphires. He enjoyed the scents of fine perfumes and incense. He was highly refined in his food, drink, and dress. He loved to observe flowers and fruit trees, and was inclined to prefer the company of Persians. He enjoyed planting shrubs, engaging in physical exercise. He delighted in the singing of birds, the scent of blossoms. He used gold cups even for water. Eating gave him undue pleasure. As we have related, he ruled over Egypt in luxury.

His word was undisputed, his authority uncontested. Officers, governors, and soldiers he held in his grip; none dared oppose him—until his ill-fated encounter with Selim Shāh. Then he suffered an unparalleled catastrophe, without precedent in the history of Egypt's kings.

Al-Ghawrī possessed both good and bad qualities, but his defects outweighed his positive traits. Among the latter, his character was sound. He controlled his temper and rarely yielded to impulses arising from his nature. He profoundly revered pious and spiritual figures. He knew how to appraise the populace according to their social stations. He could rein in his tongue from insulting the masses during outbursts of anger. He understood poetry and appreciated fine music. He actually wrote verses in Turkish. He was acquainted with works of history, biography, and poetry. He retained a degree of familiarity with the people, enjoying pleasantries and banter during conversations. He possessed common sense and a certain amiability of character—contrary to the natural Turkish disposition. He rarely displayed insolence, arrogance, or grossness—in contrast to the typical behavior of kings.

Yet his faults were legion. The sultan put his hand on money deriving from familial estates and seized the patrimony of orphans unjustly. If children, male or female, of deceased parents claimed their inheritance, he denied them their rights according to religious law. The sultan appointed prefects and shaykhs over the local provinces, charging them large sums for their offices. In turn, these officials assessed the fief- and trust-holders double. The army consequently declined, and the decay of the countryside worsened. The sultan installed governors of the Syrian provinces in like fashion, demanding large sums every year at a set level. These governors proceeded to extract their dues from the populace in cruel and oppressive ways. Thus did the commons consider fleeing their districts to find refuge elsewhere.

The prefect of Jidda collected from the Indian merchants a tenth of their income, an act discouraging them from entering the port at all—which thus fell idle. Their goods became scarce in Egypt, and the town was deserted. Similarly, the ports of Alexandria and Damietta were abandoned because Frankish merchants ceased entering them. European merchandise also disappeared.

All sorts of disreputable persons approached the sultan, gaining his favor and urging him to adopt unjust policies. The sultan imposed a tax on grain sales—affecting both buyers and sellers.... Indeed, he renewed taxes in a fashion unparalleled by his predecessors. No notable merchant ever received a favor without paying for it. The sultan even dared to confiscate property from the Caliph, on the pretext of reclaiming the latter's debts. The list of those who died under torture because of money is too long to recount.

He abused the sons of the military caste, depriving them of their fiefs and rents without cause—giving these over to his own recruits. He stopped pensions of orphans, even the very young, causing them great hardship. He terminated charitable distributions from the Special Bureau (*dīwān al-mufrad*) from which the people had benefited. His greed knew no limits, for he even stooped to extorting drivers of water-bearing draft animals and gardeners at the Citadel, forcing them to sell the dung of their beasts and to turn over the money to the reserve fund.

Senior officials and agents of state remained in extreme fear of him, never forgetting the threat of confiscation. When the amīr Khayrbak al-Khāzindār died, the sultan took over direct supervision of the treasury himself, checking all deposits and withdrawals. Vast sums of money held there were spent on projects of no benefit to the Muslims.

He shunned his legal duties as a child avoids school. And the few judgments he did make were unsatisfactory. He cared only for affairs of credit, ignoring murder cases or plaintiffs' suits—thus neglecting the people's rights. He loathed signing decrees and only a few received his signature. Thus was public business delayed. Indeed, old seals were purchased for an Ashrafī [dīnār] and fixed on documents. Truly, the list of al-Ghawrī's misdeeds was endless.

> Yet, in sum, he was one of the abler Circassian rulers. No one who followed him could equal his acts or surpass his lofty views and resolute spirit. He merited the sultanate.[1]

THE contrast between Ibn Iyās's rather straightforward eulogy of Qāytbāy and his tirade against al-Ghawrī bespeaks the latter's more complex legacy. Ibn Iyās spared Qānṣūh al-Ghawrī, Egypt's penultimate militarist autocrat, no censure for his misdeeds as the historian interpreted them. Ibn Iyās linked al-Ghawrī's policies to Egypt's decline and minced few words on the issue. Yet his obituary was no unrelieved denunciation, a diatribe listing random abuses inflicted on the sultan's hapless subjects without rationale. Ibn Iyās concluded his assessment by reaffirming al-Ghawrī's stature as an impressive ruler despite his "legion defects." Ibn Iyās's obituary to al-Ghawrī typifies the subtle perspective historians of the later Muslim Middle Ages brought to the craft of kingship. In their eyes, al-Ghawrī behaved like a tyrant and suffered God's punishment for his sins. Yet his crimes did not obscure his intelligence, his refined tastes, his personal force, or his pragmatic approach to politics. The resultant tension between al-Ghawrī's oppressive measures and his vigorous leadership presents the modern historian with an intriguing paradox.

It is tempting to make a scapegoat of Qānṣūh al-Ghawrī, branding him as an embodiment of all the ills beleaguering the Mamlūk state on the eve of its demise before the armies of Selim I in 1516. Yet, although al-Ghawrī was intimately involved in implementing policies deleterious to his society's well-being, he was more than a selfish dictator bent on personal indulgence. Both al-Ashraf Qāytbāy and Qānṣūh al-Ghawrī came from the same background, both regarded their realms as patrimonies they guarded with their own lives and exploited as they saw fit. Neither entertained any concept of shared authority with subordinates in critical policy

[1] *Badā'i'* 5, 87, l. 19–95, l. 9.

matters. Nonetheless, Qāytbāy and al-Ghawrī received vastly differing treatment from the pens of contemporary chroniclers. The first was honored as a magnanimous hero, the latter reviled as a greedy despot. Both were considered paragons of bravery; neither would have reached the top as anything less. It is therefore the antithetical legacies of these two eminently successful representatives of the Mamlūk institution that capture our attention. Were al-Ghawrī's acts of predation at the root of Ibn Iyās's condemnation and that of others who observed him at close range? Or was the stridency of their censure impelled by al-Ghawrī's covert motives behind his predation? Was al-Ghawrī vilified because of his tyranny or because of his deviance from accepted patterns of behavior established by his predecessors centuries earlier and now perceived as violated? Did God bring down his vengeance on this man for sins of gross oppression or pernicious innovation? And if he were guilty of both, which warranted the more vehement reprobation?

If Qāytbāy, prior to his enthronement, could be judged an ideal team player who progressed steadily through the ranks with little interest in the sultanate, al-Ghawrī emerges rather suddenly from virtual obscurity. A dark horse, who attracted nothing more than passing mention of his appointments, al-Ghawrī seems to have combined enough sagacity with martial ability to earn his promotion. But no details on his equestrian skills, personal interests, or factional alliances drew the attention of biographers or chroniclers. Like Qāytbāy, he dictated no memoirs nor did he instruct a personal secretary to keep a diary before his reign. Unlike Qāytbāy, he endowed no monuments or charitable institutions prior to his enthronement, nor did he draw up any waqf writs before 906.

Ibn Iyās wrote that Qānṣūh al-Ghawrī, like most of his comrades, originated in Circassia.[2] He was purchased

[2] *Badā'i'* 4, 2, l. 3.

for military service and imported into Egypt during the early years of Qāytbāy's reign. Installed in the barracks of al-Ghawr, where he received his intitial drilling, Qānṣūh chose his place of tutelage for his only agnomen. Disinterest in titles is typical of al-Ghawrī's future attitude. While obsessed with personal luxury, he cared little for official approbation and never sought to impart a formal stance encapsulated in throne-names. He received his first significant office in Dhū'l-Qa'da of 886/December 1481–January 1482, when Qāytbāy named him inspector (*kāshif*) of Upper Egypt.[3] Since he was sixty years old when he accepted the sultanate, he was already forty when he assumed his first command. If al-Ghawrī commenced his career as part of Qāytbāy's first corps of recruits, he must have attained his late twenties when he arrived in Cairo. His relative maturity at the time of his manumission qualifies the impression we have of recruits uniformly initiating their service while adolescents.[4] Qānṣūh al-Ghawrī presumably left Circassia as an adult, his predispositions and values already shaped before he was subjected to the powerful acculturating forces of the Mamlūk training system. In any case, we have no comments about his participation in the tumultuous rivalry between competing coteries of recruits, each backing officers jockeying for power or influence. Nothing more was said about al-Ghawrī until he was promoted to the rank of amīr of ten in Rabī' II 889/April–May 1484, and designated to ride in the abortive Ottoman expedition of that year.[5] Soon thereafter, he began an extended tour of duty in Syria and southeastern Anatolia when Qāytbāy assigned him the governorship over the march town of Ṭarsūs.[6] From this time on we hear more of al-Ghawrī, who appears to have been a reliable, if somewhat ruthless, provincial administrator.

3 *Badā'i'* 3, 190, l. 20.
4 Ayalon, "Studies on the Structure of the Mamluk Army," pt. 1, 208–209.
5 *Badā'i'* 3, 207, l. 12.
6 *Badā'i'* 4, 2, l. 5.

In Rabīʿ II of 894/March 1489, al-Ghawrī was transferred from this outpost to the chamberlainship (*ḥajaba*) of Aleppo.[7] There he won Qāytbāy's respect for his staving off disaster when, in Dhū'l-Qaʿda of 896/September–October 1491, a riot broke out against the city's viceroy, Azdamur. Caught off guard, the nā'ib lost control of the mob over all districts outside the citadel. Seventeen of his retainers were murdered and several staff burned alive.[8] Qānṣūh took charge, fought the rebels back from the citadel gates and then restored order in the town itself—inflicting bloody reprisals for the insurrection. The sultan, gravely alarmed by this unexpected upheaval during the Ottoman campaigns, dispatched an agent to investigate the riot's causes. Neither Ibn al-Ḥimṣī nor Ibn Iyās reported the consequences of this inquiry, but Qānṣūh's own prestige emerged considerably heightened from the affair.

The interfactional tensions following Qāytbāy's death drew al-Ghawrī inexorably into the rivalries of grand amīrs jostling for the succession. During the brief tenure of Qāytbāy's heir, al-Nāṣir Muḥammad (901–903/1496–1498), al-Ghawrī joined the elite clique of commanders of a thousand and was sent off to assume the governorship of Malaṭya, on the Anatolian frontier. Al-Nāṣir's successor, al-Ẓāhir Qānṣūh, recalled al-Ghawrī to Cairo and bestowed on him the guard captaincy on the third of Dhū'l-Qaʿda 905/31 May 1500.[9] Al-Ghawrī had apparently developed a close association with al-ʿĀdil Ṭūmānbāy, the current dawādār, because he elected to participate in his Damascus expedition in 906 to crush a revolt by the city's governor against the next ephemeral sultan, al-Ashraf Jānbalāṭ. When Ṭūmānbāy assumed control

7 *Badā'iʿ* 3, 264, l. 21.

8 *Badā'iʿ* 3, 284, l. 18.

9 *Badā'iʿ* 4, 2, l. 18. This al-Ẓāhir Qānṣūh was the grand amīr Qānṣūh Khamsmi'a who coveted the sultanate during Qāytbāy's waning years. The name Qānṣūh was extremely popular with this generation of Circassian Mamlūks, and several prominent officers bore it.

over Damascus, he declared against his patron, Jānbalāṭ, proclaimed himself sultan, and raised his khushdāsh al-Ghawrī to his own former post of executive secretary.[10] Thus did this officer, who had served in Syria competently but in relative obscurity for years, now emerge as adjutant to the reigning monarch. When al-ʿĀdil was deposed by his own troops back in Cairo during Ramaḍān of 906/April 1501, al-Ghawrī found himself squarely in the midst of an uneasy oligarchy of amīrs who once again faced the task of deciding who among them should assume the imperial office, which now seemed to ensure only ignominous removal.[11]

Before unraveling the maze of events preceding al-Ghawrī's elevation to the sultanate, a lesser-known chronicler's views about al-Ghawrī's doings in Syria should be examined for their contrasting perspective on his motives. These were offered by an Aleppo-based compiler of necrologies, Muḥammad ibn Ibrāhīm al-Ḥalabī al-Ḥanbalī, whose lengthy entry on al-Ghawrī depicts a shrewd, calculating figure who played for high stakes in dangerous circumstances and almost lost his head in the process.[12] Al-Ḥalabī relates that, following al-Nāṣir Muḥammad's assassination, al-Ghawrī was still serving as chamberlain in Aleppo when open rebellion

[10] Ibn Ṭūlūn, *Iʿlām al-warā bi-man wulliya min al-Atrāk bi-Dimashq*, ed. ʿAbd al-ʿAẓīm Ḥāmid Khaṭṭāb (Cairo 1973) 121, l. 15; 130, l. 8.

[11] The preceding skeletal outline of the extended succession crisis following Qāytbāy's death does little more than list contenders who clawed their way to the throne only to be supplanted soon thereafter. The unhappy al-Naṣir Muḥammad found himself a pawn in the hands of his erstwhile supporters, and was assassinated two years after his enthronement. Several grand amīrs among the oligarchy Qāytbāy left behind either connived to secure their acclamations as autocrats or were grudgingly compelled to assume the high-risk position by their comrades. Unassuming as he was, al-Nāṣir Muḥammad did attract at least one biographer. The Topkapı Saray Library contains the anonymous *Kitāb ithbāt al-dalālāt Muḥammad ibn al-marḥūm al-malik al-Ashraf Qāytbāy* (ms. 2960), which dwells more on machinations of Qānṣūh Khamsmi'a than on any aspirations the puppet sultan may have harbored. For an overview of these succession crises, see Gaston Wiet, *L'Egypte arabe*, 607–612.

[12] *Kitāb durr al-ḥabab fī ta'rīkh aʿyān Ḥalab*, Vienna, Codex Vinobonensis Palatinus, Mxt. 667, f. 177b, l. 5.

erupted against al-Nāṣir Muḥammad's successor, al-Ẓāhir Qānṣūh. The incumbent governor, one Īnāl, renounced his allegiance to the usurper in Cairo, Jānbalāt. Al-Ghawrī received a secret edict from Īnāl's opponent in the capital calling for the governor's arrest during one of his biweekly audiences at the Justice Hall. But Īnāl managed to outmaneuver his would-be captor and threatened him with execution. Al-Ghawrī fled Aleppo by night and sought refuge in the home of a Jew in Ḥamā.

When Jānbalāt was deposed by al-'Ādil some months later, al-Ghawrī emerged from hiding and returned to Cairo in triumph as the new autocrat's amīr kabīr. Al-Ḥalabī claims that al-'Ādil so valued al-Ghawrī's services that he designated him "Conciliator of the Realm" (*muṣāliḥ al-dawla*). But since few counted on al-'Ādil's staying power, many rumors circulated as to his imminent replacement. Diviners foretold al-Ghawrī's accession as the inevitable choice of his comrades. But so hazardous did al-Ghawrī regard such prophecies that he departed Cairo for a tour of the Upper Egyptian fiefs.

> His fellows than assassinated the sultan while he was absent and confirmed *him* to sit on the throne, whether he willed it or not. Al-Ghawrī vigorously protested upon his return, fearing that they would murder him, as they had done to his predecessors. But they told him confidentially, "Sit until we decide on our [final] choice for the sultanate." His colleagues then did obeisance before him and he occupied the throne. But God willed that he retain his grip over the sultanate. He degraded the veteran officers (*qarāniṣa*), and the might and power of the Circassian amīrs began to fade. He killed them off, one by one.

This account, while questionable for its facts, provides an insight to al-Ghawrī's own sense of his tenuous position. Accepting the sultanate only under duress, he surprised everyone by holding onto it. Fearing treachery from all quarters, he had no scruples about terminating rivals, real or imagined, and began to institute ad hoc changes in the power structure for the first time in the Circassian period.

According to Ibn Iyās's and 'Abd al-Bāsiṭ's soberer versions of the succession crisis, al-'Ādil Ṭūmānbāy was deposed in Ramaḍān. He eluded his traitorous followers, went into hiding and attempted flight from the capital on the eve of 'Īd al-Fiṭr.[13] Several amīrs who remained neutral, including al-Ghawrī, rode to the residence of al-Ẓāhir Qānṣūh, under house arrest since his own deposition. There they enjoined the current marshal, Tānibak, to accept the throne. The latter agreed, but when he reached the Chain Gate at the foot of the Citadel, he found too few amīrs or squadrons of soldiers willing to commit themselves to his candidacy. What conspiracies the redoubtable al-Ẓāhir Qānṣūh might still have up his sleeve unsettled everyone, and the majority of officers and troopers elected to spend the feast day at home awaiting events. Ibn Iyās noted the low opinion of Tānibak held by many members of the military hierarchy. "Most troopers were opposed to the atābak Tānibak and not a single one came out for him. The marshal was unlucky and given to unsound actions. He lost his judgment when he aspired to the sultanate. And thus he ended a failure, never attaining it. Rather, he unwittingly advanced the cause of Qānṣūh al-Ghawrī."

When the makeshift council of amīrs realized that Tānibak's candidacy was hopeless, two future backers of al-Ghawrī, Qāyt al-Rajabī, the armaments minister, and the muqaddam Miṣirbāy, proposed him openly for the first time. Qānṣūh reacted with a public show of surprised alarm. He protested so vehemently, weeping and rending his clothes, that the two closeted themselves with their recalcitrant nominee, remonstrating with him for some time. Their shouting could be heard by all those waiting outside. Miṣirbāy allegedly

[13] *Badā'i'* 4, 3, l. 12; 'Abd al-Bāsiṭ, *Al-risāla al-laṭīfa tashtamalu 'alā dhikrin man waliya Miṣr min al-Salaṭīn* (Istanbul, Laleli, 2044) ff. 8b, l. 20; 9, l. 18.

seized al-Ghawrī by his collar and demanded that he accept for the regime's survival. As the haggling dragged on, other officers summoned the Caliph and the four qāḍīs to prepare documents of installation. But neither the Shāfi'ī nor Ḥanafī judges were prepared to set their hands to such an instrument, claiming that no genuine consensus had been reached by a majority of officers.

Nonetheless, the Caliph prepared for the enthronement ceremony while the Ḥanbalī qāḍī wrote an edict charging al-'Ādil with malfeasance. An arrest warrant was taken out on him and amnesty was offered al-Ẓāhir Qānṣūh in return for his sworn allegiance to al-Ghawrī. Many witnesses from the populace stepped forth to denounce al-'Ādil as a bloody tyrant. The Shāfi'ī and Ḥanafī judges now decided that prudence outweighed principle and confirmed al-Ghawrī in office. We are not informed of the secret bargaining that occurred behind the facade of elaborate protest, but al-Ghawrī finally stepped forth in the company of Qāyt al-Rajabī and Miṣirbāy and agreed to sit upon the throne. The ceremony took place on Monday the first of Shawwāl 906/20 April 1501. As the turban was wound around his head and the sword girded around his waist, he muttered that such symbols counted for little if the office remained the plaything of perfidious officers. Offered his new titles of al-Ashraf and Abī'l-Naṣr, he scorned them as hollow tokens of false dignity. But nonetheless, Qāyt al-Rajabī persuaded him to mount his horse, which bore the sultan's golden saddle, for his acclamation procession down to the Rumayla. Qāyt carried the royal parasol and bird over his head as he descended. When al-Ghawrī reached the square, the amīrs and troops had assembled to pledge themselves. Qāyt was the first to kiss the ground before him. He had been promised the marshalship (*atābakīya*) in Tānibak's place and would brook no further resistance from his unwilling colleague. Miṣirbāy received the dawādārīya and vizierate in place of the new sultan.

Ibn Iyās observed that the masses responded to al-Ghawrī's installation with relief in the aftermath of so much strife. Still, many predicted that al-Ghawrī would soon follow his predecessors into oblivion or worse. Later, Qānṣūh joked openly about his early nay-sayers, but at this juncture he brooded over the perils ahead. Indeed, the intensity of al-Ghawrī's disavowal presents historians with the same enigma that surrounded Qāytbāy's resistance thirty-four years earlier. Neither man had openly sought the office, neither actively campaigned for nomination. Qāytbāy's protests strike the observer as more pro forma, but both men's reluctance could be interpreted as an elaborate sham, in light of the opportunism built into Mamlūk politics. Yet al-Ghawrī's deprecation is more believable because of the inauspicious circumstances preceding his accession and his disinclination to covet visible positions of authority. Al-Ghawrī had risen to the upper echelons of the Mamlūk hierarchy as a shadowy figure known for his effectiveness but otherwise intensely private. His own objectives were inscrutable at this stage in his career. Yet this man, already in his sixtieth year, clearly knew his own mind when he accepted the sultanate. If he did so unwillingly as a compromise candidate, al-Ghawrī realized that his prime goal was survival. Many of his critics would argue later that his reign never amounted to anything more. But al-Ghawrī fully appreciated the weakness of his position and was disposed from the outset to alter the ruling apparatus. In this, he would contrast sharply with al-Ashraf Qāytbāy.

Al-Ghawrī could not proceed to any meaningful coalescence of authority while his predecessor remained at large. So long as al-ʿĀdil Ṭūmānbāy was in seclusion, disgruntled officers or recruits might rally behind him. The new sultan, his colleagues, and several embittered partisans of Jānbalāṭ thus plotted to lure him from his lair by a pretended countercoup. In early Dhū'l-Qaʿda, two of al-ʿĀdil's allies, both bearing the name Jānibak, were enticed into the ruse with promises of promotion to the rank of muqaddam.[14] Since both knew al-ʿĀdil's refuge, they were to propose to him a conspiracy in which Miṣirbāy, the new dawādār, would be assassinated and al-Ghawrī deposed. Miṣirbāy was to be approached by stealth while he sat at night in his residence, recently expropriated from the estate of al-Ẓāhir Timurbughā. Upon his murder, al-ʿĀdil would ride to the Chain Gate and declare his supremacy. Al-ʿĀdil agreed to the plot and went over to the house of one of the schemers, where he was to await the news of the assassination. But of course he walked into a trap. While al-ʿĀdil sat at a sumptuous repast, Miṣirbāy was informed of his whereabouts. His fellow conspirators returned secretly with the dawādār and Jānbalāṭ's retainers and took him by surprise. Unwilling to submit tamely, Ṭūmānbāy tried escape by climbing over the house wall. But he fractured his leg when he fell into the street, and could not make good his flight. Seeking to avoid any further trouble from this "bane of amīrs" as they branded him, Jānbalāṭ's men beheaded al-ʿĀdil on the spot as he was hobbling away, and not content with his death, they hacked his body to pieces. When their ardor calmed, the assassins took al-ʿĀdil's head and conveyed it to Miṣirbāy, who awaited them within. He placed the trophy on a copper tray and had it paraded publicly across the city to the Citadel, where it was shown to al-Ghawrī. As they marched, its bearers shouted forth, "Such is the fate of him who sheds the amīrs' blood without cause!" Yet Ibn Iyās stated that, despite their antipathy for Ṭūmānbāy, many found the spectacle degrading. He had been enthroned but now suffered a lowly criminal's fate. Al-Ghawrī, while relieved by his deliverance from such a thorn, sensed their indignation and ordered the head returned to its mangled corpse for the semblance of proper burial. After the remains were washed and shrouded, they were sent to al-ʿĀdil's mausoleum under guard of the prefect of police, who watched

14 *Badāʾiʿ* 4, 7, l. 15; 9, l. 5.

out for any attempts by Jānbalāṭī troopers to desecrate the body. With al-ʿĀdil's elimination, al-Ghawrī could begin the process of conscripting his own network of followers. Yet the stain of his predecessor's end continued to haunt him through the years. When Qāytbāy ascended the throne, he offered his ousted predecessor, Timurbughā, honorable exile. But al-ʿĀdil's dismembered corpse now lay in his tomb, a stark symbol of how the new monarch dealt with opponents. The contrast was lost on no one.[15]

The Initial Period: Elusive Consolidation

Little euphoria greeted al-Ghawrī upon his enthronement, and his secretive nature inspired no tight band of followers to link their destinies with his unreservedly. This man faced an intimidating task of consolidation. Hostility was inevitable under the circumstances al-Ghawrī inherited and abetted; that he managed to deal successfully with them in the end is more remarkable than the advent of sedition. The final months of 906/late April to early July, overshadowed by the search for al-ʿĀdil, witnessed several attempts by al-Ghawrī to build a reliable oligarchy. He also began a systematic purge of all al-ʿĀdil's adherents, civil or military. Qāyt al-Rajabī and Miṣirbāy were duly installed as atābak and dawādār. Yet neither developed with al-Ghawrī the intimacy Qāytbāy had nurtured with either Yashbak min Mahdī or Azbak

[15] Ibn Iyās noted that al-ʿĀdil Ṭūmānbāy brought his violent end upon himself and spent no time lamenting the brevity of his reign. A strong-willed individual who exhibited many talents, al-ʿĀdil was driven by greed and a certain mean-spiritedness. Having usurped his position, he tried to slaughter off all possible rivals, earning the undying hatred of the amīral oligarchy. Al-Ghawrī lived with the stigma of a doubledealer because he lured a fellow ruler into assassination by the most devious of means, not because he had murdered an innocent victim. See *Badāʾiʿ* 4, 11, l. 4.

min Ṭuṭukh.[16] Although victims of al-ʿĀdil's brutality were granted amnesty, released from jail, or welcomed back from exile, few offered the new sultan their undying fealty in gratitude. Jalāl al-Dīn al-Suyūṭī, the eminent polymath, whom al-ʿĀdil had threatened with execution on grounds of questionable loyalty, acknowledged al-Ghawrī's pardon but received no particular favor.[17] Most of the ʿĀdilīya Mamlūks were exiled to Upper Egypt or the Ḥijāz, and al-Ghawrī possessed few recruits of his own to replace them. For the time being, he was compelled to live with the restive coalition of ambivalent factions that had served his predecessors until he could acquire his own soldiers. These men, devoid of any personal attachment to their sovereign, plotted their own course solely on the basis of promotions he granted and stipends he proffered. Al-Ghawrī was so daunted by the rapacity of their demands, unaccompanied by any show of camaraderie, that he contemplated abdicating voluntarily within a few weeks of his installation.[18]

Nonetheless, he got through those turbulent early months. Once al-ʿĀdil was executed, his removal allowed both commons and elite to breathe easier. When his head was displayed, his victims' families rejoiced, praising his successor as a restorer of justice, however severe.[19] Al-Ghawrī ordered Sultan Jānbalāṭ's body returned to the capital from Alexandria, where it had lain in the dungeon to which al-ʿĀdil had confined him. In this, al-Ghawrī was moved by no fraternal impulses but pragmatically acknowledged the sentiments of Jānbalāṭ's Mamlūks, who wished to see their former patron interred in his own tomb as a Muslim.[20] Most executive offices were filled with individuals willing at least to pursue their own fortunes in consort with their new monarch, if not

16 *Badāʾiʿ* 4, 6, l. 10; 8, l. 6.
17 *Badāʾiʿ* 4, 5, l. 20.
18 *Badāʾiʿ* 4, 7, l. 6.
19 *Badāʾiʿ* 4, 11, l. 19; *Iʿlām*, 146, l. 9.
20 *Badāʾiʿ* 4, 7, l. 23.

to commit themselves to a new grand design.[21] Yet the year concluded with an act of violence that boded ill for future stability or loyalty to the sultan. When al-Ghawrī reaffirmed his general amnesty for all who renounced their former allegiance to al-ʿĀdil, several officials who had served in the latter's dīwān emerged from seclusion and made their way to the Citadel, anticipating al-Ghawrī's absolution. But the sultan's promise of safe-conduct proved worthless in the case of those secretly targeted for reprisal. When the respected qāḍī Shams al-Dīn Abū'l-Manṣūr, who had served al-ʿĀdil as his steward, arrived at the Chain Gate, a gang of Mamlūks struck him down with their daggers, leaving him for dead in the street.[22] No inquiry was made into the murder, no delegation sent from the Palace to retrieve his body. Family members ultimately begged the sultan's leave to claim the corpse.

Although the new year 907 portended minimal support for al-Ghawrī's rule, the sultan himself checked sedition with decisive steps. In Muḥarram, acting upon multiple reports of conspiracy, he arrested Miṣirbāy and cast him in irons.[23] Jailed amīrs had been escaping with alarming frequency throughout the month, and al-Ghawrī feared their rallying around a major rival. Soldiers in the barracks had become so boisterous that the sultan resorted to an unprecedented show of unity by summoning all senior officers to take a loyalty oath, sworn on a copy of the Koran allegedly copied during ʿUthmān's reign.[24] This holy relic had sanctified similar rites in the distant past, but Qāytbāy had never relied on it. Now al-Ghawrī forced the amīrs to pledge themselves one by one with their hands on the cover in the presence of the Caliph and the four qāḍīs. The ceremony proved more symbolic

21 *Badāʾiʿ* 4, 9, l. 4 (enemy of al-ʿĀdil appointed amīr majlis); 12, l. 3 (officers previously exiled to Damascus allowed to return); 12, l. 13 (several amīrs promoted to rank of muqaddam alf); 12, l. 23 (eight amīrs of ten allowed to resume their status).

22 *Badāʾiʿ* 4, 13, l. 2.

23 *Badāʾiʿ* 4, 17, l. 21; *Iʿlām*, 148, l. 16.

24 *Badāʾiʿ* 4, 18, l. 11.

than substantive since it deterred no subsequent mutinies. Nonetheless, al-Ghawrī would repeatedly avail himself of it right up to his fated encounter with Selim. Once Miṣirbāy had been seized, the sultan's position became less precarious. Al-Ghawrī used his arrest as an occasion to break up other potential cells of sedition and pack squadrons of Mamlūks off to cool their heels in Upper Egypt. The dawādār was formally stripped of his office and imprisoned in Alexandria, but less than three months after his incarceration news reached the Citadel that he had broken out of his dungeon and returned to Cairo in disguise.

Miṣirbāy's stratagem did credit to the cunning that had facilitated his previous advancement. One of his aides allegedly smuggled a lime preparation past the guards into the ex-dawādār's cell. By smearing it on his chains, Miṣirbāy corroded them enough to slip loose. Climbing down the walls, he took flight for Cairo in a small vessel waiting outside.[25] When al-Ghawrī received the news, his colleagues speculated that Miṣirbāy was already plotting in seclusion to topple him. Al-Ghawrī wasted no time lamenting this turn of events. The prefect was ordered to search the city quarter by quarter, house by house. Protests by residents that their businesses were disrupted, their privacy needlessly abused, fell on deaf ears. Since a general amnesty failed to entice Miṣirbāy out, the sultan intensified the search, while meting out savage punishments for any further shows of rebellion. In Jumādā II/December 1501–January 1502, two amīrs rumored to be hatching plots in the barracks were flogged to death in the Citadel courtyard while the sultan impassively looked on. Their bodies were cast into graves without prayer services as a sign of the autocrat's ire.[26]

Days and weeks passed as the search for Miṣirbāy dragged on. An eerie calm belying the tensions lurking beneath the

25 *Badā'i'* 4, 21, l. 7.
26 *Badā'i'* 4, 23, l. 7.

facade of order settled over Cairo. In Ramaḍān/March–April, Miṣirbāy, frustrated over the stalemate, finally took the initiative. Having gathered a small band of "disreputable Mamlūks," he planned to assault officers loyal to the sultan when they descended from the evening fast-breaking at the palace.[27] The rebels wounded several amīrs but killed none. Miṣirbāy had hoped to murder his replacement, Azdamur min 'Ālī Bāy, along with his former partner, Qāyt al-Rajabī. Failing in this scheme, he retreated to the Rumayla Square, where he hoped disaffected soldiers would come over to him. But when none showed up, Miṣirbāy retreated to the Azbakīya in one last desperate attempt to rouse Sulṭānī veterans, men who had suffered the most from al-Ghawrī's purges, to his cause. But despite their resentment, few even of these aggrieved troops were prepared to side with a loser. By daybreak of the thirteenth, only twenty men had joined the ex-dawādār. Al-Ghawrī then sent the prefect of police to confront his devious colleague. The engagement was brief and bloody. Miṣirbāy was cut down and mutilated. An officer hoisted his cadaver onto his horse and bore it to the Citadel.

Once delivered of his enemy, al-Ghawrī showed himself magnanimous. He ordered Miṣirbāy's body washed for burial. Ibn Iyās ridiculed this abortive coup as a plot doomed before it began. Having recruited the least respected elements of the Mamlūk caste, Miṣirbāy could not induce more reputable groups to join him. Also, many factions were grudgingly resigning themselves to al-Ghawrī's entrenchment. Despite their antipathy, they had wearied of interminable plots and counterplots. Ibn Iyās believed the foiling of Miṣirbāy's comical adventure merited comment solely because it marked the tide's turning in al-Ghawrī's favor. Even though the sultan did not relax his vigil for several more years, he had effectively broken resistance when he crushed Miṣirbāy. But Ibn Iyās also observed that his search, drawn out over

[27] *Badā'i'* 4, 26, l. 13.

months, left abiding scars among the commons, who resented their sovereign's disregard for their own comfort. Al-Ghawrī appears to have paid their suffering no heed. He hosted his cronies to lavish soirées during the final months of 907 and celebrated the end of the polo season with a vast banquet for them—but did not invite the public.[28]

Ibn Iyās began his coverage of the year 908/1502–1503 by listing all executive officers, muqaddamūn (now numbering the full complement of twenty-four), and amīrs of forty (also a large host of seventy-five).[29] He did so partially to underscore the extraordinary turnover in the upper ranks of the military hierarchy since al-Ghawrī assumed power. He also signaled the restoration of enough stability to make such an inventory worthwhile. But the ubiquitous threat of revolt still haunted the sultan throughout the year because of the troops' dissatisfaction with their stipends. Many persisted in believing that their sovereign pleaded insolvency while hoarding money that was rightfully theirs. Factional rivalries and personal vendettas also continued to divide the ruling oligarchy. Al-Ghawrī never received the respect Qāytbāy had commanded, which during his rule counteracted these centrifugal forces. Nor did he emulate his revered predecessor.

Since al-Ghawrī's ruling style emerged from myriad acts of defiance to his authority, a calculated stance of insouciance about their inevitablity can be detected in his demeanor after 908. Al-Ghawrī dealt with opposition by playing off potential rivals against each other rather than by building coalitions. In short, the sultan became the realm's master schemer in the game of conspiratorial politics. Not seeking the adulation given Qāytbāy, al-Ghawrī imbued few even of his closest associates with a sense of mutual trust. In Rabīʿ I/September, his dawādār, Azdamur, was struck by an arrow while ascending the Citadel for morning prayer.[30] The projectile caught

28 *Badāʾiʿ* 4, 29, l. 23.
29 *Badāʾiʿ* 4, 30, l. 6.
30 *Badāʾiʿ* 4, 41, l. 15.

in Azdamur's cloak and did him no injury. But since a recruit from the royal barracks shot it, Azdamur suspected al-Ghawrī as the instigator. Livid with anger, he presented the sultan with the arrow saying, "If you intend my murder, don't assign a recruit the task!" Al-Ghawrī swore on the 'Uthmānī Koran that he had no part in the assault. Convening the barracks aghas for interrogation, he accused some of slack discipline and ordered them lashed. He then packed the others off to ferret out the guilty recruit. Their search produced a Mamlūk who was a blood relative of the atābak, Qāyt al-Rajabī. Several claimed he was the atābak's younger brother; in any case, he was rumored to be a brigand and murderer. When al-Ghawrī exiled him to Syria, Azdamur was at least partially mollified. But both now suspected the atābak's intentions. Incidents of this kind occurred frequently during the initial period of al-Ghawrī's reign. Ibn Iyās's roster of events for 908 is replete with descriptions of abortive revolts, escapes, recaptures, and rumored conspiracies. He reported no positive decree for public welfare until late in the year. Only in Shawwāl was an officer dispatched to supervise the dredging of an irrigation canal near the capital.[31] By the end of Qāytbāy's third year, the sultan had sponsored many beneficial projects.

The years 909 and 910 saw little change in the situation, but the sultan steadily whittled away at remaining knots of sedition. After the attempted assassination of Azdamur, al-Ghawrī harbored gnawing suspicions about his atābak, Qāyt al-Rajabī, although he was never formally implicated. The marshal and sultan eyed each other warily while publicly manifesting their mutual esteem. Al-Ghawrī waited some sixteen months before he produced proof of Qāyt's treason. In Rajab of 910/December 1504–January 1505, the sultan was presented with correspondence between Qāyt and Sībāy, the semiautonomous governor of Aleppo (and later Damascus),

[31] *Badā'i'* 4, 51, l. 6.

in which the marshal urged the viceroy to renounce his allegiance to Cairo.[32] As field commander, Qāyt would then request the sultan's permission to march against Sībāy; once he reached Aleppo he would declare his own candidacy for the sultanate. Sībāy would presumably be free to establish his independent control over northern Syria. Leading an army strengthened by Syrian contingents, Qāyt would then return to Cairo as a deliverer liberating the city from a despot.

Al-Ghawrī arrested Qāyt on the sixteenth/3 January while the latter was presiding over a weekly muster of officers in the Citadel courtyard. When the marshal was called to account for his audacious plot, he denied any knowledge of such an affair. Qāyt protested his innocence even after al-Ghawrī produced the incriminating evidence, insisting that these letters were forgeries. In fact, the missives' authenticity was never ascertained by any judge, notary, or historian. The possibility that al-Ghawrī or an aide concocted them cannot be dismissed. Nonetheless, the atābak stood condemned before the assembled court. Stripped of his office, he was sentenced to life imprisonment in Alexandria. His escort was chosen from among grand amīrs whom al-Ghawrī had recently promoted. Several bore grudges against Qāyt and relished his downfall. Ibn Iyās depicted this man as an opportunist who had readily devised wicked, albeit ingenious, means of extracting money from the masses. Yet he pointedly observed that none of these crimes against the people brought on Qāyt's downfall; the sultan removed him only in consequence of his suspected treason. By contrast, Qāytbāy, Azbak, and Yashbak had coexisted for years as a powerful triumvirate, curbing the excesses of a turbulent military caste because none challenged the others' status. The sole tie that bound al-Ghawrī and Qāyt al-Rajabī was the guarded respect of conspirators who recognize a kindred spirit.

[32] *Badā'i'* 4, 73, l. 1; 74, l. 8.

In the aftermath of Qāyt's removal, demonstrations erupted sporadically within the barracks. Amīrs were routinely jailed or exiled. But few now predicted any serious challenge. Indeed, al-Ghawrī decided that his own security warranted his wife's transfer to the Citadel.[33] Her formal entry to the palace in Ṣafar of 911/July 1505 was an elaborately staged event. Al-Ghawrī's fears of a coup in which his household might be victimized had delayed his wife's relocation for almost five years. All this time she had dwelt in a former officer's townhouse at the Bayn al-Qaṣrayn, visited by her husband when he could safely depart the Citadel confines. Now her ascent to the palace signaled the sultan's confidence that his reign had a future. Her procession was modeled after al-Khawand Fāṭima's triumphal return from the pilgrimage in Qāytbāy's time. She rode in a litter embossed with gold. The royal parasol and bird were carried over her head by senior officers. Assembled courtiers cast gold and silver pieces before her. A silk tapestry demarcated her path from the Bāb al-Sitūra to the Hall of Columns, which her husband had decorated for her. We know nothing about this princess's personality or influence, as chroniclers rarely commented on al-Ghawrī's family or personal life. Unlike the vivid presence posed by Fāṭima, al-Ghawrī's wife is an elusive figure, who attracted little of the popular affection Qāytbāy's spouse had enjoyed.

In the flush of security, the sultan made his first public gestures as benefactor of the populace. In Muḥarram of 912/June 1506, on the Festival of 'Āshūrā', al-Ghawrī summoned the poor and indigent of Cairo to assemble at the Citadel staircase, where he would grant them largesse.[34] When the sultan descended on his horse, he began to give each supplicant an Ashrafī dīnār. Such a windfall had not occurred in living memory, since even Qāytbāy had not

[33] *Badā'i'* 4, 81, l. 1.
[34] *Badā'i'* 4, 94, l. 9.

provided a dīnār to persons of the lowest order. Many of these riffraff never saw a gold coin in their lives unless they managed to pilfer one. Word of this extraordinary act of generosity spread like wildfire through the teeming warrens surrounding the Citadel, and a mob soon surged around the staircase. Three people were crushed to death in the melée. Al-Ghawrī gave away three thousand dīnārs on this occasion. But he found the prospect of fending off hundreds of outstretched hands distasteful and refused to descend again, even though he had intended a second donation.

A month later, the sultan manumitted the first contingent of Mamlūks acquired in his own name.[35] Four hundred young recruits received their first promotion certificates, mounts, and uniforms. Their unit took the title "al-Ashrafīya al-Ghawrīya" in their patron's honor. Observers of the military elite must have speculated over al-Ghawrī's protracted delay before advancing his own Mamlūks, who at least in principle bestowed their first loyalty on him. Al-Ghawrī's studied indifference to the time-honored practice of nurturing a personal corps was fully consistent with his own sense of security. He did not regard the spoiling of young trainees as a fail-safe means of ensuring his safety. Recruits were predictable only in their greed; their reliability was commensurate entirely with their patron's magnanimity. Al-Ghawrī had perceived this dilemma early in his career and therefore began toying with ad hoc means of protecting his position, enhancing his revenues, and extending his influence—few of which appealed to his soldiers.

Throughout 912 and 913, the sultan profited from the death or exile of several officers who remained from previous administrations or had participated in his accession to install men on whom he could rely. On 20 Jumādā II of 913/27 October 1507, word arrived that the dawādār Azdamur, Miṣirbāy's successor, had died in Ghazza five days

[35] *Badā'i'* 4, 95, l. 5.

earlier.[36] When Azdamur's death was announced, his colleagues mourned his loss, since he was regarded as both able and honest. His death was so unexpected that foul play was rumored. This was the officer who had accused al-Ghawrī of inducing a recruit to assassinate him, and the sultan had a long memory. No inquiry was allowed. Al-Ghawrī showed his estimation of the late dawādār by sequestering his estate, disenfranchising his heirs, and arresting his staff—all of whom paid a hefty ransom for their release. More interesting was al-Ghawrī's choice for Azdamur's replacement. The sultan picked his own nephew Ṭūmānbāy to walk in the footsteps of this dour but respected amīr whose presence had been a source of unease ever since the arrow-shooting incident.

The pattern of Qānṣūh al-Ghawrī's dealings with both colleagues and subordinates reveals a disinclination for binding ties. Yet several individuals entered the sultan's inner circle during the initial period. Aside from their capacity to mold their objectives from al-Ghawrī's, they differed radically in background or temperament. The closest to al-Ghawrī personally was his nephew. Many family groups or at least siblings were imported together into Egypt as Mamlūks throughout the Circassian period. Their cohesion after years of training as novices counters statements made by commentators on the classic system of slave-soldiers that prior lineage ties were intentionally weakened in the barracks.[37] Ṭūmānbāy was identified as the son of al-Ghawrī's brother. The brother was himself never mentioned in the narrative sources, and indeed may never have served in Cairo. But his son might have been sent to the capital to join his uncle at some time. In any case, nephew and uncle had developed a positive relationship well before al-Ghawrī's accession. By any standard, Ṭūmānbāy was impressive. Highly skilled in military arts, he cut a dashing

36 *Badā'i'* 4, 119, l. 19.

37 See Ayalon, "Studies on the Structure of the Mamluk Army," pt. 3, 74–75; id., "The Circassians in the Mamluk Kingdom," 135–147.

figure as an officer, in a way his uncle had not. He advanced rapidly on his own through the ranks of the khāṣṣakīya and the amīrship of ten. Ṭūmānbāy exhibited the kind of charisma, the ability to lead men by inspiration, which was wanting in al-Ghawrī. Yet strangely enough al-Ghawrī chose not to resent his nephew's popularity but rather turned it to his own advantage. Ṭūmānbāy became renowned for his integrity. A man whose word was sacred, he never broke a pledge. Al-Ghawrī, who went back on his whenever circumstances warranted, found a special satisfaction in cementing a bond with his nephew, whose honesty was impeccable.

Ibn Iyās first mentioned Ṭūmānbāy on his betrothal to the daughter of Qāytbāy's last dawādār, Aqbirdī min 'Alī Bāy.[38] The sultan's nephew had already attained the commandership of one thousand and held the superintendancy of the royal larder (*shurabkhānāh*), with responsibility for the stewardship of food supplies in the royal household. The nuptials occurred at the end of 912. When Azdamur died a few months later, al-Ghawrī installed Ṭūmānbāy in the dawādārīya, where he would remain until his uncle's ill-fated campaign against Selim.[39] That al-Ghawrī would declare Ṭūmānbāy regent in his absence surprised no one. Only the sultan's nephew, bound to his patron by blood and fealty, enjoyed al-Ghawrī's absolute confidence. Over the years Ṭūmānbāy grew in stature until he became al-Ghawrī's alter ego. The sultan bestowed office after office on him in a manner reminiscent of Qāytbāy's beneficence to Yashbak min Mahdī. Certainly the two dawādārs exhibited the unswerving loyalty so essential to their reliability. But they differed sharply in other ways. Yashbak's lack of scruple was more like al-Ghawrī's deviousness than the probity of Ṭūmānbāy. Ultimately, Yashbak could not balance his lust for power

38 *Badā'i'* 4, 99, l. 23; 107, l. 1.
39 *Badā'i'* 4, 12, l. 12.

against his devotion to his patron, so pursued his fortune abroad. Ṭūmānbāy remained content with his adjutant status to al-Ghawrī's death. He accepted the regency fully intending to relinquish it when his uncle returned. After fate placed final responsibility on his shoulders, he accepted his new authority with a sense of resignation rather than exhilaration.

As dawādār, Ṭūmānbāy rarely deviated from straightforward administrative practices. Soon after his appointment, he forbade his retainers to accept excessive bribes from supplicants bringing petitions to his gate.[40] No one was to take more than two half-faḍḍas (a silver coin worth approximately 25 per dīnār) in return for arrangement of a hearing. Petty officials depended on modest bribes to make ends meet, and Ṭūmānbāy prudently allowed the practice to continue—but only at a level consonant with past traditions of acceptability. He had no interest in collecting kickbacks himself. Of course, his own vast income relieved him of the need, but his example moved the commons nonetheless. Ibn Iyās noted that Ṭūmānbāy personally enforced his ban on excessive tipping for several days, and thereafter periodically checked on his staff randomly to assure compliance. Because of such behavior, his stature grew enormously. His repute greatly outshone that of his uncle, but al-Ghawrī never bridled at it. He gave his nephew almost free rein to administer his offices as he saw fit. When Ṭūmānbāy's staff committed serious crimes, the sultan referred their cases to the Sharī'a court, knowing that the oral testimony required to sustain a conviction would never be secured.[41] No one cared to stand forth as a witness against a client of the dawādār, even when he was accused of murder. Ṭūmānbāy tacitly accepted his uncle's ploy in protecting his retainers, a blight in his otherwise blemish-free record. To his credit, such incidents were rare. The dawādār

40 *Badā'i'* 4, 131, l. 6.
41 *Badā'i'* 4, 168, l. 9.

compelled his subordinates to eschew most of the corrupt dealings endemic in the Mamlūk system of clientage.

Al-Ghawrī's other intimates came from civilian origins. Certainly the most distinguished belonged to a respected juristic family. Sarī al-Dīn 'Abd al-Barr ibn al-Shiḥna al-Ḥalabī was the son of a learned Ḥanafī qāḍī, Muḥibb al-Dīn, who served Qāytbāy as chief justice of his madhhab in Cairo. The family had achieved such fame in Aleppo that their services as teachers and jurisconsults were in demand throughout Syria and in the imperial capital itself.[42] Sarī al-Dīn was inclined early on to dabble in politics at the summit of the royal hierarchy. During a sojourn in Aleppo forced on him by untoward dealings in Cairo, he behaved as if he were the sultan's personal envoy.[43] Upon his return to Cairo on 1 Jumādā II 876/16 October 1471, Sarī al-Dīn took on the airs of a royal confidant. In fact, Qāytbāy regarded him with ambivalence, tolerating his pretensions only because of his esteem for the man's father. Upon Muḥibb al-Dīn's solicitation, Qāytbāy reluctantly admitted Sarī al-Dīn to the fraternity of Ḥanafī judges in Cairo and installed him in a deputyship at the Ṣāliḥīya Madrasa, seat of the highest civil court.[44] Al-Ṣayrafī related, somewhat wryly, that the brash young jurist immediately embroiled himself in disputes smoldering among rival judges at the college. He sided with one shaykh, Shams al-Dīn al-Amshāṭī, who challenged a despised colleague's setting up of a dais in the mosque's outer court to hear cases, against the express prohibition by the waqf deed of such an act near the entryway. Sarī al-Dīn secured the colleague's dismissal on these grounds, an ironic twist, since he later attained a measure of notoriety for his own

[42] K. S. Salibi, "Listes chronologiques des grands cadis de l'Egypte sous les mamlouks," *REI* 25 (1957): on Muḥibb al-Dīn: 105–107, nos. 41, 43, 45; Sarī al-Dīn: 108–109, nos. 51, 53; C. Petry, "Geographic Origins of Academicians in Cairo during the Fifteenth Century," *JESHO* 23 (1980) 137 n. 30.

[43] al-Ṣayrafī, *Inbā'*, 279, l. 2; 359, l. 11; 361, l. 4.

[44] cf. Petry, *Civilian Elite*, 330–331.

manipulation of waqf laws to facilitate his royal sponsor's designs.

Sarī al-Dīn's father died in Muḥarram of 890/January–February 1485, leaving the son with an illustrious name but a modest patrimony.[45] He acceded to his father's rectorship of the Ḥanafī academy of al-Shaykhūnīya near the Ṭūlūnid Mosque, a sinecure providing a comfortable if not lavish living. But Muḥibb al-Dīn had not occupied the senior Ḥanafī qāḍīship for years, and the sultan would not dislodge the current incumbent on his son's behalf. Sarī al-Dīn's career is therefore obscure in the period between 890 and 906. In Shawwāl of the latter year, however, he reemerged to prominence when al-Ghawrī finally appointed him to the Ḥanafī justiceship because the incumbent, Burhān al-Dīn ibn al-Karakī, had earned al-Ghawrī's ire for allegedly sheltering al-ʿĀdil.[46] Sarī al-Dīn instantly perceived that the road to a long and profitable tenure lay in winning the autocrat's favor rather than upholding strict interpretations of Sharīʿa.

He soon found the opportunity to demonstrate his talents. In Muḥarram 907/July–August 1501, al-Ghawrī found himself pressed for money to meet the demands of his recruits for a bonus increase. He convened the Caliph and four qāḍīs in extraordinary session to debate the feasibility of tapping waqf yields to make up the shortfall.[47] Sarī al-Dīn alone elected not to participate in the formal session, in which his three colleagues denounced the plan and chided the sultan for considering it. Sarī al-Dīn then ascended to consult with his sovereign later in the afternoon, and not only concurred with the sultan's need but presented him with legal justifications for his action. Al-Ghawrī summoned all the qāḍīs back the next day and compelled the three recalcitrant ones to acknowledge the validity of Sarī al-Dīn's arguments, even if they rejected the proposal on moral grounds. The sultan

45 *Badāʾiʿ* 3, 214, l. 6.
46 *Badāʾiʿ* 4, 7, l. 3.
47 *Badāʾiʿ* 4, 14, l. 13.

immediately charged his atābak, Qāyt al-Rajabī, with seizing the Cairo waqf yields for the year, the first of many such measures during his reign. There were, as Ibn Iyās relates, abhorrent consequences of this confiscation for both scholars and the indigent, but Sarī al-Dīn steadfastly upheld the ruling—which al-Ghawrī did not forget.

Over the following years, Sarī al-Dīn augmented his stature as the sultan's most favored jurist, if not the most respected legal authority in Cairo. On Friday the first of Rabīʿ II 909/24 August 1503, the sultan formally dedicated his tomb mosque, which he had erected at the southern quarter of the Bayn al-Qaṣrayn.[48] The savant selected to preach a commemorative khuṭba was one publicly recognized as a master of rhetoric and elocution. For this occasion, al-Ghawrī chose the Shāfiʿī qāḍī of Damascus, Shihāb al-Dīn ibn Farfūr, on the advice of academic and religious notables in Cairo who acknowledged the Damascene's oratorical skills as peerless. Sarī al-Dīn, who dutifully attended along with his colleagues and the Caliph, raised not a word of protest, although he would later defame Ibn Farfūr when the latter was appointed to the Shāfiʿī justiceship of Cairo. Al-Ghawrī himself regretted the decision of the learned community, even though he accepted it, for he allowed Sarī al-Dīn to cite the charitable principles motivating construction of the edifice and bestowed a robe of honor on him matching Ibn Farfūr's. The very next week, Sarī al-Dīn preached the second khuṭba in the mosque at the sultan's behest. He apparently outdid himself during the event, for even his enemies recognized his sermon as superior to Ibn Farfūr's. From this time on, he would regularly deliver Friday homilies in the sultan's mausoleum.

Sarī al-Dīn's growing eminence, accompanied by commensurate pomposity, did not escape the scorn of popular satirists in Cairo, who often derided the antics of the rich and powerful, to the masses' delight. In Muḥarram of 913/May–

48 *Badāʾiʿ* 4, 58, l. 10.

June 1507, one of these cynics, Jamāl al-Dīn al-Salmūnī, wrote an ode ridiculing Sarī al-Dīn, after the latter had sided with a previous recipient of his sarcasm, the chancellor of the exchecquer (*wakīl bayt al-māl*) Mu'īn al-Dīn ibn Shams.[49] Incensed by this satire, which was widely circulated and chortled over throughout the capital, Sarī al-Dīn ascended to the Citadel and requested his patron's condemnation of the poet who had mocked him. But in this incident, the ambivalent status of a client in the Mamlūk hierarchy, no matter how high, was starkly revealed. According to Ibn Iyās, al-Ghawrī secretly admired al-Salmūnī's biting wit, so long as it slandered someone else. Reluctant to punish the satirist outright, he duly summoned al-Salmūnī to a hearing in which he confronted him with the "ignoble ode." Al-Salmūnī denied that he had concocted its criticisms, which he claimed were on everyone's tongue. He had but arranged them to highlight their aptness. The sultan then elected not to appease his minion with an execution, but rather turned al-Salmūnī over to the judgment of all four senior qāḍīs, including that of Sarī al-Dīn, at the Ṣāliḥīya. Since the civil court could not render a death sentence, the four could only order al-Salmūnī's imprisonment. The poet was incarcerated briefly, with no writ of censure to still his pen. Sarī al-Dīn was privately outraged but let the matter pass. The sultan may have responded to widespread protests over al-Salmūnī's arrest simply because a haughty judge found his writings offensive. Sarī al-Dīn still retained his patron's favor, but his awareness of where true authority lay had been bluntly reinforced.

The second individual who would wield exceptional influence as a royal client—and survive to savor it—served al-Ghawrī as his master inquisitor.[50] This person, one Zayn al-Dīn Barakāt ibn Mūsā, rose from the humblest origins

[49] *Badā'i'* 4, 112, l. 7; 125, l. 18.

[50] No official title approximating this function was ever granted Zaynī Barakāt. But his fame as a master of extraction via exquisite tortures was attested so repeatedly by Ibn Iyās that use of the term is appropriate.

to inspire terror in the hearts of even his wiliest competitors. Zaynī Barakāt's father was a Bedouin who had worked as a groom in the stables of sultan al-Mu'ayyad Aḥmad ibn Īnāl. His son, an alert boy with a knack for charming his superiors, caught the monarch's eye and became a court page who capped royal falcons during hunting excursions. Zaynī Barakāt survived al-Mu'ayyad's deposition (19 Ramaḍān 865/28 June 1461) but never captured Qāytbāy's fancy. He remained a shadowy figure in the court throughout Qāytbāy's rule. It was al-Ghawrī who found a resonant quality in Zaynī Barakāt's cupidity and offered him the chance to refine it to an art. In Shawwāl of 908/March–April 1503, the sultan surprised his entourage of lofty amīrs and distinguished jurists by appointing this Bedouin's son his bailiff (*bardadār*) and spice dispenser (*bahhār*) in place of 'Alī ibn Abī'l-Jūd, a monster of greed whom Barakāt would abuse after his own installation.[51]

The career of Ibn Abī'l-Jūd merits comment at this juncture because it illustrates how a civilian procurer might step over the fine line separating service from aggrandizement, a distinction Zaynī Barakāt intuitively grasped. Ibn Iyās labeled this man contemptuously a "petty marketeer" whose father had labored as a carpenter and then sold confections in a shop at the entry to the Bath of Shaykhū.[52] He took the name "Liberality's Father" (*Abū'l-Jūd*) to enhance his business, a title the chronicler found vulgar in the extreme but well-suited to this boor and his progeny. When Abū'l-Jūd died, his son inherited his stall and fried Ramaḍān pastries, which he dusted with sugar by his own hand. Although Ibn Abī'l-Jūd prospered modestly at his calling, he aspired to loftier enterprises. When a clerkship opened in

51 *Badā'i'* 4, 50, l. 7. This exceptional man's career has attracted notice from modern novelists. See Jamāl al-Ghayṭānī's *Al-Zaynī Barakāt*, 3d ed. (Cairo, Dār al-Mustaqbil al-'Arabī, 1985), English translation by Farouk Musṭafā (New York, Penguin Books, 1989).

52 *Badā'i'* 4, 45, l. 11.

the wazīr's ministry, he jumped at it and rapidly gained the reputation of a skilled manipulator of assets, even though he had received no formal education. Ibn Abī'l-Jūd ultimately served al-'Ādil Ṭūmānbāy as his bailiff, and when the latter won the sultanate he transferred over to the new dawādār, Qānṣūh al-Ghawrī. Al-Ghawrī recognized Ibn Abī'l-Jūd's fiscal adroitness and as sultan elevated him to a series of high offices. By Jumādā I of 908/November 1502, he had accumulated the supervision of pious endowments (*naẓrīyat al-awqāf*), agency of the treasury (*wakālat bayt al-māl*), bailiffship (*bardadārīyat al-sulṭān*), supervision of the viziral bureau (*dīwān al-wizāra*), the majordomoship (*ustādārīya*), the market inspectorship (*ḥisba*), and supervision of the special bureau (*dīwān al-khāṣṣ*). Ibn Abī'l-Jūd's appointment to these influential positions dismayed both civil and military notables. His deportment soon became a matter of public scandal. But al-Ghawrī found his slippery client's antics amusing and winked at the posturing of this parvenu, who donned the robes of a sophisticated savant and purchased a horse with expensive trappings usually reserved for amīrs. Ibn Abī'l-Jūd faithfully turned over twelve thousand dīnārs a month to the sultan from his diverse embezzlements, which al-Ghawrī used to supplement the stipends for recruits. Not until this man aroused al-Ghawrī's suspicions that he was hoarding more than his allotted share from their mutually agreed corruption and was becoming excessively rich did the "sultan's wrath fall upon him."

Ibn Iyās observed that Ibn Abī'l-Jūd's power went to his head since he "managed the realm's affairs according to his own whims." "Neither merchant nor official could oppose his will. He devised schemes of extraordinary wickedness in Egypt. All the populace dwelt in mortal fear of him."[53] Ibn Abī'l-Jūd excelled in whitewashing the trumped-up claims of plaintiffs who in fact had violated the law, and

[53] *Badā'i'* 4, 44, l. 7.

collected a percentage of their settlements from falsely argued suits. Some hundred agents stood at his gate to handle the onslaught of petitions. Indeed, so lucrative were the prospects of employment in Ibn Abī'l-Jūd's dīwān that artisans abandoned their crafts to join his staff. Ibn Iyās claimed that Ibn Abī'l-Jūd's reputation reached as far as Istanbul and "realms of the East" because of the antipathy he incurred among foreign merchants, who loathed the special fees he extracted from them for their right to trade in Egypt. Customs collectors complained over the precipitous decline in revenues formerly generated by European and Ottoman merchants arriving in Alexandria and Damietta. They blamed Ibn Abī'l-Jūd's undue beleaguering of these traders for their decision to dock elsewhere. Toward the close of his career, Ibn Abī'l-Jūd began to forget who sanctioned his affairs. He took to rebuking the most senior officials and state dignitaries—including several amīrs, who presumably expressed their outrage to al-Ghawrī.

Ultimately, the sultan could no longer overlook the mounting charges against his favorite, and on 30 Ramaḍān 908/29 March 1503 he summarily stripped him of all offices and cast him into a dungeon in the Khāzindār's barracks.[54] All Ibn Abī'l-Jūd's retainers were arrested for their "crimes against the people." His goods and residences were impounded, and even "his women" placed under surveillance in order to ferret out hidden caches of wealth he had stashed away. Ibn Abī'l-Jūd remained imprisoned at the barracks until mid-Shawwāl/late April, when he was turned over to Zaynī Barakāt's exquisite torments. The sultan's new inquisitor, who had assumed several of Ibn Abī'l-Jūd's posts, had become well versed in the more refined dimensions of torture, specializing in techniques that preserved life while inflicting such excruciating pain that the sufferer could not conceal even his darkest secrets. Ibn Iyās feigned disgust while describing the

[54] *Badā'i'* 4, 49, l. 11.

sordid details of torture sessions that became legendary in Zaynī Barakāt's house of horrors over the years. But he had little pity for an upstart like Ibn Abī'l-Jūd, who got what he deserved. One wonders what the historian resented more, the lout's fiscal excesses or his social presumption. He certainly found both odious. In any case, Zaynī Barakāt subjected Ibn Abī'l-Jūd to a variety of afflictions, of which wedges driven under his fingernails and skull clamps bound so tightly that his eyes popped out loosened his tongue most readily. After Ibn Abī'l-Jūd divulged the whereabouts of his closeted fortune and implicated his accomplices, he was dragged before the sultan on the twenty-first. Al-Ghawrī reviled him for his transgressions and had him whipped.[55] That he clung to life after such abuse was considered remarkable enough to obviate any further punishment, and he was turned loose, broken and penniless. Zaynī Barakāt, on the other hand, rose in stature because of his service to the sultan. Unlike his crude rival, he assumed no pompous airs. He remained in the background as al-Ghawrī's loyal aide, prepared to take on the most cunning of officials. In all his years of clientship, he never failed to fulfill the sultan's expectations. Despite his dreadful treatment of fallen favorites, he was to enjoy a high level of popularity among the commons, from whom he had risen. After all, Zaynī Barakāt perceived a fundamental axiom early in his career: cruelty was resented only if applied to the innocent. When the sufferer merited his fate, the torturer rose in the public's estimation.

With the ensconcing of men such as the amīr Ṭūmānbāy, the qāḍī Sarī al-Dīn, and the inquisitor Zaynī Barakāt, al-Ghawrī had shaped his own network and stamped his regime with his peculiar style of governance. All three were firmly in place at the end of 912/1507, when the sultan could regard his position as secure. The support he received remained tenuous at best, never approaching the allegiance Qāytbāy won. But

55 *Badā'i'* 4, 50, l. 23.

despite the endemic threat of conspiracy, few now took it seriously. Al-Ghawrī held off participation in martial reviews or recreational excursions until Dhū'l-Qa'da of 909/April–May 1504, the month of his first polo matches.[56] From then on, however, he indulged himself with the same relish Qāytbāy had displayed, and with less formality—paying scant regard to traditions of dress and deportment, mingling informally with officers who had so recently challenged him.

Such relaxed behavior, however, could not dispell portents of unrest following so many years of chaos. Because the regime focused so much energy on neutralizing opposition, it was compelled to neglect urgent matters of local security. Incidents of brigandage throughout the countryside and in the capital itself increased markedly during the formative period, in comparison with the relative peace of Qāytbāy's reign. Ibn Iyās reported numerous instances of enterprising street thugs (*zu'ar*), Bedouin marauders, and even Mamlūk recruits disguised as rabble assaulting caravans by day or terrorizing city quarters by night.[57] Al-Ghawrī denounced these acts and charged his prefects with quelling them, but they

[56] *Badā'i'* 4, 63, l. 14. In subsequent years al-Ghawrī ceased conforming with traditional dates for changing from winter woolens to summer cottons. He tended to dress according to the day's temperature, especially when engaging in the rigors of polo matches. See above: 79, l. 8; 93, l. 3 (sultan dons summer whites early); 94, l. 6 (sultan gives amīr one of his own mounts when latter's horse collapses and dies during match); 95, l. 4 (sultan hosts amīrs to impromptu post-match banquet); 100, l. 9 (sultan changes to winter outfit prematurely); 108, l. 18 (sultan helps amīr remount after bad fall during match); 115, l. 13 (sultan hosts amīrs to post-match banquet, encouraging them to stay the entire afternoon); 130, l. 17 (sultan initiates festive martial reviews to coincide with polo season).

[57] *Badā'i'* 4, 20, l. 5 (robbers pillage markets unopposed); 30, l. 3 (arsonists set fires to cover up thievery); 39, l. 22 (brigands pillage Chamberlain Bridge district, night of terror for residents); 41, l. 4 (pension money stolen by Mamlūk recruits disguised as Bedouins); 51, l. 8 (Ṭūlūn market robbed, some thieves apprehended); 51, l. 18 (Bedouin raiding in Upper and Lower Egypt increases); 86, l. 3 (shepherds parading draft animals before sultan rob shops); 96, l. 5 (riot between rabble [*zu'ar*] gangs put down with difficulty); 107, l. 21 (person accused of setting fire to grain reserve captured and almost burned alive).

continued to erupt sporadically. Many among the least fortunate elements of society seem to have taken their cue from the sultan's own example to profit from the unease he was prepared to manipulate. Since the autocrat had "spread his oppression throughout Egypt," few among the lower orders saw any reason to endure their poverty by obeying the law.[58]

The Medial Years: Indulgence and Innovation

The period extending from the close of 912 to mid-918—the accession of Selim I in Istanbul (May 1507–July 1512)—was the happiest of al-Ghawrī's reign and quite possibly his life. Already in his late sixties, this heretofore private man had guarded his personal feelings during the arduous years of consolidation. Now that he could face the future with a certain air of confidence, al-Ghawrī revealed a new side of himself that reveled in the luxuries of supreme power. He also felt free to experiment with novel forms of fiscal accumulation, troop recruitment, and military techniques. The times were auspicious for this change of posture. Despite residual opposition to the sultan's authority and his rapacious extortions, 912 was a year of widespread prosperity in the Nile Valley.[59] The river crest had been high without undue flooding and crops were abundant, with consequent lowering of prices. The sultan and his coterie of officers were, admittedly, neither able nor willing to curb the marauding recruits, but the populace was temporarily spared the trauma of full-scale riots. And the victory of al-Ghawrī's governor in the Ḥijāz over regional Bedouins had once again rendered the annual pilgrimage safe for mass participation, after several years of restrictions. Several Ḥijāzī tribes, and in particular the Banū

58 Al-Ḥalabī, *Durr*, f. 177, l. 1.
59 *Badā'i'* 4, 111, l. 5.

Ibrāhīm, had exploited the early weakness of al-Ghawrī's administration in Cairo to dissolve their allegiance and pillage pilgrimage caravans arriving from Cairo or elsewhere. Their raids had been widely interpreted as an evil omen, a sign of God's displeasure with the new sultan's policies. Now that the Bedouins were defeated, the regime could formally declare the Ḥajj open to all who wished to go. The sultan chose the festival of a local saint to signal the new era of prosperity and security. In Muḥarram of 913/May–June 1507, he lavishly observed the Mawlid of Sīdī Ismā'īl al-Anbābī on the Būlāq shore.[60] Some five hundred tents were set up on the island across from the port to house confectioners, merchants, and entertainers from all over the country. The fair attracted thousands of merrymakers from the city and environs who frolicked from dusk till dawn over several days with no fear of robbery by local brigands or Mamlūk recruits.

Two months later, with the clearing of marauders from the pilgrimage routes, al-Ghawrī sanctioned preparations by the general populace for the annual journey to the shrines of western Arabia.[61] Men and women were free to make their plans, confident of a safe trip. Both elite and commons responded to this proclamation with praise, seeing in it a renewal of the imperial peace prevailing under Qāytbāy. Indeed, the Ḥajj of 913 proved an exceptional event, marked by the highest level of participation since Qāytbāy's death more than ten years before. In Shawwāl/February, al-Ghawrī presided over a spectacular showing of the Ka'ba mantle (*kiswa*) and the tent (*maqām*) to enclose Abraham's tomb in Hebron.[62] The sultanate customarily sent these beautiful tapestries, the work of hundreds of artisans, as annual gifts to these shrines in Palestine and the Ḥijāz during the pilgrimage month. A caravan known as the mahmal

60 *Badā'i'* 4, 114, l. 10.
61 *Badā'i'* 4, 117, l. 10.
62 *Badā'i'* 4, 127, l. 10; 128, l. 10.

was organized to transport them.[63] Al-Ghawrī had already renewed the custom of ceremoniously escorting the mahmal with his lancers as it departed Cairo. This year, the sultan ordered public viewings of the mantle and tent at several locations in the capital, enabling all who so wished to see them. The tapestries were unusually fine and required hundreds of bearers, marching between the lancers, to carry them across the city. The mantle supervisor (*nāẓir al-kiswa*), army comptroller ʿAbd al-Qādir al-Qaṣrawī, had so effectively discharged his obligation that the sultan bestowed a magnificent robe of honor on him. When the mahmal set out from the Pilgrim's Lake for the Ḥajj Road, a vast throng accompanied it in a festive mood. Many civil and military notables expressed their trust in the regime's protection by joining the pilgrims' ranks. Their lavish cortèges, supported by swarms of servants, contributed a sumptuous flair to the caravan unseen for years. Several princesses, including wives and daughters of former monarchs, made the Ḥajj, guarded by a special squadron at the sultan's behest. Al-Ghawrī actually sought to relieve himself of their presence, since these women, as living symbols of past reigns, often reminded restive Mamlūk factions of more generous patrons. Aṣilbāy, mother of Qāytbāy's heir, had become particularly onerous to him because of her popularity with both recruits and ambitious officers. Al-Ghawrī thus refused to permit her return from the Ḥijāz upon completion of her devotions. The former royal concubine was compelled to reside for the rest of her days in Mecca, a town that for eleven months of the years appealed only to pious mendicants.[64] But aside from this draconian ruling, the pilgrimage of 913 was a resounding success, an ideal harbinger of the harmonious future this administration hoped to promote.

63 J. Jomier, *Le mahmal et la caravane égyptienne des pèlerins de la Mecque, XIIIe–XXe siècles* (Cairo, IFAO, 1953).

64 *Badāʾiʿ* 4, 131, l. 11; 159, l. 15.

Al-Ghawrī's closest military adjutants in the medial period were his new atābak, Qurqumās min Walī al-Dīn, and his nephew, the dawādār Ṭūmānbāy. Qurqumās, who succeeded Qāyt al-Rajabī, was in character much like his predecessor Azbak. A soldier of undisputed valor, Qurqumās inspired the army with his commitment to discipline. An early supporter of al-Ghawrī's enthronement, he had declined any involvement in subsequent plots and won the esteem of all factions as an officer true to his loyalty oath. Following his appointment, al-Ghawrī drew Qurqumās into his intimate circle and the two became quite close. Qurqumās shared Ṭūmānbāy's growing distinction as a queller of boisterous Bedouin rebels, and led several expeditions to Upper Egypt in search of these troublesome marauders.[65] But Qurqumās' tenure, which showed promise of duplicating Azbak's career, was cut tragically short by his premature death in Ramaḍān of 916/24 December 1510.[66] The entire court mourned his loss, and every notable marched in his funeral procession. The four qāḍīs led the cortège, preceding amīrs of all ranks. Ibn Iyās, who attended the ceremony, mentioned touching rites performed during the procession. Penitential offerings, including bread, dates, and sheep, were conveyed in front of Qurqumās's bier. When the cortège arrived at the Madrasa of Sultan Ḥasan, these were distributed to the crowd in memory of the atābak's beneficence. The onlookers themselves cast silver coins on the bier as it passed by. The chronicler marveled at this mass outpouring of grief, rare for an officer who wielded such enormous power over the commons. Qurqumās had been revered for his restrained temper and personal modesty, and the throng wished to show their respect.

When the cortège arrived at the Mu'minī prayer hall at the south end of Rumayla Square, the sultan rode out from the Hippodrome to express his condolences. Dismounting,

[65] *Badā'i'* 4, 125, l. 6.
[66] *Badā'i'* 4, 197, l. 13.

he approached the bier on foot. Tears streaming down his face, al-Ghawrī bowed over the coffin to kiss the corpse of his colleague. He then took the unprecedented step of joining the pallbearers in lifting Qurqumās's casket and transporting it several paces. After remounting, the sultan followed the procession to the atābak's tomb in the Desert Plain to oversee his interment. Al-Ghawrī's sorrow, at a time when cruelty had become a leitmotif of his reign, was genuine. Qurqumās had never dabbled in the clandestine procurement of funds that so preoccupied the sultan. His refusal to entangle himself in the web of plots and counterplots spun by rivals earned him a special kind of gratitude in the eyes of his sovereign, who assumed treachery from every subordinate. Such an adjutant was rare in these times and difficult to replace.

Ṭūmānbāy was not mentioned among the mourners at the atābak's funeral. The two were neither enemies nor comrades, but each pursued activities that rarely infringed on the other's sphere of influence. Ṭūmānbāy spent many months during these years away from Cairo as the sultan's chief inspector. He may have found provincial duties more congenial than responsibilities in Cairo that would have drawn him inexorably into the corruption his uncle nurtured. Ṭūmānbāy might therefore have been absent when Qurqumās died, and so spared attendance at the funeral of his esteemed counterpart. Ṭūmānbāy proved himself a redoubtable field commander, who struck terror among Bedouin raiders on the fringes of the Delta and Upper Egypt. Fully in keeping with the assumption of superiority and proprietorship ingrained in his caste, he ruthlessly squeezed produce and revenues from the peasants whom he delivered from their Bedouin despoilers during his progressions up and down the Nile. When he returned to the capital, he invariably presented his sovereign with booty in excess of anything tax collectors could extract.[67] The dawādār thus reinforced his

[67] *Badā'i'* 4, 160, l. 10; 206, l. 15.

indispensability to al-Ghawrī throughout the medial period. He became in effect the sultan's regent outside Cairo, and to the rural populace he was a far more vivid, albeit formidable, presence than the monarch himself. Al-Ghawrī's affection for Ṭūmānbāy knew no bounds, and when the dawādār's three-year-old son, the offspring of a concubinal relationship, died in Shawwāl of 915/January–February 1510, al-Ghawrī ordered the child buried in his own mausoleum.[68]

In the medial part of his reign, al-Ghawrī belatedly began to inspect pious and public works. He first visited a shrine in Ramaḍān of 913/January–February 1508, almost seven years after his accession.[69] The venerated Mālikī qāḍī, Burhān al-Dīn al-Damīrī, who served several terms under Qāytbāy, had died that month and al-Ghawrī decided to attend his funeral at the Azhar. On his way back to the Citadel, the sultan stopped at the tombs of Imāms al-Shāfi'ī and al-Layth, both located in the Qarāfa cemetery. Local residents were pleasantly surprised by al-Ghawrī's unheralded arrival. Touched by their spontaneous acclamation, al-Ghawrī subsequently made impromptu visitations at local shrines a part of his tours. Later the same month, he traversed the length of the aqueduct he had commissioned to water the gardens he had planted below the Citadel.[70] Before examining the work, he prayed at the tomb of Azdamur al-Dawādār and then paid his respects to a holy man, one Shaykh Abū'l-Sa'ūd, who dwelt at the Kūm al-Jāriḥ. When he reached the pumping station at the river shore, he ceremonially bathed his face in Nile water, praising its life-giving qualities. Al-Ghawrī then went on to the shrine of al-Sayyida Nafīsa. At each site, he distributed largesse to the intendants and construction workers. The latter received one hundred dīnārs on that day alone, a hefty gratuity in light of prevailing wage levels for

68 *Badā'i'* 4, 168, l. 1.
69 *Badā'i'* 4, 126, l. 10.
70 *Badā'i'* 4, 126, l. 21.

laborers.[71] Over the following years, until he became obsessed with the Ottoman menace and incessant demands from his own soldiers, al-Ghawrī made the rounds to Cairo's sanctuaries whenever he departed the palace. Because formal religious observances bored him, these brief appearances suited his restless inclinations. The spiritual renewal al-Ghawrī experienced seems to have been sincere, for he found the company of local divines and mystics quite comforting, provided he did not linger to attend their interminable prayer vigils.

For much of the medial period al-Ghawrī risked no sojourns beyond the capital and its vicinity. But upon his initial forays to examine ships bringing naval stores from Istanbul and elsewhere, he found the Nile vistas at Būlāq and the lower section of Rawḍā Island especially appealing.[72] Cairene aristocrats had built summer residences along the Nile shore, as it then existed, since the Ayyūbid era. Their villas were interspersed among gardens and orchards on both sides of the river. Rawḍā Island was given over largely to plantations during the fifteenth century, but the Nilometer (*miqyās*), first installed at its southern tip during early Islamic times, caught the sultan's particular fancy after 912. The site commanded a spectacular view of the main channel as it swept up from the valley proper. To the east, the lower spurs of the Muqaṭṭam Hills caught the afternoon light. To the west, the Giza Pyramids diffused the sun's rays as it set. Al-Ghawrī ordered restoration of the Nilometer tower and began construction of several pavilions in its vicinity. The site became his favorite place to visit, a refuge from the cares of office.[73]

Contemporary historians faulted al-Ghawrī for his incapacity to win his troops' adulation—or obedience—even if

[71] Eliyahu Ashtor reports that wages for a manual laborer in Egypt during the fifteenth century varied between two and four Ashrafī dīnārs per month. See his *Histoire des prix et des salaires dans l'orient médiéval* (Paris 1969) 373.

[72] *Badā'i'* 4, 202, l. 4; 212, l. 2; 215, l. 15.

[73] *Badā'i'* 4, 212, l. 19.

he received their grudging respect. His failure to intimidate his recruits left the entire metropolis open to their excesses. Even though the medial years were relatively prosperous, the commons lived under the shadow of petty arson, assault, and theft inflicted by the Julbān, who flaunted their behavior arrogantly in the regime's face with little fear of reprisal. Ibn Iyās noted that the lowest orders of society, who eked out a marginal existence under the best of circumstances, seized upon the sultan's studied indifference to Mamlūk waywardness to plague the city with their own disorders. Many of these "rabble and riffraff" had organized themselves in gangs that operated extortion rings under the aegis of rival amīrs, who took a share of their proceeds. When these gangs infringed on each other's turf, riots broke out that often resulted in the burning or looting of a whole district.

One such incident occurred in Jumādā II of 913/October 1507, when hooligans under the patronage of the atābak Qurqumās clashed with their counterparts under the amīr akhūr Qānibāy Qarā.[74] The two mobs devastated much of Būlāq's market district as they battled over control of local collection rights. Al-Ghawrī reacted to this outburst with alarm, but dared not intervene and risk alienating either Qurqumās or Qānibāy, on both of whom he relied. Whether the populace suffered more from the wanton destruction of such internecine disturbances or from insecurity for which they saw little chance of amelioration is hard to judge. That they despaired of ever finding surcease is apparent from the comments of Ibn Iyās and other observers. Al-Ghawrī himself continued to march all his new recruits through the oath-swearing rituals on the 'Uthmānī Koran, which required several new bindings to replace leather soiled by hundreds of palms placed on it.[75] His strident pleas for restoration of

74 *Badā'i'* 4, 122, l. 16.
75 *Badā'i'* 4, 180, l. 5.

law and order in the aftermath of such strife were received by the masses with the same contempt as that exhibited by his recruits to the oaths. When, in Rajab of 915/October–November 1509, al-Ghawrī urged the commons not to arm themselves for self-defense against rioters and to find solace in prayer at the mosques, "his injunction went in one ear and out the other."[76]

Indisposed to confront these perennial problems, al-Ghawrī experimented with novel kinds of military technology and draconian means of alleviating his fiscal straits. On the matter of new weaponry, al-Ghawrī had studied reports of artillery units introduced by Ottoman rulers to their armies from the reign of Mehmet the Conqueror. Manned by European engineers lured into their service by the offer of high wages, these units had aided the Ottomans in their spectacular victories.[77] Whether al-Ghawrī feared an invasion by his northern neighbors before the accession of Selim I is difficult to know. Relations between Cairo and Istanbul had remained cordial ever since Qāytbāy's stunning defeat of the Ottomans, but no prudent commander could rule out the possibility of renewed hostilities. More relevant to his internal situation, al-Ghawrī toyed with options that would lessen his dependence on the intrenched bastion of military power in his realm: the Mamlūk cavalry soldier equipped with bow, lance, and sword.

Al-Ghawrī's awareness of the increasingly outmoded effectiveness of this mounted warrior in the changing conduct of warfare throughout the Mediterranean basin cannot be ascertained. But regardless of his motives, he initiated his attempts at establishing a cannon foundry in Rajab of 913/November–December 1507.[78] Casting proceeded intermittently for three years before the first pieces were ready

76 *Badā'i'* 4, 161, l. 7.

77 See H. Inalcik, "The Socio-Political Effects of the Diffusion of Fire-arms in the Middle East," 195–217; V. J. Parry, "La manière de combattre," 218–256.

78 *Badā'i'* 4, 123, l. 9.

for testing. The results of preliminary trials hardly gave al-Ghawrī and his colleagues cause for optimism. On the sixth of Jumādā II 916/10 September 1510, some fifteen cannons, all unwieldly juggernauts of great weight, were transferred from the foundry to the mausoleum of al-ʿĀdil Ṭūmānbāy in al-Raydānīya.[79] Simply hoisting the cannons onto their carriages proved hazardous, and several laborers were injured in the process. On the thirteenth, the first ignitions took place. Ibn Iyās, who looked askance at the experiment from a professional point of view, reported the fiasco that ensued. All fifteen pieces exploded when their tinder was lighted. Brass fragments flew in every direction, terrifying both igniters and observers, who rushed for cover. Al-Ghawrī was depressed at this failure, and departed for the Citadel immediately. A banquet planned to celebrate the debut of his new weapons was summarily canceled.

Yet the sultan doggedly persisted. A second trial later in the month turned out more positively, since at least some pieces held together when detonated.[80] By the end of 917/March 1512, al-Ghawrī's fledgling artillery unit could construct a device that withstood the force of a discharge. No pieces had been tried in mock battles to determine their viability in the field, but the precedent for their use had been set.[81] Since all ranks of the regular army, from raw recruit to senior officer, contemptuously disdained incorporating an artillery unit into their service, al-Ghawrī moved cautiously. But he never abandoned his experiment, continuing to refine construction and firing techniques until the period of intensified hostilities with Selim I after 918. To the best of our knowledge, what progress his casters and igniters achieved resulted from their own ingenuity, because no references to European advisers appear in the chronicles.

79 *Badāʾiʿ* 4, 191, l. 17; 192, l. 10.
80 *Badāʾiʿ* 4, 194, l. 16.
81 *Badāʾiʿ* 4, 229, l. 12, 23; 238, l. 1; 243, l. 13.

Al-Ghawrī's penchant for confiscation of money and property was so fundamental a dimension of his ruling style that a political narrative cannot do justice to the intricacy of his ploys. Al-Ghawrī hardly initiated this approach to solvency. His illustrious predecessor Qāytbāy had seized a substantial portion of the funds he required for his military expeditions. Fiscal dilemmas stemming from simultaneous declines in formal sources of revenue and increased hoarding of assets by property holders had already reached crisis levels when al-Ghawrī was enthroned. From a practical perspective, he therefore simply responded to hard reality when he squeezed money from recalcitrant officials or affluent institutions. But al-Ghawrī earned an abiding reputation as a master thief even by contemporary standards—one who exceeded his troopers' demands by exploiting confiscations to indulge his luxurious whims.

Al-Ghawrī resorted to bribes and extortion soon after his accession. He first toyed with the sale of offices to raise bonus money for his rebellious troops, and also placed in office individuals who promised him a reliable share of their graft in lucrative bureaucratic posts. As early as Jumādā I 907/November–December 1501, al-Ghawrī gave the controllership of pious endowments to one Muḥammad bin Yūsuf, an accountant whose name was already tainted by rumors of his embezzling assets held by the mosque of al-Mu'ayyad Shaykh.[82] Once ensconced, this Muḥammad subjected other prominent waqf supervisors to harrowing inquisitions in order to ferret out hidden trusts, which presumably had escaped formal taxation. Ibn Iyās noted that at these sessions the controller was attended by "an amīr of ten whom no one dared oppose"—a hired enforcer who lent muscle to Muḥammad's interrogations. This man so callously abused the waqf-holders' rights that al-Ghawrī soon dismissed him, but not before he had collected his own share from the

[82] *Badā'i'* 4, 21, l. 23.

controller's confiscations. Ibn Yūsuf's successors would follow his example in their own schemes.

The sultan's treatment of a respected princess illustrates his lack of regard for hallowed tradition. Eminent women of the Mamlūk court, and in particular venerated dowagers who had survived their royal husbands' deaths, enjoyed a special status as living symbols of continuity in a volatile military hierarchy. Few widows of sultans enjoyed the prestige that accrued to al-Khawand Fāṭima, Qāytbāy's spouse. When her husband died in 901, she became the executrix of his vast estate, while administering her own ancestors' assets. Ibn Iyās's obituary of Fāṭima, dated 22 Dhū'l-Ḥijja 909/6 June 1504, extols her position and wealth, unequaled by any female contemporary.[83] But he also dwelt on indignities she endured after Qāytbāy's death. Harassed by soldiers belonging to factions jockeying for power in the extended interregnum following her husband's death, Fāṭima sought security by marrying at least one ephemeral successor and possibly more. Al-Ghawrī ultimately extended his own protection to her, but only on condition that she consign all her remaining property over to him. Fāṭima spent her declining years in penury, brooding over the knowledge that this despot would seize what remained of the holdings she and her husband had amassed. Al-Ghawrī himself believed that he had dealt as fairly as this woman could expect. No royal estate was secure from expropriations in the Mamlūk period, and in the absence of surviving heirs Fāṭima could not anticipate a better fate.

Once al-Ghawrī had consolidated his power by the end of 912, he stepped up the frequency of his extortions so that they provided a major portion of his income. His tactics ran the gamut from confiscations imposed on individuals he accused of crimes to acceptance of bribes for offices, mulcting of skilled procurers, seizures of iqṭā'ʿs and waqfs, and arrests

[83] *Badā'iʿ* 4, 64, l. 6.

of close associates who had grown excessively rich. This last ploy statistically outweighed all the others, and served to remind every ambitious civilian who sought his fortune through clientage that this patron was totally without scruple. Ibn Iyās's entries for the medial years are rife with variants on the phrase: "the sultan's displeasure fell upon so-and-so."

Al-Ghawrī rarely struck randomly when he denounced an official who had provided him with lucrative sums, but usually waited until cries of protest had been raised by the masses over his corruption. When the hapless accomplice was arrested, he was subjected to a public trial in which his offenses were enumerated at length. But the sultan never returned the assets his client had been accused of extorting. Nor did the aggrieved victims dare to protest their monarch's confiscation of money previously stolen from them. The immense sums taken from these persons relative to prevailing salary levels for even the upper levels of the civilian elite bear witness to the importance of extortion in al-Ghawrī's fisc. Ibn Iyās regularly reported amounts in excess of one hundred thousand dīnārs in a society where an annual income of a thousand represented substantial wealth.[84] Al-Ghawrī's

[84] *Badā'i'* 4, 114, l. 22 (sultan arrests procurer accused of abusing populace; offender placed in custody of Zaynī Barakāt who is praised for racking him); 134, l. 19 (sultan exiles prefect of Old Cairo who had previously tortured the chancellor, Badr al-Dīn ibn Muzhir); 134, l. 21 (sultan mulcts assistant to director of the arsenal of ten thousand dīnārs for shortfalls in weapon supplies); 136, l. 21 (sultan mulcts treasury officials of one hundred thousand dīnārs because of their corruption during reign of Muḥammad ibn Qāytbāy); 147, l. 8 (sultan arrests moneylenders, primarily Christians and Jews); 158, l. 5 (sultan executes counterfeiter who failed to convert base metal to gold); 161, l. 15 (suicide of treasurer's father to avoid sultan's demand for money); 166, l. 18 (dispute between previous nāẓir al-awqāf and current nāẓir al-khāṣṣ over countercharges of corruption); 169, l. 2 (sultan fines senior bureaucrats six hundred thousand dīnārs to make up arrears in their payments to him); 184, l. 21 (sultan flogs procurer guilty of torturing rival officials to verge of death); 185, l. 16 (sultan banishes former spy and intimate when other associates warn of his deviousness); 235, l. 2 (sultan tortures Jewish moneylender and extracts five hundred thousand dīnārs); 235, l. 6; 250, l. 2 (sultan arrests one of his most astute extorters "detested by the populace").

propensity to strip a former intimate of his assets and his brutal methods of compelling his divulgence of hidden caches was so routine that any civilian who drew close to him faced the virtual certainty of abuse. Yet the sultan never lacked for adept procurers during his reign. Persons whose reputation for fiscal adroitness reached the royal ear eagerly accepted the risks they knew for the wealth they coveted.

For all the calumny heaped on al-Ghawrī for behavior of this kind, the context of his acts must be recalled. The majority of his extortions occurred when he confronted his officers and recruits over stipend demands. The noose the army tightened around their sovereign profoundly influenced his conduct. Because of al-Ghawrī's paranoia over rebellion, he was loath to stand firm against these ultimatums. Nonetheless, despite the genuineness of his monetary woes, al-Ghawrī never stinted himself. His lifestyle stood out for its lavishness at a time of widespread destitution. Chroniclers condemned al-Ghawrī more for his greed than his brutality.[85] If the brutality served a genuine need in turbulent times, it could have been condoned. But as the Syrian biographer al-Ḥalabī somberly observed: "His sultanate wallowed in luxury, focusing on procurement of assets, food, drink, and women ... with but a few literary colloquia."[86]

Al-Ghawrī neither desired nor sought the companionship of revered clerics, who figured so prominently in Qāytbāy's circles. He nonetheless founded several edifices ostensibly dedicated to religion and the public interest that were impressive for their scale and opulence. Yet his avarice was evident even in his generosity, since he resorted to the same extortion that tarnished his reputation in finances. Nowhere was al-Ghawrī's intent more blatant than in the construction

[85] When the 'Īd al-Fiṭr occurred in Shawwāl of 912, al-Ghawrī distributed robes of honor so shoddy that recipients were embarrassed to accept them. Cotton had replaced silk and no fine furs appeared on the hems. See *Badā'i'* 4, 104, l. 10.

[86] al-Ḥalabī, *Durr*, f. 177, l. 11.

of his mausoleum mosque, admittedly one of the noteworthy structures of the later middle ages in Egypt. When work on the building was finished in Dhū'l-Ḥijja 908/May–June 1503, al-Ghawrī hosted the Caliph, the senior qāḍīs, the grand amīrs, and their retainers to a banquet in the mosque courtyard, followed by a spectacular show of fireworks.[87] While the guests publicly extolled the exceptional marbles gracing the mausoleum's walls, they privately smirked over their origins. Al-Ghawrī had stripped these marbles from palaces and tombs of arrested notables, often without compensating their families. Ibn Iyās mentioned the hall of the moneychanger, Shamwāl al-Yahūdī, as especially attractive to the sultan. When he seized Shamwāl's assets, he included his home—and off came its lovely marbles. Even the site of al-Ghawrī's mausoleum was expropriated under trumped-up charges. The lot had been purchased as the final resting place of a wealthy eunuch named Mukhtaṣṣ, who had served as guardian of Mamlūk novices trained by al-Ẓāhir Qānṣūh. When al-Ghawrī took power, this Mukhtaṣṣ fell to his purges. Faced with an insurmountable payment demand, he was compelled to offer al-Ghawrī his property. Although secular assets of notables were fair game for seizure in this era, personal religious foundations remained sacrosanct for the most part—especially if their donors planned to be interred there. So reprehensible was al-Ghawrī's eviction that a local pundit dubbed his mausoleum the "Mosque of Shame" (*al-masjid al-ḥarām*). Ibn Iyās observed that criticism of him abounded "because the people could not hold their tongues before such a flagrant violation of property rights." When al-Ghawrī sought to enhance his edifice's prestige by placing sacred relics in it from other shrines, against the prohibition of such transfers by their waqf deeds, he heightened indignation over his arrogance.

[87] al-Ḥalabī, *Durr*, 52, l. 19. This passage describes the removal of Shamwāl's marbles and expropriation of Mukhtaṣṣ's burial site.

Undaunted by the condemnation of backbiters, al-Ghawrī squandered large sums on a variety of pet projects, never hesitating to expropriate appointments from existing structures if they struck his fancy. In Ṣafar 909/July–August 1503, he began to redesign the Hippodrome square at the base of the Citadel.[88] Since the existing field was barren and scorched by the midday sun, al-Ghawrī decided to render it more pleasing to the eye and comfortable for both polo players and spectators. Its casement walls were razed, the arena surface enlarged. On its western side, al-Ghawrī built a palace, a belvedere for viewing events, and a reflecting pool watered initially from local cisterns and later from his new aqueduct from the Nile. He then planted a garden adorned with fruit trees, flowering shrubs, and aromatic plants from all over the Mediterranean, southwest Asia, and even the Orient. This garden became an instant showpiece of the Egyptian capital and source of delight to many foreign visitors. Yet the project cost more than eighty thousand dīnārs, most wrung from special taxes imposed on the commons. The sultan indulged himself in several building sprees of this nature, until his preoccupation with the Ottoman menace after 918. Ibn Iyās's roster of al-Ghawrī's projects is striking for its length, but the historian was sober about how they were funded.[89] That the sultan often kept these projects for his private use also provoked the historian's ire: Qāytbāy had certainly built lavishly in his day, but his edifices had served to glorify God's commonwealth; al-Ghawrī's structures, by contrast, smelled of corrupt money and for the most part served his own pleasures. When he went to face his nemesis at Marj Dābiq, the All High recalled his servant's offenses.

Al-Ghawrī passed progressively larger portions of his daily routine escaping the duties of his offices by departing the Citadel on recreational outings. His self-indulgence when

88 *Badā'i'* 4, 56, l. 3.
89 *Badā'i'* 5, 93, l. 23.

absent from Cairo increased noticeably from 917 on, encouraged in part by his growing worry over developments abroad. Ibn Iyās commented on popular resentment about the frequency of al-Ghawrī's excursions. On Tuesday, the ninth of Shawwāl/30 December 1511, when the sultan descended from the Citadel for an impromptu examination of his renovations at the Khān al-Khalīlī Bazaar, he deliberately canceled his biweekly audience. Indeed, forty days had elapsed since the sultan last held a pen or fixed his seal to a document. That a backlog of petitions from anxious supplicants had built up disturbed him not at all, "for the sultan resented spending time on judgments and signings, preferring riding tours every day, attending festivals, and reviewing military exercises."[90] These he certainly relished. Al-Ghawrī's sojourns exhibited a predictable pattern by 917, which emphasized recreation over work. The sultan would depart the Citadel at sunrise accompanied by a modest escort, or at midday in formal procession. He would make his perfunctory rounds of inspections that inevitably ended with a visit to either the Nilometer or a belevedere at Būlāq. There, one or more of his intimates, in particular Zaynī Barakāt, would host him and his retinue to a banquet. The sultan would then board his royal barque for a sail up or down the river. If he headed downstream toward Maṭarīya, he would often disembark to witness an artillery test or lancers' drill. He then returned to the Citadel at sunset. Ibn Iyās observed many of these progressions, and commented on the colossal scale of these feasts served up by the monarch's clients. Dozens of fatted sheep and hundreds of chickens, ducks, or geese might be roasted and portioned out with huge quantities of rice, followed by an enticing array of confections, fruits, and sweetened beverages.

Al-Ghawrī himself held soirées at his favorite retreat, the Nilometer, of such grandeur that they were recalled as a hallmark of his reign. After dinner, the sultan would entertain

90 *Badā'i'* 4, 248, l. 19.

his guests, who often included visiting dignitaries and even royalty, with singers, instrumentalists, fireworks, and illuminated vessels plying the river in the vicinity of his pavilions. Ibn Iyās described one such extravaganza on the thirteenth of Jumādā II 918/26 August 1512.[91] Al-Ghawrī planned to spend this hot night of late summer at the Nilometer. When the sun sank below the horizon, a procession carrying castles and fantastic structures, all festooned with candles, flares, and torches, set out from the Rumayla toward the Nile shore. The Nilometer tower, mosque, and belvedere were illuminated so that the southern tip of Rawḍā glowed "like a celestial constellation." When the procession reached the riverbank, the devices were placed on waiting vessels that transported them in review before the sultan and his guests in the pavilion. Bugle, drum, and tambourine corps set their progress to music. Ibn Iyās asserted that no previous ruler had surpassed al-Ghawrī's exhibition, a show that, incidentally, cost thousands of dīnārs for a single evening's diversion. But while Ibn Iyās chided the sultan for such an outpouring of cash in pursuit of display, he could not criticize him for idle frivolity as he did for his buildings. These spectacles were gripping public affairs, thrilling thousands of spectators. Al-Ghawrī's multifaceted style of governance was clearly apparent in his desire to delight the masses with enchanting celebrations while he simultaneously pressed them for funds. His predecessors may have behaved with more restraint, but they provided less enthralling entertainments. For the masses certainly enjoyed al-Ghawrī's shows and eagerly awaited to see what he would devise in future months.

Al-Ghawrī shared little of Qāytbāy's pride in his physical vigor or guardianship of the people while on excursion. He traveled at leisure with his retinue and scheduled all stages of a journey for maximum personal comfort. He made few extended trips away from the capital. His first, to the Giza

91 *Badā'i'* 4, 275, l. 23.

Pyramids, Fayyūm, and the Caliphal estates at Dahshūr, occurred in Dhū'l-Qa'da and Dhū'l-Ḥijja of 918/February–March 1513.[92] He ordered a luxurious bivouac set up at the Pyramids, where his favorite lyricists and musicians awaited his evening arrival after the formal procession through Cairo and Nile crossing in the royal barque. The sultan spent two days at Giza before setting out with his retainers, amīrs, and guests for the Fayyūm districts. His ostensible purpose was to inspect repairs he had ordered for the dykes and canals conveying water to the huge oasis. But in fact, he spent little time checking such worthy projects. Hunts, exercises, and games preoccupied him throughout the trip. His progression must have overawed local residents, for he had brought along several ceremonial cavalry units, with their mounts wearing the golden saddles and crystal bridles normally reserved for state occasions in Cairo. These he intended to deploy in a spectacular review sponsored jointly with the Caliph, who awaited him in Dahshūr. When al-Ghawrī arrived, he and the Commander of the Faithful exchanged gifts of such value that all in attendance marveled at the motive. Robes lined with ermine, sable, and Russian squirrel were bestowed on the officers accompanying the sultan. Ibn Iyās recalled al-Ghawrī's previous flippant distribution of crudely stitched cotton robes to eminent literati during the 'Īd al-Fiṭr, and allowed the reader to speculate whom he sought to impress more. The entire trip was noteworthy for "its squandered revenues and gross show of pomposity." While on the road, al-Ghawrī's cooks "prepared succulent repasts for the army *four* times a day." "But grooms, pages and staff were forbidden to partake of these repasts," and had to make do with their marching rations. This progression through the Fayyūm epitomized al-Ghawrī's deportment. Elaborately disinterested in official business or coddling scholastics who might condone his costly antics, this ruler enjoyed the fleeting years of peace

92 *Badā'i'* 4, 290, l. 9–293, l. 7.

fate ordained for him as he wished. His opulent tastes were brandished for all to see with little regard for popular carping. And perhaps al-Ghawrī rightly gauged the brevity of this serene interlude. Forces were converging abroad to disrupt it.

Foreign Affairs in the Medial Period: Persian Belligerence, Ottoman Entente

The interregnum preceding Qānṣūh al-Ghawrī's accession owed its tortuous protraction in part to the peace that prevailed in the eastern Mediterranean and southwest Asia during the early tenth/sixteenth century. The Mamlūk regime could afford the luxury of a prolonged competition for supremacy at this time. Following Qāytbāy's successful blockage of Ottoman aggression, this most formidable rival remained quiescent for the next two decades. No other power in the central Muslim world posed a challenge to Mamlūk authority until the year 908, when a charismatic figure meteorically erupted on the political stage in Iran. So unforeseen were Shāh Ismā'īl Ṣafawī's initial forays against his western neighbors that al-Ghawrī and his advisers reacted with alarm. During the medial years, the Mamlūk and Ottoman regimes shared a common interest in containing this new menace, and their joint concern for maintaining the status quo certainly contributed to the positive relations between Cairo and Istanbul that lasted until the supplanting of Sultan Bāyazīd II by his choleric son, Selim, in 918.

Word first reached Cairo from Aleppo of Ismā'īl's breaching the frontier in Ṣafar of 908/August–September 1502, and his despoiling of districts in southeastern Anatolia.[93] Al-Ghawrī and his colleagues were caught off guard, with little knowledge of who this person was or what he intended.

93 *Badā'i'* 4, 39, ll. 7–19.

But since memories of past disturbances from this region lingered, disquiet was widespread in the capital, and al-Ghawrī immediately announced preparations for an expedition. When follow-up reports made it known that the Ṣafavid raiders had returned to Iraq, mobilization exercises were canceled, although none of the dīwān officials got any of the money back they were compelled to offer for expenses. No further rumors of Ismā'īl's expansionist designs plagued al-Ghawrī for five years. But in Rabī' II of 913/July–August 1507, the governor of Aleppo sent a message confirming a second, more serious incursion. Ismā'īl's army, having probed deep within Mamlūk territory, now threatened Malāṭya.[94] Al-Ghawrī called his amīrs in council to debate a response. They unanimously advised a massive expedition, presumably to demonstrate for the first time since the sultan's accession the regime's commitment to guard its borders. Al-Ghawrī duly called for a full-scale muster of officers and troops. He invited the visiting Ottoman ambassador to attend, as he did the prince of a regional Turkmān confederation, Khalīlbak ibn Ramaḍān. Both shared al-Ghawrī's worry over Ismā'īl's bellicose posture and applauded his response. The sultan designated some fifteen hundred Mamlūks under the command of no less than five muqaddamīn. The expedition's size demonstrated al-Ghawrī's anxiety over the situation in Anatolia.

Yet once again, lucky chance relieved al-Ghawrī of this problem. While the expedition was being organized and couriers dispatched to the Syrian capitals ordering them to muster their own contingents, emissaries from Ismā'īl arrived bearing a conciliatory missive.[95] Ismā'īl apologized for his army's act of trespass, claiming his officers had done so inadvertently. As soon as he had learned of their error, he recalled them. Al-Ghawrī accepted Ismā'īl's excuses,

94 *Badā'i'* 4, 118, l. 6.
95 *Badā'i'* 4, 123, l. 15.

disbanded the expedition, and hosted the Ṣafavid ambassadors to a reception in the Citadel courtyard. The affair gave the court an opportunity to observe representatives of this new Persian ruler at close range. They struck most as rustic and peculiar. Ibn Iyās described them as extremely coarse (*fī ghāyat al-ghilāsa*),[96] with odd red headgear (*ṭarāṭīr*). "They could not compare with the Ottoman ambassador's elegance." Yet Ismā'īl's contingents persisted with their sporadic forays. Al-Ghawrī now dismissed them as an irritant and planned no subsequent mobilizations. When, in Rabī' I of 916/June–July 1510, the nā'ib of Aleppo informed him that a Ṣafavid detachment was raiding villages near al-Bīra and pillaging sheep herds of Kurdish tribesmen, al-Ghawrī ordered the local prefect to deal with it. Yet the sultan apparently decided that some degree of reciprocal contact was warranted and dispatched his own emissary that month.[97] He appointed only an amīr of ten, showing his low esteem for the Ṣafavid upstart, whom he scorned to regard as a peer. But this upstart showed himself capable of grandiose schemes. Soon after al-Ghawrī's emissary had departed for Tabrīz, a courier arrived posthaste from the prefect of al-Bīra, bearing missives of a most extraordinary nature that had been seized from Ṣafavid messengers captured during the prefect's counterattack.[98] They were addressed to several European monarchs, offering cooperation in a joint operation against the Egyptian sultan. The Europeans were to attack Egypt by sea while Ismā'īl invaded from the east. Whether any similar proposals had already reached the courts of Europe, al-Ghawrī could not guess. But in light of the harassment continually inflicted on his coastal ports by Frankish corsairs, he could not discount this conspiracy.

Subsequent events kept the Ṣafavid issue alive. In Dhū'l-Ḥijja/March 1511, news came to the sultan that Ismā'īl had

96 from the literary "*ghilāẓa*."
97 *Badā'i'* 4, 184, l. 16.
98 *Badā'i'* 4, 191, l. 5.

defeated Azbak Khān, ruler of the Caucasus Ṭaṭars, in personal combat. He had beheaded his enemy and set his skull in silver as a pledge cup.[99] When al-Ghawrī convened his colleagues to assess this new development, he was informed that Ismā'īl's apparent willingness to coexist with the Mamlūk regime derived from his preoccupation over the Ṭaṭar chieftain rather than from any respect for his western neighbor. But all in attendance counseled restraint, since the Ottoman monarch was face to face with this menace and would be compelled to respond. Cairo would be well advised to wait upon events. Al-Ghawrī thus decided to bide his time. For several months no further news of disturbances in Persia reached Cairo. Then, in Rabī' I of 917/May–June 1511, an ambassador from Ismā'īl arrived at the capital's outskirts and requested an audience with the sultan.[100] Al-Ghawrī agreed, but placed the emissary under close guard while he bivouacked at al-Maṭarīya. So consumed with curiosity about the ambassador's ulterior mission was al-Ghawrī that he descended from the Citadel by stealth to spy on him unobserved. Ibn Iyās found this behavior demeaning, a violation of diplomatic protocol. But the sultan evidently hoped to discover whether Ismā'īl's messenger planned to spread sedition among his own officers.

In any case, the emissary was received on the twentieth/17 June. Al-Ghawrī sought to impress his unwelcome guest with the grandeur of his own position, and sat on a golden dais in the courtyard. While he personally scorned to don full royal regalia, al-Ghawrī ordered the arsenal gate festooned with imperial standards, blazons, and armaments to underscore his military power. When the ambassador ascended from the lodging assigned him in the Rumayla quarter, he bowed to kiss the sultan's feet. He then read his patron's greeting and presented al-Ghawrī with a prayer rug and copy

99 *Badā'i'* 4, 207, l. 18.
100 *Badā'i'* 4, 218, l. 23; 219, l. 11; 220, l. 17; 221, l. 5.

of the Koran. Al-Ghawrī did not stand when he received these tokens of peace, but kissed the holy scripture, acknowledging the common faith both rulers revered. The ambassador then produced an elegant wood chest and opened it before the assembled courtiers. They were aghast to behold Azbak Khān's skull set in silver. This blatant insult shown al-Ghawrī by the Persian ruler appalled the spectators but the sultan reacted coolly. He took possession of the head as if it were presented by a supplicant in recognition of his loftier status and ordered it buried after a proper service. Thus he, defender of Orthodoxy, would grant a decent funeral to this fellow Muslim whose right of faith Ismā'īl had so shamefully defiled.

While al-Ghawrī granted Ismā'īl's ambassador the safe-conduct due an emissary, he restricted him to his lodging with no civilian contact whatsoever. Receptions were hosted and robes exchanged. But al-Ghawrī had cause to suspect his guest's agenda, not to mention the designs of his master in Tabrīz. Fancying himself something of a rhymer, Ismā'īl often included satirical verses mocking his rivals in letters to be delivered by his ambassadors. The verse he composed to commemorate his gift of Azbak Khān's head to al-Ghawrī went as follows:

> The sword and dagger are our perfumes.
> Sniff the narcissus and myrtle, therefore.
> *We* are intoxicated by our enemies' blood,
> quaffed from their skulls made into cups.[101]

Al-Ghawrī had no intention of allowing Ismā'īl's minion to spread such inflammatory lines as these among Cairo's pundits, who already delighted in circulating homegrown poems slighting the royal honor. Al-Ghawrī had found out

101 Al-Ḥalabī, *Durr*, f. 177, l. 23, provided a variant on this verse, which Ismā'īl also sent to Istanbul: The sword and dagger are our lances, / turned against suppressor and captor. / We drink of our enemy's blood, / for our cup is fashioned from his skull.

that this emissary derided his love of beauteous vistas and aromatic plants, while Ismā'īl allegedly ridiculed the sultan's new Hippodrome garden and his Nilometer belvederes as signs of effeteness.[102] Al-Ghawrī requested several eminent Cairene poets, including Ibn Iyās, to compose lines equally derisive of the Persian ruler. He found verses offered by one Ṣafī al-Dīn al-Ḥillī most suitable, since they compared Ismā'īl to the Mongol conqueror Hūlāghū. This thirteenth-century founder of the Il-Khānid regime in Iran was depicted as a barbarian by Egyptian historians. He was a pagan animist with a Christian wife, who induced her husband to desecrate mosques and synagogues when he stormed Baghdād in 1258. Comparing Ismā'īl to him brought into question Ismā'īl's status as a true believer. And Hūlāghū's forces had gone down to defeat at the hands of Quṭuz and Baybars when they dared set foot in Mamlūk territory. Ibn Iyās found al-Ḥillī's lines inappropriate, for "of course, the Ṣafavid ruler could not be compared to Hūlāghū in any way." Quite possibly, the historian resented al-Ghawrī's preference for his rival's composition.

Early in Jumādā I/July, Ismā'īl's ambassador departed Cairo. He left at daybreak to avoid public notice of his passage through the streets.[103] Al-Ghawrī had in the end decided against incorporating al-Ḥillī's verses, or any others, into his response, which Ibn Iyās assumed was deliberately obtuse if not openly obsequious. But al-Ghawrī invariably opted for caution in his diplomacy and avoided any phraseology that might induce Ismā'īl to renew hostilities. Fortune itself was to resolve this matter, however: it would be Bāyazīd's successor who was to decide Ismā'īl's fate and the future of southwest Asia for centuries to come.

Prior to Selim's accession, few could have predicted the reversal of Mamlūk–Ottoman relations after he was on the

102 *Badā'i'* 4, 222, l. 1.
103 *Badā'i'* 4, 230, l. 13.

throne. Al-Ghawrī's contacts with emissaries from Bāyazīd II were uniformly cordial, and he spared no turn of protocol to demonstrate his own good will. From the year 908, coinciding with the first reports of Ismā'īl Ṣafawī's raids, the two regimes exchanged a series of embassies reaffirming their mutual respect.[104] Al-Ghawrī showered Bāyazīd's representatives with the highest honors permitted a foreign dignitary. Upon his arrival, each ambassador was personally received by the sultan, who draped a splendid velvet robe lined with sable from his own wardrobe over his shoulders. At the receptions that followed, the sultan's guests were invariably treated to some extraordinary show of hospitality. Often, the Hippodrome's central fountain was completely filled with a sweetened beverage or perfumed water to be served after the main meal. When Bāyazīd's emissaries presented their missives, al-Ghawrī would stand to accept them personally, as if he were taking them from his peer's own hand. He would press the packet against his eyes before handing it over to his chancellor, Ibn Ajā, for public reading. Since the Ottoman wars against Christian kingdoms in Europe were followed avidly in other Muslim capitals, visits of famous battle heroes elicited a royal welcome. In Jumādā I of 913/September–October 1507, one such paladin, named Kamāl, presented himself at court. Ibn Iyās referred to him as a veritable "paragon of holy warriors" (*mujāhid al-murābiṭīn*), so ferocious were his exploits against the Franks.[105] Al-Ghawrī received Kamāl as if he were a revered officer from his own army. That this man enjoyed his sovereign's special favor certainly contributed to the splendor of al-Ghawrī's reception.

A fundamental dimension of al-Ghawrī's foreign policy was to keep the peace with Bāyazīd. Qāytbāy's Ottoman campaigns had drained the treasury, and al-Ghawrī sought to husband the state's resources in the long run by entertaining

104 *Badā'i'* 4, 9, l. 12; 46, l. 5; 47, l. 7; 107, l. 6; 122, l. 8.
105 *Badā'i'* 4, 119, l. 10.

Ottoman visitors lavishly when they arrived. That they extolled the luster of his court when they returned home enhanced his reputation as a great king worthy of respect and even deference. Al-Ghawrī attached such importance to Bāyazīd's good will that he was profoundly dismayed by tidings of his death after an illness in Muḥarram of 915/April–May 1509.[106] Wishing to show his esteem for both the deceased and his successor, whoever he might be, al-Ghawrī ordered special prayers to be offered in Cairo's cathedral mosque, the Azhar. When the rumors were discounted, the sultan dispatched 'Alān al-Dawādār, an officer with diplomatic experience in Istanbul, to offer his personal congratulations for Bāyazīd's recovery. Indeed, so long as Bāyazīd reigned, the two empires remained at peace.

In Ṣafar/May–June, Prince Qurqud, Bāyazīd's eldest son, arrived at Damietta and requested permission to meet al-Ghawrī in Cairo.[107] This man's presence placed al-Ghawrī in something of a quandary. Hints of rifts between Bāyazīd and his offspring had circulated in Muslim courts for years, and al-Ghawrī feared being asked to intervene in a family quarrel. Al-Ghawrī had, to this point, avoided any entanglement in such squabbles. But now this prince of the Ottoman house had placed a claim on his hospitality, a request the sultan could not refuse without losing face. Yet sheltering this man as a guest might be interpreted in Istanbul as endorsement of his right to the succession. Al-Ghawrī made a decision to welcome Qurqud with full honors, while maintaining a stance of strict neutrality whatever his entreaty.

Qurqud arrived at Shubrā on the eighteenth/7 June.[108] A delegation of grand amīrs escorted him to his hostel at the Barābakīya Hall in Būlāq. Here he was to remain until the twenty-third, when he would be formally received at

106 *Badā'i'* 4, 152, l. 4.

107 *Badā'i'* 4, 152, l. 11. Bāyazīd had three sons: Qurqud, Aḥmad, and Selim, who was destined to supplant his brothers and all other possible competitors.

108 *Badā'i'* 4, 153, l. 14.

the Citadel. Qurqud's safekeeping was placed in the hands of the atābak Qurqumās, who presented him with twenty horses from the sultan's own stock for his retainers' use during their stay. On the day of his procession to the imperial court, al-Ghawrī ordered his officers and troops to line the route in formal dress uniforms to display the splendor of the Egyptian army. Qurqud sat on a golden saddle al-Ghawrī had provided him, a gesture Qāytbāy had not extended Prince Jem when he came calling. Al-Ghawrī's show of respect hardly stopped with his guest's mount. The prince's route from the Chain Gate to the royal courtyard was hung with brocade of gold silk, and the dais itself, where the sultan would greet him, was covered with gold satin. Yellow was the color of Egyptian royalty, and its ceremonial use for a visitor signaled the sultan's acknowledgement of his coequal status. After Qurqud made his way up the several ramps leading to the Citadel in the company of the receptionist (*mihmandār*), he dismounted at the Ḥawsh Gate to greet al-Ghawrī on foot. But the sultan himself broke protocol by leaving the throne to embrace him at the foot of the dais. No obeisance beyond hand-kissing was called for: the two met as equals. Qāytbāy had refused even to stand when Jem was presented, much less descend to his guest's level on the Ḥawsh pavement.

Al-Ghawrī and Qurqud spent one hour of this initial meeting talking over the reason for the impromptu visit. Ibn Iyās recounted only that Qurqud, having quarreled with his father and brother Selim, sought the sultan's aid as an intermediary. The historian noted his appearance: "a young man in his forties, of medium height, Arabic features, light complexion, slender frame, black mustache—overall attractive." He wore exquisite but not flashy garments for his presentation, including a small Turkmān turban. The sultan gave him the first of several splendid robes of honor, which Qurqud donned. Ibn Iyās marveled at the scope of al-Ghawrī's reception, comparing it with the studied austerity shown Jem by Qāytbāy. Here again, we see the differences in style between the two rulers. Neither sought to insult the reigning Ottoman autocrat by favoring his prodigal sibling or son. But Qāytbāy made Jem keenly aware that his presence compromised his host's standing in Istanbul. Al-Ghawrī, on the other hand, showered Qurqud with honors, while carefully sidestepping the matter of his dispute with his father. No one in Istanbul could accuse the Egyptian sultan of slighting his royal guest, yet none could find any cause for accusing him of clandestine support. The respective statuses of Jem and Qurqud contrasted markedly, of course. Jem arrived as a fugitive with his mother and children; Qurqud came confident of his royal position at home, to which he could return at will. Nonetheless, Ibn Iyās found al-Ghawrī's gifts to a prince with no record of personal achievement inordinate: twenty thousand dīnārs, half in silver, half gold, and several chests containing wardrobes of Skandarī and Manzalāwī cloth, in addition to the riding horses. Qurqud's reciprocal gifts to his host "were reputed to be of great value," but Ibn Iyās could not provide a precise inventory. They could hardly have matched al-Ghawrī's largesse. Restraint marked Qāytbāy's approach, excess al-Ghawrī's.

Prince Qurqud passed more than a year in Cairo before leaving in Rabīʿ II of 916/June–July 1510. During his protracted stay, al-Ghawrī invited him to attend every religious festival, military review, or court ceremonial that took place over these months.[109] At all such events, al-Ghawrī treated Qurqud almost as a brother or nephew, breaking the Ramaḍān fast with him in private, requesting his company

109 *Badāʾiʿ* 4, 157, l. 1 (Qurqud pleads case for return of Azbak al-Mukaḥḥil from exile, pardoned for conspiring with Qāyt al-Rajabī); 157, l. 9 (al-Ghawrī celebrates Prophet's birthday with Qurqud, wears formal uniform in his honor); 158, l. 2 (sultan and Qurqud play polo together); 158, l. 21 (sultan fines governor of Damietta for offending Qurqud when he arrived); 160, l. 20 (sultan and Qurqud attend battle exercises and artillery demonstration); 163, l. 23 (lancers drill before Qurqud); 164, l. 9 (concerned for his winter comfort, sultan transfers Qurqud to Jānbalāṭ's city palace); 166, l. 8 (sultan and Qurqud break fast).

on recreational outings, and admitting him to his circle of intimates. When Qurqud exhausted his initial subsidy, al-Ghawrī granted him a monthly allowance of two thousand dīnārs drawn from the reserve fund over the protests of several officials who warned of other exigencies that might go unfunded.[110] When the Maḥmal caravan prepared to depart for Mecca in Shawwāl/January–February 1510, Qurqud's senior aide professed his desire to make the pilgrimage himself.[111] The prince gave him forty thousand dīnārs for distribution to the pious in his name and that of his family. Whether Qurqud had brought this sum expressly for charitable purposes Ibn Iyās did not say, but al-Ghawrī almost certainly donated part of it.

When Qurqud announced his intention of returning to Istanbul to resolve his dispute, al-Ghawrī insisted that he travel in the royal barque all the way back to Rosetta.[112] Once again, Ibn Iyās remarked al-Ghawrī's unprecedented beneficence to this prince. No previous sultan had granted such a reception to a foreign guest, even if he were royal. This Qurqud was, after all, only one among three Ottoman heirs, and who could predict which would emerge victorious after their father's death or deposition? What would al-Ghawrī stand to gain, therefore, from this extravagance? Ibn Iyās had no answer, and we can only speculate on al-Ghawrī's inner motives. Certainly his reception exceeded the requirements of royal protocol under such circumstances. Qurqud's personality may have enhanced his standing. By all accounts, he was a bon vivant, whom the sultan and amīrs found engaging. By contrast, Jem's presence remained a thorn in Qāytbāy's side he longed to be rid of. Jem tediously reiterated his need for military support; Qurqud requested only the sultan's good word with his father. Yet even if we acknowledge their differences, al-Ghawrī's lavishness bespoke

110 *Badā'i'* 4, 167, l. 11.
111 *Badā'i'* 4, 168, l. 4.
112 *Badā'i'* 4, 186, l. 11.

his peculiar impulse toward extremes when dealing with a favorite. As with his pet projects and personal pleasures, al-Ghawrī would spare no expense to show his fondness for someone he admired. Did al-Ghawrī also seek to display the wealth he possessed to this representative of the Otttoman House? Quite possibly. Still, the opinion astute observers reached about the episode was that Qurqud got far more than he gave.

Whatever the opinion of it in Cairo, the affair did not sour al-Ghawrī's relations with Qurqud's father. Bāyazīd remained al-Ghawrī's ally, prepared to support his defense against common enemies. Soon after Qurqud's departure, in Rajab of 916/October 1510, al-Ghawrī's own ambassador to Istanbul returned with pleasant news confirming Bāyazīd's magnanimity. This emissary, Yūnus al-ʿĀdilī, had traveled to the Ottoman court with a request for naval supplies, iron, gunpowder, and timber.[113] The Egyptian sultanate needed these resources, in extremely short supply at home, to ward off European corsairs who terrorized its ports and vessels. Yūnus informed al-Ghawrī that Bāyazīd would indeed fulfill the sultan's plea but would accept no payment. In Shawwāl, all the supplies arrived by ship at Būlāq. Soon thereafter, Bāyazīd's emissary arrived seeking confirmation of their safe transfer. Truly, the Egyptian and Ottoman sultans, though never meeting, enjoyed a harmonious relationship, prized by each in this turbulent age. Indeed, al-Ghawrī's exceptional treatment of Bāyazīd's son, even if he were temporarily estranged, may have played a positive role in nurturing this cordiality. Al-Ghawrī regarded Qurqud as an extension of his father, whom he profoundly respected but never came to know. Perhaps the other ambitious son, Selim, resented his brother's reception at al-Ghawrī's court and nursed this favoritism among his private slights when he ascended the throne two years later.

113 *Badāʾiʿ* 4, 196, l. 4; 201, l. 5; 202, l. 21.

The Final Years: Scorning Old Tensions

Selim Yavūz's succession year in Istanbul, 918, presaged a reversal in al-Ghawrī's fortunes. The sultan's greed for confiscated wealth set an ominously appealing example for both civilian robbers and Mamlūk recruits, who stepped up their own pillaging of Cairo's markets.[114] The Julbān found al-Ghawrī's greed particularly galling since he refused to share his gains with them. The immorality of expropriation itself never entered their minds, but their patron's inclination to secrete his wealth, when they were lacking, eroded their respect for his edicts. The recruits therefore seized foodstuffs and commodities from the merchants when they went short on their rations. That their lawlessness ran rampant in a period of prosperity highlighted the lapse of al-Ghawrī's personal authority over the military establishment. Ibn Iyās concluded his summation for the year 918 with a statement on its bountiful productivity.[115] A high flood, abundant crops, and an interval free from pestilence all contributed to a sense of well-being among the populace. Yet revival of the insecurity that marred al-Ghawrī's early years dampened any widespread rejoicing over God's generosity this year. The All High, regardless of his mercy, remained remote. Reawakened tensions within the military caste posed a menace that was alarmingly tangible.

114 *Badā'i'* 4, 259, l. 21 (markets robbed, no culprits apprehended); 260, l. 5 (sultan confiscates large block of Sharīfī waqf properties); 279, l. 22 (robbery of Zarbīya Quarter, lasts all night with no police response); 283, l. 20 (sultan refuses to release debtors); 286, l. 15 (distribution of shoddy festival robes during Ramaḍān).

115 *Badā'i'* 4, 295, l. 13.

The following year saw no diminution of these tensions or the popular irritation over the sultan's fiscal ploys. On the fourteenth of Ṣafar/21 April 1513, al-Ghawrī descended from the Citadel to inspect a pavilion he had commissioned near the Qubbat Yashbak in al-Maṭarīya and repair work on his mausoleum dome at the Bayn al-Qaṣrayn.[116] As he made his way toward his tomb, crowds hurled epithets at him decrying his purchasing wheat in Egypt to sell in Syria, where it drew higher prices. Resultant scarcities in Cairo drove up the cost of bread and flour. When al-Ghawrī heard such curses as "God will destroy him who causes famine among the Muslims!," he was visibly shaken and returned to the Citadel via back alleys rather than the Bāb Zuwayla and Darb al-Aḥmar in full public gaze. These outpourings of discontent increased markedly throughout al-Ghawrī's latter years. Coupled with his growing alarm over brigandage and the heightening militancy of troopers, such demonstrations revived al-Ghawrī's earlier paranoia. Yet he focused his creative energies on ensuring his own safety rather than alleviating the problems themselves. Few thievery cases were vigorously prosecuted, and the sultan vacillated between spiteful obstinacy and sullen capitulation when his soldiers defied his orders.

Revolts had now become routine expressions of the recruits' dissatisfaction with their monthly stipend and bonus allotments.[117] Al-Ghawrī repeatedly lined up his officers and troops to reconfirm their wavering ties of fealty by oaths on the 'Uthmānī Koran. Even al-Ghawrī's senior adjutants, who worked closely with him, questioned his constancy and demanded that he promise to uphold their own rights and the integrity of their estates. The image Ibn Iyās depicts of al-Ghawrī at these sessions was poignant if not demeaning. The sultan was himself compelled to place his hand on

116 *Badā'i'* 4, 302, l. 12.

117 On revolt threats during 919: *Badā'i'* 4, 313, l. 6; 315, l. 5; 316, l. 3; 318, l. 12; 337, l. 13.

the relic and reiterate his commitment to the tenure of his amīrs in office and their safety from assassination attempts by his own henchmen. When, on the twenty-fifth of Rabīʿ II/31 May, al-Ghawrī learned that recruits were plotting his confinement in the palace precinct with no fear of opposition from his amīrs, he convened the latter in the Hippodrome. Reviling them for their indifference to his plight, al-Ghawrī threatened abdication on the spot. "If there is any among you whom you wish to enthrone, I shall relinquish the Citadel to him and retire to my mosque, where death will be welcome." Fearing the chaos of a succession crisis, the amīrs prostrated themselves before him and begged his forgiveness. This little comedy was to be staged repeatedly up to the sultan's departure for his confrontation with Selim in 922. While the posturing in these mock threats was obvious, the underlying gravity of conditions promoting them was equally apparent. Al-Ghawrī doubled the guards assigned to the prison in Alexandria where the former sultan al-Ẓāhir Qānṣūh languished, still nursing hopes of restoration. Despite al-Ẓāhir's tyrannical behavior during his abortive reign, he posed a threat as a surviving member of the executive club. Officers convinced of al-Ghawrī's incapacity to maintain order might attempt his reinstallation.

In the face of mounting dissension, al-Ghawrī did not retreat into the inner sanctum of his palace. His penchant for excursions was, if anything, strengthened by his growing revulsion against his retainers' company at home. Al-Ghawrī now abandoned the Citadel confines as often as he could to escape rumors of sedition.[118] His refusal to curtail his mobility, in contrast with his fear of assassination during the early

[118] *Badāʾiʿ* 4, 311, l. 9; 327, l. 20 (sultan inspects pavilion in Maṭarīya); 328, l. 8 (sultan sojourns at Nilometer); 330, l. 10 (sultan hosted to banquet at Maṭarīya); 337, l. 18 (sultan sojourns at Rawḍā Island); 338, l. 12 (sultan inspects pavilion at Maṭarīya); 339, l. 19 (sultan back again at Rawḍā); 340, l. 8 (sultan relaxes at Nilometer); 340, l. 19 (sultan overnights at Qubbat Yashbak).

period, suggests his confidence that he had become indispensable, if not beloved. Rather than risk a civil war with no charismatic rival capable of rallying disparate factions, the amīrs were resigned to retaining the old despot they knew so well. Al-Ghawrī flaunted his love of grand living in their faces during these excursions. He savored all the attention his cronies fawned upon him, often carousing into early hours of the morning over wine, sham battles, musical performances, and poetry recitals. When he planned an excursion to the desert oasis of Wādī al-'Abbāsa in Dhū'l-Qa'da/January 1514, he departed "with baggage and provisions sufficient for an expedition to Syria."[119] Later the same month he made an eight-day tour of the eastern Delta. His agents preceded him, demanding obligatory gifts from local iqṭā' stewards in the villages he planned to visit.[120] At year's end, al-Ghawrī journeyed once again to the western Nile shore in high style. The troops escorting their sovereign grumbled openly about the trip, which served no practical purpose.[121] The sultan had laid out an elaborate itinerary of inspection sites, followed by a trip to the Fayyūm or Alexandria. But once he arrived, he spent his time relaxing at Anbāba. Since the soldiers had been compelled to transport even his sedan chair for this trivial outing, they resented such needless fuss. Ibn Iyās wryly remarked later that al-Ghawrī rapidly squandered whatever stature he had built up in the medial period by these frivolous outings, undertaken when the troops regarded themselves as impoverished.

The year 920/1514–1515 exhibited the same pattern of latent mutiny and escapist excursions. The show of revolt had now become so routine that al-Ghawrī anticipated it before every stipend review and often circumvented the ceremony by departing early, relegating the burden of distribution to some hapless subordinate who was left to face the recruits' wrath.

119 *Badā'i'* 4, 352, l. 14.
120 *Badā'i'* 4, 354, l. 4.
121 *Badā'i'* 4, 356, l. 6.

Al-Ghawrī took pains to treat his personal bodyguard well, granting them silver-embossed weapons and fine uniforms in addition to their salaries, which never fell short.[122] Soldiers who served other amīrs or had been promoted under previous sultans fared worse, often doing without their stipends and having to repair their worn-out arms. Such treatment did little to promote the cohesion Qāytbāy had attempted to instill. When, in Ṣafar/April 1514, al-Ghawrī chastized his dīwān agents over shortfalls in their accounts, several soldiers awaiting their stipends denounced his duplicity to his face.[123] "It is you who have caused delays among the dīwāns by instituting your new Fifth Corps[124], and by usurping stipends of orphans and widows to support it. This unit is comprised of Turkmān nomads, effete Persians, shoemakers (*asākifa*), and second-generation infantrymen—a hodgepodge of rags and tatters!" The sultan replied, "I created this new corps to relieve *you* of travel and expeditions abroad—which you protest against so vigorously." The khāṣṣakīs responded, "This was not al-Ashraf Qāytbāy's policy at all. You have beggared the dīwāns so that for five months meat and fodder rations have been delayed. The granaries hand us wheat so rotten our horses won't touch it. Our stipends from you do not suffice to rent a house or stable, to pay a groom, or to buy either clothing or uniforms—all of which are costly. Throughout your reign we have never been properly provisioned. We are now famished and go naked!" Al-Ghawrī sat silent a long moment and then acknowledged their grievance, paying out their salaries and lowering the price of ration

122 *Badā'i'* 4, 358, l. 11.
123 *Badā'i'* 4, 369, l. 3.
124 Al-Ghawrī was experimenting with the formation of a new unit of soldiers recruited from outside the Mamlūk hierarchy and trained in the use of firearms. Because they were paid on a special fifth stipend session, following the four days during which the regular troops and reservists (*awlād al-nās*) received theirs, they were called "The Fifth Corps" (*al-ṭabaqat al-khāmisa*). See *Badā'i'* 4, 100, l. 15; David Ayalon, *Gunpowder and Firearms in the Mamluk Kingdom* (London 1956) 71–83

staples on the spot. Yet Ibn Iyās noted that this knuckling under pressure merely amounted to a temporary stopgap, for the sultan had no intention either of disbanding his Fifth Corps or of raising stipends for soldiers whose loyalty was suspect.

The rhythm of sedition and pleasure jaunts in 920 was broken by two major trips the sultan planned, one to Suez in Ṣafar, the other to Alexandria in Dhū'l-Qa'da. Al-Ghawrī organized the first to check on the shipyards he had built in concert with the Ottomans to deal with incursions of Portuguese corsairs in the Red Sea.[125] Ibn Iyās dwelt more on al-Ghawrī's ceremonial procession upon his return to Cairo than the expedition itself, since he put on such an elaborate show.[126] Although the sultan dispensed with the traditional parading of the royal parasol and bird, he was preceded by forty riderless horses wearing gold saddles and crystal bridles. Even his pack mules were decked out in saffron silk.

Al-Ghawrī's progression to and from Alexandria, however, dwarfed any previous pageant he had concocted. Ibn Iyās devoted the bulk of his comments for the year to this single venture lasting the entire month.[127] Al-Ghawrī intended to duplicate Qāytbāy's visits to the seaport, even though he could justify the expense with no imposing edifice to compare with his predecessor's fortress on the site of the Pharos lighthouse. On the twenty-fifth of Shawwāl/13 December 1514, al-Ghawrī ordered the troops of four barracks to muster for his selection of officers and khāṣṣakīs who would accompany him. Ever since he first planned it, al-Ghawrī considered only

[125] The appearance of the Portuguese in the Indian Ocean and Red Sea heralded the end of Egypt's effective monopoly over the trade in south and east Asian commodities prized in European markets. See Eliyahu Ashtor, *Levant Trade in the Later Middle Ages* (Princeton 1983) 200–210; Subhi Labib, *Handelsgeschichte Ägyptens im Spätmittelalter (1171–1517)* (Wiesbaden 1965) 337–440; R. B. Sergeant, *The Portuguese off the South Arabian Coast* (London 1963).

[126] *Badā'i'* 4, 367, l. 8.

[127] *Badā'i'* 4, 412, l. 13; 425, l. 13.

the spectacle he could create when he departed and returned to the capital. The trip itself became incidental to its formal inception and conclusion. At least so concluded Ibn Iyās, who of course observed only these phases. Al-Ghawrī decided to stage a full-blown display of military regalia for the departure procession, even though the journey entailed no expeditionary function. He took two palanquins with him for use during his stay in the seaport. All the royal standards were to appear with the escort, and all the royal cavalry trappings embossed with gold and gems were to be shown off. After the initial review, the sultan conducted an inventory of the imperial magazines and armories of the Citadel to locate famous items designed as far back as the Ayyūbid era for inclusion in this extravaganza.

Over the following three days, al-Ghawrī chose his retainers for the progression. Since the weather had turned cold and damp, the Rumayla Square was covered with a film of mud the troops found unappealing. The men resented this special tour of duty, since they would march in mid-winter. Even the prospect of wearing finery most had never seen before failed to spark their enthusiasm. Many apparently found the trip a garish parading of outmoded trappings that provided no real measure of the regime's fighting capacity. Nonetheless, al-Ghawrī proceeded with his preparations, scheduling his departure for midday the first of Dhū'l-Qa'da/18 December 1514. The Caliph and the four qāḍīs ascended to the palace to present their monthly greetings. Al-Ghawrī accepted their felicitations summarily since he was impatient to be off. After signing a few decrees, the sultan closed his pen box with relief and mounted his grey charger for the descent down to the Hippodrome. He was preceded by his escort battalion, decked out in their lustrous uniforms and seated on their gold saddles. The royal drummers, flutists, and trumpeters sounded their marching beats as they went down. When the unit reached the Rumayla, thirteen lines of dromedaries draped in velvet and bearing the monarch's copious baggage commenced their swaying pace toward the Cross Street and the Nile shore. More than one hundred horses, similarly decorated and wearing ostrich plumes in their bridles, followed the camels. Behind them came the litters and palanquins, then the khāṣṣakīs, the companion officers, and finally the sultan himself. The old man wore a magnificent robe of purple velvet trimmed with Russian squirrel and a small turban from which ceremonial horns projected. Before the sultan rode out of the Rumayla, he bestowed the regency on his nephew Ṭūmānbāy, who assumed full executive authority in his absence.

Al-Ghawrī ultimately made his way to Anbāba, where a vast encampment (*wuṭāq*) arranged around Qāytbāy's bivouac tent had been set up in advance. Here he remained relaxing at polo matches and lance-casting drills until the sixth, awaiting news about his wife and son, who had joined the Ḥajj. When he received missives reporting their safe passage, he advanced toward the coast in stages, rejoicing in both his family's welfare and the prospect of a pleasure jaunt "on the road." Upon his arrival in Alexandria a week later, the city's minarets were illuminated for his visit. "From each niche in the casement walls was suspended an oil lamp" flickering in the evening's waning light. The effect was spellbinding, and al-Ghawrī spent his first night outside the port at his camp to savor the scene. The sultan had no impulse to rush his inspection tour. The next morning he journeyed to the seashore, where he invited the city's garrison officers to a polo match. In the afternoon, the sultan paid his respects at tombs of local saints. Only then did he examine Qāytbāy's watchtower. The next day, the seventeenth, al-Ghawrī reserved for inspecting other fortresses in Alexandria's vicinity and attending an artillery demonstration. That evening he dazzled the populace with a fireworks display on the shore, having brought his famous pyrotechnic experts with him for this purpose. The sultan intended to return to Cairo on the eighteenth, after only two days in the seaport. Before he left he made a rare gesture of magnanimity to two former opponents. He sent his director of provisions (*muhtār al-ṭishtakhānāh*) to the dungeons where al-Ẓāhir Qānṣūh and Qāyt al-Rajabī languished in solitary confinement chained to their cell floors. Henceforth, both were to remain in prison but freed of their shackles and at liberty to move about, although still isolated from any visitors. Each received a grant of one thousand dīnārs and new vestments befitting their former rank. "The two kissed the ground before the muhtār and swore to obey the sultan's command."

Al-Ghawrī intended to spend at least a week traversing the Delta before his formal reentry to the capital. When he arrived at the town of al-Manṣūrīya, he sent word ahead to Ṭūmānbāy forbidding any reception until he himself reached al-Raydānīya, where his procession would begin. He scheduled the event for the first of Dhū'l-Ḥijja/17 January to coincide with the commencing of pilgrimage rites in the holy cities of the Ḥijāz.

Ibn Iyās describes the event in detail as a wonder unequaled in the annals of the Mamlūk regime.[128] The sultan personally arranged his escort battalion (*ṭulb*). It contained one hundred and eighty horses, eighty of which were riderless. Sixty of these wore chain mail mantles padded with multicolored velvet and embossed with gold and silver. Twenty, draped in yellow silk buckled with jeweled clasps, bore the royal saddles and bridles. The drums were set in silver cases decorated with crystal. Some fifty horses, also clad in yellow silk, carried the percussionists and trumpeters. Preceding the escort battalion filed sixteen lines of camels divided into two units, one with gold and silver trappings, the other with velvet capes. Even the sultan's pet elephants, presented as gifts by visiting ambassadors, were called into service, bearing silk-wrapped howdahs containing the sacred relics taken along to shed *baraka* on the excursion. Al-Ghawrī followed this host

128 *Badā'i'* 4, 417, l. 16.

mounted on his charger, wearing his purple cloak and horned turban. When his peers, the muqaddamīn who had remained in Cairo, learned of his finery, they immediately donned their own best not to be outshone when they joined him for the procession across the city. The atābak Ṣūdūn al-ʿAjamī rode on the sultan's left, holding the parasol and bird aloft over his head when the battalion reached the Bāb al-Naṣr. To his right rode the Caliph al-Mutawakkil, wearing the black Baghdādī turban of his office and a white robe lined with green wool. Behind came the four senior qāḍīs. Ibn Iyās stated that their participation was unplanned, but they refused to be left out since they felt snubbed when the sultan had brusquely dismissed their monthly greetings as he was setting out. The historian also contrasted al-Ghawrī's midday procession with Qāytbāy's return to the Citadel from his two Alexandria trips. The latter had bypassed the city, going by the eastern tombs route and ascending to his palace only in the morning. "None of the populace had therefore observed him—but each to his own style." Al-Ghawrī had ordered all his escort khāṣṣakīs, almost five hundred in number, to don their full complement of mail and weaponry for the procession. When the host passed through the northern gate, they were received by delegations from the Christian and Jewish communities of the city, who presented them with special gifts of welcome.

The extravaganza did not go off without blemish. When al-Ghawrī passed by the entrance to the fodder (*darīs*) market, the atābak, riding at his side, struck a hanging lamp filled with oil. Its contents spilled onto the parasol and spattered down on the sultan. Al-Ghawrī was plainly discomfited and would have rebuked Ṣūdūn's clumsiness on the spot but for his concern over his dignity before the masses. Many interpreted the accident as an ill omen. Ibn Iyās dismissed this superstition but mused over the propriety of such ostentation. Since the dawādār Ṭūmānbāy had ordered the city's merchants to decorate their shops along the parade route, the general effect was certainly impressive. The populace was appropriately awed, "and both elite and masses raised their voices in acclamation. No other Egyptian ruler had mounted such a procession. Indeed, al-Ghawrī made only this one formal traversal of the city in full regalia, accompanied by his amīrs and khāṣṣakīs." When the host reached the Rumayla, they were formally received by Ṭūmānbāy, who handed his emblems of authority back to al-Ghawrī and then hosted the assemblage to a banquet in the Hippodrome garden. Ibn Iyās summed up this procession as the most grandiose event of the year 920 and penned twenty verses to commemorate it. Yet when the sultan's Mamlūks rioted soon after, ostensibly over the death of an amīr who they suspected had been pushed from his observation post, Ibn Iyās blamed the procession as the root cause of their rancor. "The sultan's affairs went from bad to worse after his return from Alexandria and his life was soured. The consequences of this event plagued him to the end."[129]

Why was al-Ghawrī motivated to stage such a show? A man singularly unmoved by the accumulation of titles or personal honors was driven to parade the trappings of his worldly wealth before both domestic populace and foreign visitors. And under law and tradition this treasure did not belong to him. It remained the regime's property, many of its most precious objects dating to earlier and far more prosperous reigns. Al-Ghawrī was charged with custody over this hoard rather than exploiting it for his own grandeur and possibly as a facade to hide defects of his administration. Whether the sultan's raw recruits or even his seasoned bodyguard saw through the ceremonial to his flawed sense of propriety cannot be known. But they assuredly sensed the irony of so much expensive finery riding on their own backs while their patron pleaded his poverty when they came calling for stipend increases or timely rations. Al-Ghawrī never lacked

129 *Badā'i'* 4, 428, l. 11.

the wherewithall to finance a parade or soirée, but he stubbornly refused to indulge his own troops.[130] The procession thus stood out as a symbolic watershed of his reign. Few subsequent events signaled a positive future.

Although al-Ghawrī exhibited the longevity and resilience noteworthy in his fellow Circassians, he suffered from numerous minor ailments. Few of these were memorable enough to merit a chronicler's mention. But an infection of his eyelids beginning in Rabīʿ I of 919/May–June 1513 posed a serious threat to his executive competence. Al-Ghawrī responded to the omnipresent risk of illness with more hypochondria than Qāytbāy or others of his royal precursors had shown in similar misfortunes. He was also keenly sensitive to public disclosure of any ailments he might be enduring. In Muḥarram of 918/April 1512, he jailed his masseur for revealing to courtiers that he was afflicted with unsightly boils and a scrotal hernia (*qillīṭ*).[131] In Shaʿbān that year, he sought to cover up a severe attack of dysentery by appearing at Friday prayer even when he was acutely indisposed.[132]

Al-Ghawrī also relied on the advice of soothsayers and magicians when he feared illness, a trait many of his contemporaries found unmanly. When the pestilence menaced Cairo in Muḥarram of 919/March–April 1513, al-Ghawrī took to wearing several ruby rings offered him as a protective device to ward off contamination.[133] Consulting geomancers after an earthquake had rocked the Citadel, al-Ghawrī was informed that the tremors heralded a new epidemic and that he should take all precautions to remain immune. Rather than submitting to God's providence, the sultan stooped to using petty

130 These tensions flaring up between al-Ghawrī and his Mamlūk troops over pay represented the culmination of tendencies evolving from two centuries of militarist government in Egypt. See David Ayalon, "The System of Payment in Mamluk Military Society," *JESHO* 1 (1952) 37–65, and *Orient* 1 (1958) 257–296.

131 *Badāʾiʿ* 4, 254, l. 1.

132 *Badāʾiʿ* 4, 281, l. 19.

133 *Badāʾiʿ* 4, 297, l. 11.

talismans. A month later al-Ghawrī dreamed that the stars and moon fell from the firmament to the earth. When he demanded an explanation from his forecasters, they told him the vision portended his imminent demise. Stunned by this interpretation, the sultan canceled a series of special taxes he had earlier imposed, hoping that the resultant acclamation would nullify the omen.[134] In light of al-Ghawrī's record, his eagerness to spare his subjects only under the threat of death seemed selfish rather than beneficent.

But this dream proved dramatically prophetic. On the seventeenth of Rabīʿ I/25 March, the sultan bruised his eyelids and retired to the Duhaysha Palace.[135] Both lids soon swelled and festered, impairing his vision. Initially predicting a rapid recovery, he refused to preside over monthly stipend distributions. Fear of his troops' reaction to his infirmity impelled him more than any worry over long-term debility. But as the infection worsened during the next several weeks, al-Ghawrī's vexation gave way to mortal terror. By mid-Rabīʿ II, he had become almost completely reclusive, eschewing most of his formal duties and spending his days and nights trying remedies ranging from poultices concocted from occult substances to magical spells offered by sorcerers. He refused the remedy his physicians advised him as the only sure way to alleviate his inflammation: lancing of the lids to promote drainage.[136] Even when servants suffering from similar infections were dragged before him and surgically treated to prove the cure, al-Ghawrī declined. As the swelling persisted, the court sat paralyzed, awaiting the sultan's fate. Since he now conducted no public business, a backlog of decrees and procedural edicts built up with no prospect of their being signed. Despite al-Ghawrī's paranoia over his image, all sorts of rumors about his behavior spread from the Citadel into the city and even foreign capitals. Ibn Iyās picked up on one of

134 *Badāʾiʿ* 4, 304, l. 5.
135 *Badāʾiʿ* 4, 307, l. 8.
136 *Badāʾiʿ* 4, 310, l. 12.

these when he described the sultan pacing his chambers in the wee hours pleading with God to spare him. "O you who is never unjust or tyrannical, have mercy on your wretched servant. Truly, we have shown wickedness but if you, the All Compassionate, disdain to pardon us, we are surely lost!" Ibn Iyās noted that "the sultan had forgotten all his earlier oppression inflicted by his own hand, fearing only what his enemies alleged against him."[137] By month's end, al-Ghawrī still rejected his physicians' admonitions for surgery, but instead began to empty his jails of prisoners incarcerated for debts, plot-mongering, or even criminal assault. Some eighty-one were released on the twenty-ninth alone in a gross show of clemency.[138]

Yet no act of mercy alleviated his affliction. The infection persisted unabated throughout Jumādā I, and, as gossip spread of deposition, al-Ghawrī reversed most of his previous fiscal and legal policies. Public appeals tribunals that had been closed for much of his reign were now reconvened. Claimants with the flimsiest of grievances rushed to the Citadel gates, since word had spread that the sultan would copiously reward any supplicant who presented himself. All pensions to orphans and widows, previously revoked, he now restored.[139] Finally, in early Jumādā II/August, the swelling began to recede slightly. Al-Ghawrī attended his first Friday prayer in six weeks on the third/17 August, although only an anti-inflammation balm enabled him to see.[140] But though the swelling subsided somewhat, festering continued. Al-Ghawrī procrastinated out of dread of the knife for five months until, on the twenty-second of Rajab/23 September, he finally allowed a lancing. Amazingly enough, given the length of the infection, the sultan rebounded rapidly.[141] By

137 *Badā'i'* 4, 312, l. 17.
138 *Badā'i'* 4, 316, l. 12.
139 *Badā'i'* 4, 320, l. 14; 321, l. 9, 22; 323, l. 14.
140 *Badā'i'* 4, 325, l. 4.
141 *Badā'i'* 4, 330, l. 19.

the fourth of Sha'bān/5 October, he received all the grand amīrs in his first formal audience since the injury. Al-Ghawrī sumptuously rewarded the surgeon who drained his lids, a lucky turn of events for this oculist, who must have feared for his life if the operation failed.[142] The sultan showered his gratitude on all his attending physicians. The whole court rejoiced in his cure. Zaynī Barakāt ordered several days of public celebration in Cairo to commemorate the autocrat's recovery.[143] Al-Ghawrī showed himself less magnanimous when he reconsidered his previous acts of clemency. All the canceled fiscal extractions and taxes he reimposed with a vengeance, claiming that the masses had not properly appreciated his anguish.[144] Al-Ghawrī's deportment throughout this taxing episode hardly moved observers, who compared his inconstancy with the stoic resignation past monarchs had shown in the face of adversity. His summary abandonment of charity once he recovered implied a fundamental shallowness of faith. Al-Ghawrī's antics during this episode haunted him until his death on the battlefield three years later.

The Road to Marj Dābiq: Inexorable Conflict

Rabī' II and Jumādā I of 918/May and July 1513 witnessed a flurry of diplomatic exchanges at the Citadel in Cairo. No

142 *Badā'i'* 4, 331, l. 22.
143 *Badā'i'* 4, 333, l. 14; 334, l. 5. These included gaudy decoration of Cairo's streets with banners and tapestries (all paid for by property owners), the sounding of drums and trumpets day and night, and the presentation of a tableau at the gate of Baybarsīya Khānqāh depicting the sultan's recovery from blindness. Ibn Iyās deemed these observances as excessive for "never was a sultan's or amīr's recovery so elaborately commemorated in Egypt." The qāḍīs even decked out the Ṣāliḥīya Madrasa entry with tapestries, over the protests of staff, who claimed the academy served to disseminate God's Law, not to glorify his earthly penitent who had formerly set his hand against charitable endowments.
144 *Badā'i'* 4, 328, l. 20.

fewer than fourteen emissaries presented their credentials to the sultan in the audience hall, signaling a shift in the political order of the central Islamic lands.[145] The failing health of Bāyazīd II was widely known, and possible consquences of his demise were pondered in capitals throughout southwest Asia. Even though Selim was the youngest of Bāyazīd's sons, he had already seized control over the military apparatus. Fearing for their lives, his two brothers, Qurqud and Aḥmad, had fled Istanbul along with their progeny. Several of the ambassadors who presented themselves before al-Ghawrī represented sovereigns or chieftains with a vital interest in the Ottoman succession. All the Turkmān dynasties in southeastern Anatolia, who depended on the Mamlūk sultanate to ensure their autonomy from Istanbul, sent agents. Al-Ghawrī attempted to bolster their confidence in his regime's military might by regaling them with a display of lance-casting in the Hippodrome.[146] While his guests were impressed by the spectacle, they may well have questioned its effectiveness. Selim had revived his grandfather's experiments in gunpowder technology with a vengeance, and who could predict how cavalrymen employing traditional weaponry would fare?[147]

The Ottoman emissary held the court in suspense until the beginning of Jumādā I before disclosing his missive after all the others.[148] He announced the imminent death of al-Ghawrī's long-time ally and the certain accession of the third son. Fast on the heels of this messenger arrived a second courier confirming Bāyazīd's death on Friday, the second of Jumādā II/15 August. Bāyazīd had followed the Conqueror to the throne of 'Uthmān on the nineteenth of Rabī' II 886/15 July 1481, during Qāytbāy's reign. He had

145 *Badā'i'* 4, 268, l. 21.
146 *Badā'i'* 4, 269, l. 6.
147 The Ottoman Janissaries were trained in the use of the arquebus. See supra n. 77, and D. Petrovič, "Firearms in the Balkans on the Eve of and after the Ottoman Conquests of the Fourteenth and Fifteenth centuries," in *War, Technology and Society in the Middle East*, 186–194.
148 *Badā'i'* 4, 269, ll. 18, 22.

governed his polyglot realm with studied restraint for almost thirty-three lunar years. His impetuous son Selim found his father's penchant for political equilibrium stifling, an affront to the dashing exploits of his ancestors. For his part, al-Ghawrī sincerely lamented the loss of his partner in coexistence, and donned mourning garb. He ordered special obsequies to be offered in the Citadel Mosque. When news of Bāyazīd's death spread among the populace of Cairo, spontaneous services were held in local mosques since the Ottoman sultan's respect for harmony in God's commonwealth had won him widespread admiration. Ibn Iyās mentioned prayers in the Azhar, the mosques of al-Ḥākim and Ibn Ṭūlūn, the Ghawrīya, and elsewhere. After his stalemate with Qāytbāy, Bāyazīd had focused his military operations on infidel Europeans, acknowledging the rights of his fellow Muslims. Selim's ambitions, on the other hand, were rumored to be boundless. He paid little heed to the prerogatives due his coreligionists. Nonetheless, al-Ghawrī courted the new sultan. He immediately dispatched a senior officer as his ambassador to Istanbul.[149] The second dawādār, Aqbāy al-Ṭawīl, departed Cairo on the tenth of Dhū'l-Qa'da/17 January 1513 bearing a flowery letter of congratulations. He had been instructed to negotiate a treaty of friendship (*muwadda*).

The Citadel court soon received living manifestations of Selim's ruthlessness, however. Even before Aqbāy departed, one of Selim's nephews, Sulaymān, Aḥmad's elder son, arrived at the royal gates.[150] He presented himself as a fugitive who had fled for his life before his uncle's murderous sweep of all possible competitors. Al-Ghawrī made him welcome and draped a robe befitting a royal guest over his shoulders. Yet he was profoundly disturbed over Sulaymān's presence, fearing it would incur Selim's personal animus against him. The problem was compounded soon thereafter when Sulaymān's

149 *Badā'i'* 4, 289, l. 11.
150 *Badā'i'* 4, 289, l. 5; 291, l. 5; G. Wiet, "Deux princes ottomans à la cour d'Egypte," *BIE* 20 (1938) 137–150.

brother 'Alī appeared with a similar claim for sanctuary. Fate relieved al-Ghawrī of this immediate dilemma when the plague carried off both brothers within a few months of their plea for refuge.[151] But during the early part of 919, disquieting reports of Selim's attempts to eliminate all blood rivals reached Cairo.[152] According to these, Selim had enticed his brother Qurqud, al-Ghawrī's former guest, back to Istanbul with promises of a truce and adjudicated settlement of their differences over the succession. Yet when Qurqud presented himself, Selim had him strangled. The remaining brother, Aḥmad, had tried escape to Persia but had been apprehended and executed. Aḥmad had sent his two sons to Cairo with hopes of saving them from their uncle's homicidal designs. Now, God seemed to have thrown His support behind Selim's consolidation of absolute power, since Selim succeeded in eliminating all his opponents descending from the imperial lineage. Such drastic measures were hardly unique to the Ottoman dynasty, especially since the Sharī'a recognized only partible inheritance of equal shares with no principle of primogeniture. But the cold-blooded savagery of Selim's behavior stunned his peers throughout the Muslim world, who with good reason pondered their own fates.

The remaining months of 919 passed without further incident, as Selim rehoned the Ottoman army and dealt devastating blows against the Europeans. Yet the megalomania of Ismā'īl Ṣafawī in Iran was certain to draw Selim's attention eastward. On the twenty-third of Rabī' I 920/18 May 1514, Selim's emissary arrived at the Citadel requesting a private audience over "pressing foreign matters" with the sultan.[153] Selim had sent no reply to al-Ghawrī's earlier request for a treaty of friendship, but instead demanded al-Ghawrī's support for his impending campaign against the Shah. Al-Ghawrī drafted a carefully worded response that

[151] *Badā'i'* 4, 303, l. 2; 306, l. 2.
[152] *Badā'i'* 4, 306, l. 15.
[153] *Badā'i'* 4, 372, l. 21; 373, l. 11; *I'lām*, 229, l. 12.

left him impartial to either side and sent it back with the courier. Although Ismāʿīl had given the Mamlūk regime ample cause for irritation over the past two years, al-Ghawrī steadfastly maintained his time-tested policy of nonalignment. Unfortunately for him, Selim was not disposed to honor it. Ismāʿīl's red-caps (*qizilbāsh*) had renewed their raids across the Mamlūk frontier at the beginning of 918/March 1513.[154] During a review of Mamlūk contingents to put down Bedouin revolts in outlying parts of the Nile Valley, al-Ghawrī was interrupted by reports that the Ṣafavids were besieging al-Bīra near the Euphrates. This operation ended in ignominous failure for Ismāʿīl's warriors, since the prefect of Sīs drove them off and sent ten severed heads complete with scarlet turbans to Cairo as tokens of his success.[155] But the menace continued, and Ismāʿīl's arrogance was glaringly apparent in the tone of his missives, written by his own hand.

When al-Ghawrī's ambassador to the Ṣafavid court, Timurbāy al-Hindī, returned to Cairo in mid-Rabīʿ II/June, after an absence of two years, he reported gross humiliation by Ismāʿīl's minions.[156] Ismāʿīl had scorned to entrust his message to him but instead packed him off in the company of his own emissaries, who would deliver it personally. Two Ṣafavid representatives thus accompanied Timurbāy when he ascended the Citadel. They came attended by one hundred armed retainers, unseemly for ambassadors already protected by diplomatic immunity. Their reputation for incivility had preceded them, since they had insulted the governor of Aleppo when he accorded them an audience. In any case, al-Ghawrī received them with the honors required by protocol, although he laid emphasis on his regime's martial power by displaying its weaponry on the arsenal gates. Ismāʿīl's messengers did not come cap in hand but presented an extraordinary array of gifts. So eager was the

154 *Badāʾiʿ* 4, 257, l. 8; 258, l. 4.
155 *Badāʾiʿ* 4, 262, l. 3.
156 *Badāʾiʿ* 4, 265, ll. 7, 21.

Shah to show even a rival his beneficence that forty bearers were necessary to transport his largesse to the Duhaysha. The gifts struck observers as remarkable for their diversity and even their eccentricity, since they included live panthers (*fuhūda*) decked out in silken mantles, horses with peculiar mane and tail croppings, silver vessels of outlandish shape, coats of mail, and a dazzling variety of carpets, robes, and tapestries.

Yet this bizarre gesture hardly belied the tenor of Ismā'īl's letter, which reeked with "blatantly hostile statements framed in crude language" the sultan and his associates found unsuited to either tradition or etiquette. Despite his anger, al-Ghawrī treated the two emissaries hospitably while he and Cairo pundits pored over a response of equivalent vulgarity. The ambassadors attended Friday prayers in the Sultan's Mosque, although they were compelled, as Shī'īs, to sit through a khuṭba preached by the Mālikī Qāḍī, Muḥyī al-Dīn ibn al-Damīrī, who extolled the virtues of the first Caliph and guardian of the Sunna, Abū Bakr (before whom the Prophet's cousin 'Alī had been passed over).[157] They subsequently were hosted to a reception and banquet. Al-Ghawrī had no intention of being outdone by Ismā'īl and sought to overawe his guests with his own lavish display. Upon summoning the ambassadors for their departure ceremony, he bestowed fur-lined robes on them for delivery to their patron. He also read aloud his reply to Ismā'īl, couched in abusive phrases befitting the other's insults. Because Ismā'īl intimated his innate supremacy, the sultan had ample reason to regard the Shah as an enemy when he received Selim's demand for an alliance against him. But al-Ghawrī remained the equivocator, who refrained from responding in kind to shows of aggression. Since his stance had spared the regime the grueling campaigns that had so beleaguered Qāytbāy, he clearly hoped it would preserve his neutrality now.

[157] *Badā'i'* 4, 268, l. 1, 15; 271, l. 9.

Al-Ghawrī procrastinated throughout the early months of 920, evading any decision on either the Ottoman or Ṣafavid issues. When Selim showed his displeasure with the sultan's demurral by sending another emissary demanding a more concrete reply, however, al-Ghawrī convened the amīrs to discuss how he should proceed.[158] True to his habit of mixing business with pleasure, he invited his colleagues to a refreshing bathe in the Hippodrome pool before addressing this knotty problem. The officers advised al-Ghawrī to strengthen his garrison at Aleppo with a larger contingent of Mamlūks, to be stationed there indefinitely. No threatening gestures or forays into territories north or east should be allowed once they arrived. Rather, they should await the Ottoman–Ṣafavid confrontation. When one or the other had succumbed, the Egyptian army could seize the advantage. Finding this advice sound, al-Ghawrī laid plans forthwith for the Aleppo venture. He also decided to sound his own intelligence gatherers in Istanbul, so dispatched an agent who took service ostensibly as an adjutant with the Ottoman ambassador upon his departure.[159] The agent, an officer of medial rank, received a special purse from al-Ghawrī to defray his expenses and "contingencies" while he sojourned at the Ottoman capital. Once he determined Selim's real intentions he was to hasten back, "allowing no impediment save road blockades to deter him."

In mid-Jumādā I/July 1514, al-Ghawrī finally mustered his troops.[160] He designated three separate units, each given a distinct mission. One, comprised mainly of reservists (*awlād al-nās*), was to patrol the roadways, barrages, and canals of the Delta, protecting them from Bedouin raiders. Another was to prepare for a long period of duty far away in al-Hind (literally "India," but probably Aden at the southern end of the Red Sea). These soldiers, members of the new Fifth

158 *Badā'i'* 4, 376, l. 9.
159 *Badā'i'* 4, 378, l. 7; 381, l. 15.
160 *Badā'i'* 4, 381, l. 20; 383, l. 2.

Corps, were to guard the straits against Portuguese corsairs who had made their appearance in the Indian Ocean. The third and largest contingent was to proceed to Aleppo. This review required several days, since more than two thousand Mamlūks were designated. The sultan placed four muqaddamīn in charge of the Aleppo contingent alone. Once he made his plans, al-Ghawrī moved resolutely to implement them. But he seems to have harbored nagging doubts over making any provocative sign. A few days after presiding over the muster, he visited the shrines of al-Shāfiʿī and al-Layth, where he dispersed votive offerings to their staffs and pious mendicants—presumably in return for their prayers in support of his venture.[161]

Soon after the review, yet another deputation from Istanbul arrived. On the twenty-seventh of Jumādā I/20 July, one of Selim's most senior officials requested the sultan's ear in private audience.[162] Impressed with his rank, al-Ghawrī received him with full honors. Although the missive he brought from Selim remained confidential, he presented gifts that might signal either his esteem for al-Ghawrī—or a contemptuous warning to a potential enemy who should not be bought by Ismāʿīl. The ambassador's bearers marched into the courtyard with a rich collection of furs, Burṣā velvets, and Samarqandī weaves. Twenty-five novice Mamlūks were also proffered. These gifts pointedly underscored the Ottoman realm's commercial importance to the Mamlūk sultanate in straddling the trade routes through which the latter's manpower and luxury goods flowed. Al-Ghawrī readily perceived the message implicit in these gifts and treated the emissary as visiting royalty. But subsequent events disclosed how labyrinthine the diplomatic scene had become.

On the twelfth of Jumādā II/15 August, a second emissary claiming to represent the Ottoman monarch sent word

161 *Badāʾiʿ* 4, 382, l. 20.
162 *Badāʾiʿ* 4, 383, l. 13; 384, l. 7.

from al-Ṣāliḥīya that he had been waylaid while proceeding to Cairo by Bedouins, who had made off with his document pouch containing another letter from Selim.[163] So shaken was al-Ghawrī that he reacted hysterically before corroborating this story. After tearing at his beard and casting off his turban, the sultan sent a courier posthaste to the local Bedouin shaykh with orders to apprehend the culprits. The shaykh did succeed in capturing the offenders and returned the satchel with its missive intact. Palace gossip dwelt on al-Ghawrī's dismay over this affair. He allegedly "swore on his own head that if the shaykh failed to produce the pouch with all its contents, he would have him cut in half." The incident starkly revealed the sultan's alarm over any interference with one of Selim's deputies during these delicate exchanges. Two self-styled representatives of al-Ghawrī's potential enemy had converged on Cairo just when his Aleppo contingent was departing to wait upon the outcome of Selim's confrontation with the Ṣafavids. Al-Ghawrī was walking a tightrope when he hosted the senior ambassador to military drills, permitted him to observe troop reviews for the expedition, and still proclaimed his neutral stance.[164] He may have hoped these displays of martial readiness, combined with his unswerving refusal to pledge himself to either side, would dissuade Selim from traversing his northern marches on the way toward Tabrīz. Such maneuvers were rendered almost comical when the first Ottoman emissary denounced the second as a fraud.[165] On the eighteenth of Rajab/8 September, upon their first face-to-face encounter, the senior ambassador disavowed any knowledge of the second, claiming he held no position on Selim's staff and bore no genuine message from him. Al-Ghawrī was baffled by this unforeseen development but hesitated to jail the second emissary on the word of a possible rival. He granted him permission to leave, and

163 *Badā'i'* 4, 385, l. 3.
164 *Badā'i'* 4, 391, l. 6; 392, l. 8.
165 *Badā'i'* 4, 394, l. 14.

even gave him a sum of money. So outraged was the first ambassador that he launched a tirade at al-Ghawrī, asserting that the second was in fact a spy sent by one of Prince Aḥmad's surviving sons, Ḥasan, who had sought sanctuary with Shah Ismā'īl. Now convinced of being duped, al-Ghawrī sent the prefect of Cairo after the false emissary, who caught up with him before he reached Ghazza. The sultan paraded him through the steets shackled with an iron collar and preceded by heralds who shouted: "Behold the fate of him who lies before kings!" Al-Ghawrī apparently mollified the senior ambassador, who declared his intention to depart. As a gesture of reconciliation, the sultan bestowed on him a mantle embroidered with gold thread and lined with sable. He then draped him with a second tunic of green silk containing a purse filled with no less than eight hundred mithqāls of gold.[166] Yet he still desisted from pledging his support for Selim's vendetta against Ismā'īl. The emissary thus left with no resolution to the impasse.

Scorning to curb his own plans while the Egyptian monarch equivocated, Selim forged ahead with his campaign. In Ramaḍān/October–November, couriers from Aleppo arrived in Eygpt with news of Selim's dramatic victory over Ismā'īl at a site near Tabrīz called "Iskandarān" (Chaldirān).[167] Wild stories had already circulated among the populace that Selim had captured Shah Ismā'īl at this battle and placed him in an iron cage for public display throughout Anatolia. "Of course, such rumors proved false," but their persistence caused foreboding in the Citadel court. When official reports arrived, they did confirm a staggering triumph for Selim's army. The Ottoman and Ṣafavid forces, both of vast size, had met on the second of Rajab/23 August and engaged in combat "fit to bleach one's hair white!" Both sides suffered heavy casualties; the Ottomans registered at least thirty thousand.

[166] *Badā'i'* 4, 395, l. 9. A mithqāl in Egypt equaled 24 qīrāṭ or 4.68 grams.
[167] *Badā'i'* 4, 396, l. 3; 398, l. 1; 400, l. 15; 402, l. 6.

Ismāʿīl's qizilbāsh had shown the reckless valor that carried the day so many times before, and initially shattered the Ottoman lines when battle was joined. Selim almost fainted in a paroxysm of rage over this setback, but recovered to galvanize his cavalrymen and infantry to a fresh assault. Goading them on with the admonition "Better to die seeking vengeance than to survive in disgrace!" Selim led charges in which his troops "rushed upon the Ṣafavids like devouring lions, sacrificing themselves for the higher cause." Nonetheless, the outcome teetered in the balance until Selim's corps of twelve thousand arquebusiers began firing into the Ṣafavid host. Their attack produced pandemonium among the Iranians, who were totally unprepared for this exigency. Ismāʿīl's forces panicked, broke discipline, and began to bolt in all directions.

Therefore, in an extraordinary turn of fate, the Shah's previously invincible military apparatus, his "scourge of backsliders and deviators," was wiped out in a single day. Suffering only superficial wounds, Ismāʿīl himself escaped with a remnant of his followers. Ibn Iyās observed that no previous Ottoman autocrat could lay claim to such a victory. After all, Selim's ancestor who shared so many of his militant traits, Yilderim Bāyazīd, had suffered defeat at Timur Lenk's hands on the plain of Ankara and had found suicide preferable to public humiliation.[168] Who could now foretell the outcome of any future confrontations between this formidable warrior and other rulers unlucky enough to arouse his ire? Al-Ghawrī certainly pondered Selim's own description of the battle when he got it from his courier. The sultan showed the messenger courtesies required by protocol, but allowed no public acknowledgment of this event. Ibn Iyās mused that such a holocaust among Muslims "pleased neither God nor his Prophet," but this thought would provide

[168] *Badāʾiʿ* 4, 403, l. 12. Ibn Iyās's version of Bāyazīd's self-inflicted death is not uniformly corroborated in other sources.

al-Ghawrī and his colleagues scant comfort. Having won a decisive battle, Selim appropriated most of Ismāʿīl's western territories. No buffer now lay between him and the sultan's northern provinces.

Compounding al-Ghawrī's despondency over the outcome of Chaldirān were reports that arrived in Ramaḍān and Dhū'l-Ḥijja/December, February of rioting in Aleppo by his reinforcements.[169] Soon after their arrival, the expeditionary troops had fallen out with those of the city's governor. Their quarrels degenerated into strife that left the city paralyzed, its civilian populace terrified. Bitterly resenting their assignment, the Cairo troops vented their pent-up spleen against al-Ghawrī on Aleppo's hapless citizens. They justified their pillaging on grounds of inadequate provisions provided them before they departed Cairo and ignored the sultan's admonitions to behave. Such was the conduct of the soldiers al-Ghawrī had dispatched to Aleppo for the purpose of capitalizing on the outcome of the Ottoman-Ṣafavid confrontation. Could he count on malcontents like these to support his cause when the situation worsened? He sent an order for their recall.

Selim lost no time stirring up trouble closer to home. In Muḥarram of 921/February 1515, another in the dismaying series of emissaries from Istanbul presented the sultan with a missive "soliciting" his support for the claim of a dispossessed son of Shāh Sūwār to his father's former patrimony in Little Armenia (*Ilbistīn*), a flagrant challenge to the rights of ʿAlī Dawlāt, a loyal client since Qāytbāy's time.[170] Al-Ghawrī reacted indignantly to this haughty request, which amounted to an ultimatum since Selim had already sent troops to aid Sūwār's son. ʿAlī Dawlāt's own son and grandson had already been killed, and he himself had barely escaped their fate by seeking refuge in the fortress of Zamanṭū, the same citadel to

169 *Badāʾiʿ* 4, 400, l. 1; 432, l. 3.

170 *Badāʾiʿ* 4, 435, l. 11 (this client's name is rendered ʿAlāʾ al-Dawla in some sources).

which Sūwār had retired decades earlier before Yashbak. The Egyptian monarch could hardly accept these missives with his previous reserve. Not only did they hurl a thinly veiled threat in his face, they applied openly insulting terms to him personally. Selim now referred to himself as "Our Royal Majesty" (*maqāmunā al-sharīf*), while dismissing al-Ghawrī as "Your High Majesty" (*maqāmukum al-'ālī*), a phrase reserved for princes of inferior rank. Al-Ghawrī again debated his options with the amīrs. They now seemed painfully limited. He decided to send back the troops he had recently summoned home from Aleppo, but many who had already turned up in Cairo refused to leave. The sultan finally drafted a response worded to shore up his honor while not declaring open war on the Ottoman aggressor.[171] He sent it with an emissary named Jānim, a khāṣṣakī known for his quick wits in a tight spot. He would need them in the likely outburst of Selim's wrath when he read the letter.

Events now unfolded so swiftly that the sultan and his associates were compelled to deal with new crises even before their couriers could reach Istanbul. Early in Rabī' I/April, al-Ghawrī received word from Aleppo that Selim intended to oversee a campaign against 'Alī Dawlāt and his remaining adherents.[172] The sultan's advisers interpreted this development as a ploy devised by the Ottoman to justify his trespass on Mamlūk territory. As al-Ghawrī now contemplated the likelihood of open conflict with his dreaded neighbor, he learned of treason among his own subordinates. A former intendant of granaries named Khushqadam had secretly departed Cairo for Alexandria. When he reached the port, he boarded a vessel his friends had readied for him and made off for Istanbul, where he offered Selim his services.[173] This individual was one of al-Ghawrī's own purchased Mamlūks, whom the sultan had advanced to high office over others.

171 *Badā'i'* 4, 436, l. 4; 438, l. 8; 445, l. 20.
172 *Badā'i'* 4, 446, l. 12.
173 *Badā'i'* 4, 449, l. 19; 471, l. 10; 472, l. 1.

But he had married the daughter of a senior officer who, on running afoul of al-Ghawrī's suspicions, was arrested and his property confiscated. When the sultan ordered Khushqadam either to divorce his wife or suffer her father's fate, he opted for flight. Since his brother had already gained the Ottoman monarch's favor, he apparently paved the way for Khushqadam's entry to the Topkapı Saray. Khushqadam gave Selim an extensive briefing on the unhealthy climate prevailing in Cairo.

> Khushqadam incited the Ottoman ruler against the sultan, informed him about the latter's tyrannical and oppressive acts, described his illegal monthly and weekly taxes imposed on commodity sellers, and dwelt on his forced exchanges of gold and silver currency at unfavorable rates. He told him many other stories in this vein about the sorry state of affairs in Egypt. He even reported on the unruly condition of the Egyptian armies, and how this might be exploited. He deplored the immorality of Egyptian qāḍīs, their habitual acceptance of bribes before pronouncing judgments. He urged the Ottoman ruler to march against the sultan's realm, stressing how simple its conquest would be. He explained to him how he should deploy his fleet against Alexandria and Damietta. Henceforth, the Ottoman's ambition was inspired to conquer Egypt. God remains the master of its future.[174]

Khushqadam's shift of allegiance was to become symptomatic of lapsing morale within the Mamlūk hierarchy. Al-Ghawrī was now reaping the harvest of the dissension he had sown. As he weighed his increasingly desperate situation, former clients began arriving in Cairo requesting aid he was reluctant to offer. In Jumādā I/June–July, a group of ʿAlī Dawlāt's blood relatives requested an audience with him. Realizing that they would deluge him with piteous complaints about Selim's aggression, he declined to hear them.[175] Yet

174 *Badā'i'* 4, 471, l. 16.
175 *Badā'i'* 4, 459, l. 3.

he dared not refuse the next appearance of an emissary from Selim. The Ottoman couriers now strutted before him as if they heralded their master's rule over the Citadel itself and arrogantly read out his pronouncements with little regard for protocol. On the twenty-fifth of Jumādā II/6 August, one such envoy ascended bearing the heads of 'Alī Dawlāt, several of his sons, and his wazīr.[176] When they were held aloft for all the court to behold, the spectators were shocked. Al-Ghawrī recovered his composure enough to demand: "Whose heads are these you have shown me? Do they belong to European kings you display to celebrate victories against the infidel?" The sultan then ordered the prefect to impound the severed heads for proper burial. They were interred in the modest tomb Qāytbāy had allowed for Shāh Sūwār following his execution. Al-Ghawrī had finally stood up against the brazen insults Selim cast at him. But he and his colleagues had to acknowledge the brutal facts behind this barbarous gesture. 'Alī Dawlāt was now dead, his principality firmly under Selim's heel, while the Ottoman busied himself constructing a series of fortresses on the northern borders of Aleppo Province.

On the twenty-sixth, as al-Ghawrī secluded himself in the Duhaysha brooding over these events, several officers admonished him to abandon his neutrality, since it had patently failed to deter Selim. "Our Lord Sultan, the Ottoman has wrested most of Aleppo Province from us. The khuṭba is preached in his name, coinage struck with his titles. He has begun work on a watchtower at the Pass of Baghrāṣ, another at Bāb al-Malik. Your hand is paralyzed [literally, "remains immersed in cold water"], while the realm's condition worsens. Most of the masses (*ra'īya*) of Aleppo and elsewhere suffer your governor's oppression and tyranny, and thus incline toward the son of 'Uthmān because he shows his commons justice."[177]

176 *Badā'i'* 4, 462, l. 15.
177 *Badā'i'* 4, 463, l. 3.

Al-Ghawrī spent the month of Rajab/August–September agonizing over how he should deal with the calamities engulfing him. None of his amīrs would agree to venture on any more Istanbul missions. When he summoned several of his former emissaries, they summarily rejected his request as a virtual death sentence. "This man [Selim] is an ignoramus (*jāhil*) who thirsts for blood. Anyone who delivers your reply to him will be executed on the spot!"[178] Al-Ghawrī belatedly accepted the futility of further diplomatic ploys. In mid-Sha'bān/late September, he called up his restive troops for their first muster against Selim.[179] The sultan seems to have undergone something of a spiritual renewal once he accepted the inevitablity of warfare. No longer would the successor of Baybars and Qalā'ūn hide from his rival's derision. Al-Ghawrī now assumed the demeanor of a commander in chief who would personally lead his troops to battle against this aggressor. From Sha'bān to the day he rode from the Citadel to meet his doom, al-Ghawrī brooked no opposition to his preparations. Early in Ramaḍān/October, he journeyed once again to Alexandria and Rosetta.[180] Selim was rumored to have readied a fleet for possible invasion of Egypt by sea, and al-Ghawrī wished to inspect the coastal defences before he left. Late the following month, as the sultan continued with his reviews, 'Alī Dawlāt's oldest surviving son arrived at the Citadel gates.[181] The governor of Aleppo, ostensibly alarmed over the prospect of an Ottoman siege, had sent him to urge the hastening of arrangements for the expedition. 'Alī Dawlāt's son was accompanied by the governor's second chamberlain, who brought Selim's answer to the governor's request that he depart Dhū'l-Qādrid territories that lay in Aleppo's domain. "I have taken these fortresses by the sword and only by its blade shall I relinquish them." Egypt's

178 *Badā'i'* 4, 467, l. 14.
179 *Badā'i'* 4, 473, l. 10.
180 *Badā'i'* 4, 474, l. 20; 476, l. 8.
181 *Badā'i'* 4, 482, l. 23.

last year of independence, 921, therefore closed under the cloud of impending invasion. Still, the crippling paralysis of indecision had been broken, and al-Ghawrī's regime finally girded itself for defense of its honor.

Al-Ghawrī preoccupied himself with musters and weapon inventories throughout the early months of 922/February–March 1516.[182] His new firmness of resolve embraced all his colleagues, civilian or military. Dīwān officials were to shoulder their share of responsibilities in this enterprise, while religious functionaries were expected to offer prayers for victory en route. When the Caliph and the four qāḍīs presented their monthly felicitations on the first of Ṣafar/6 March, the sultan informed them of their imminent departure. Reacting to allegations that he had corrupted the judiciary during his reign—which had reached Selim's ear—al-Ghawrī forbade the qāḍīs from extracting any funds from their deputies to defray travel costs. The four descended trembling and distraught but so cowed by their sovereign's severity that none dared protest. Al-Ghawrī also mitigated the tales of fiscal oppression his renegade officials had gleefully recounted to Selim. He canceled the monthly and weekly taxes he had imposed on grain and commodity merchants on the advice of Zaynī Barakāt and other "wicked counselors."[183] These taxes had crippled trade in several staples, but they also yielded almost eight thousand dīnārs a year, which the muḥtasib held in a special fund. The sultan bore a substantial loss by abolishing them. Presumably, had he triumphed over the Ottomans, he would have reimposed these imposts, but his viceroy, Ṭūmānbāy, elected to do without them in his tenure as regent and then sultan. He thereby won popular support in the troubled months following al-Ghawrī's demise.

At the end of Ṣafar, in the midst of his preparations, unexpected yet heartening news arrived from Aleppo. Two

182 *Badā'i'* 5, 15, l. 4; 17, l. 19; 19, l. 8, 12; 21, l. 20.
183 *Badā'i'* 5, 17, l. 20; 18, l. 17.

years after his crushing defeat, the Ṣafavid Shah Ismā'īl had raised a new army with the aid of his Ṭaṭar neighbors, who also feared Selim's unchecked advance to the east.[184] He had decimated an Ottoman force based at the city of Āmid, executing the governor Selim had installed there. While al-Ghawrī and his officers savored this report, they soberly pondered its consequences. Given Selim's hatred for Ismā'īl, he would certainly respond with a new campaign even more formidable than that of 920. Al-Ghawrī decided to persevere with his original plan. He would travel to Aleppo to follow the course of events at close range. If the Ottomans failed to score a second victory over the Ṣafavids, the Eygptians might yet profit from their disarray. According to al-Ḥalabī, al-Ghawrī sent off secret missives congratulating Ismā'īl and offering his own collusion in any strategies he might devise.[185] Despite the attendant risk of Selim learning about his complicity, al-Ghawrī felt bolstered by this development. He could now proceed with his mission, inspired by some glimmer of hope that his enemy's forces might be diverted and possibly crippled.

As al-Ghawrī quickened his preparations, word of his impending campaign spread from Cairo to the provinces. While the governor of Aleppo, Khayrbak, urged him to prepare with all due speed, the nā'ib of Damascus, al-Ghawrī's onetime rival Sībāy, reacted with caution. On the fourteenth of Rabī' I/17 April, al-Ghawrī received a missive from him requesting a delay.[186] "Our Lord Sultan, the Syrian Provinces are now barren. Fodder and hay are unavailable since the crop remains in the soil unripe for harvest. The enemy has shown no sign as yet. The sultan should therefore not risk his own safety but rather desist from departure. If the enemy is sighted, *we* can deal with him." Surmising that Sībāy, who had nurtured his own hegemonic ambitions for years,

184 *Badā'i'* 5, 32, l. 1.
185 al-Ḥalabī, *Durr*, f. 178b, l. 13. See also *Badā'i'* 5, 35, l. 13.
186 *Badā'i'* 5, 26, l. 11.

might well cut a deal with Selim in ways unappealing to him, al-Ghawrī summarily dismissed the letter. In no mood to quibble over bonus incentives, he threatened unhappy officials with dismissal and recalcitrant soldiers with demotion if they balked at their assignments. On the twenty-third of Rabī' I/26 April, when the sultan finished paying the troops their stipends, he ordered them to set their departure date for the first of the coming month. Already irate over their low stipends, the recruits and veterans threatened to seize their supplies from the markets.[187] Since their patron held their needs in contempt, they would despoil the populace to fulfill them. A delegation of officers warned al-Ghawrī that the forced pace of his muster would undermine the effectiveness of his overall strategy. "He had broken with policies of previous rulers when they set out on campaign. The present situation warranted no such turbulence [literally "dust cloud": *rahaj*]. No reports confirmed the Ottoman's impending invasion of Aleppo Province, nor was there any hint of his advance guard. Indeed, his realm seemed quiescent at the present time." The amīrs also rebuked the sultan for reviewing his troops in only four days and issuing their pay simultaneously, since they feared the undue speed of the muster would be interpreted by the Ottomans and Ṣafavids as a sign of weakness. If the sultan assembled his army in just four days, the enemy would surmise its minimal size; upon hearing rumors of haste, the enemy might consider an attack when they had planned none. But al-Ghawrī dismissed such admonitions, enlarging his retinue instead.

On the seventh of Rabī' II/10 May, al-Ghawrī summoned the rectors of Egypt's most revered rural shrines, the tombs of Aḥmad al-Badawī and Ibn al-Rifā'ī, and ordered them to join the host of divines who would ask God's succor for the expedition as it marched.[188] Aghast at the prospect of leaving

187 *Badā'i'* 5, 28, l. 13.
188 *Badā'i'* 5, 34, l. 4.

their sinecures for a journey fraught with danger, the two pled infirmity. No previous ruler had expected their predecessors to serve in this fashion, and the sultan risked incurring the All High's wrath by uprooting his servants. Al-Ghawrī turned a deaf ear to their protests. Since he had made up his mind to confront the most formidable adversary in the Muslim world, he would enlist the support of every prominent spiritual figure in his realm. Moreover, all the musicians, caterers, barbers, physicians, and craftsmen who constituted his traveling household were forced to serve without special compensation. When their amīr objected, his complaints were met with such responses as: "You who have devoured the proceeds of your office for years will now pay your staff from your own reserve. If you cannot, we shall find someone else to occupy your position who is able."[189]

Thus enshrouded with tension was the muster completed. The sultan's battalion (*ṭulb*) set out on Monday the tenth/13 May. Ibn Iyās observed its descent from the Citadel to the Rumayla, its passage through the city toward the Bāb al-Naṣr and bivouac at al-Raydānīya.[190] While describing the opulence of its accouterments, he also noted that these dated from earlier reigns and hearkened back to past glories rather than any recent achievements. None of this splendor could mask the modest scale of al-Ghawrī's battle units. Venerable spectators in the crowd who had witnessed Sultan Barsbāy's departure for his campaign to Āmid several decades before compared al-Ghawrī's ṭulb unfavorably. Far fewer horses and cavalrymen could be seen. Similar shortfalls were apparent in the squadrons of the fifteen muqaddamīn who rode with the sultan. Only 944 royal Mamlūks made up al-Ghawrī's contingent. All told, the army numbered approximately five thousand individuals. It might possibly have included two thousand more—"but God knows."[191] With such an army

189 *Badā'i'* 5, 34, l. 22.
190 *Badā'i'* 5, 35, l. 17–37, l. 6.
191 *Badā'i'* 5, 44, l. 17.

did al-Ghawrī contemplate facing off Selim's enormous host if they were fated to meet. He might find comfort in the adage "One Mamlūk is worth a thousand infantrymen," but the discrepancy was nonetheless blatantly apparent to the assembled observers. That the sultan dispensed with customary practice during the procession, compelling his men to march in the heat of high summer, boded ill for his expedition's success. Tradition carried weight in this culture, and those who ignored it toyed with calamity. "But al-Ghawrī heeded only his own will in all affairs."[192]

The sultan himself departed the Citadel for Raydānīya on the fourteenth/17 May.[193] He remained at the royal encampment eight days, arranging the battalions' riding order and setting the itineraries of his civilian retinue: the Caliph, the four qāḍīs, their deputies, and the religious functionaries he had ordered along. Three muqaddamīn set out for Syria with their units in advance of the main force to rendezvous with Bedouin and archer squadrons conscripted by local shaykhs. Before leaving Cairo, al-Ghawrī emptied the Citadel magazines of all the gold and silver treasures he had accumulated.[194] Bound by pledges as his regent Ṭūmānbāy might be, the sultan trusted no one with the wealth he had stashed away. The amount astounded everyone. The coins alone exceeded more than a million dīnārs, not counting ingots and bullion. And who could place a value on the fabulous trappings from the vaults al-Ghawrī had emptied? Ibn Iyās claimed that the baggage train required for transport of this hoard made a far greater impression than the combat force itself. The sultan clearly regarded his treasury as property he could not let out of his sight. Fate remained forever fickle, but money could resurrect even the sorriest of fortunes. Whether al-Ghawrī intended to fall back on his treasure as a means of negotiating his release in the event of defeat we do not know.

192 *Badā'i'* 5, 37, l. 6

193 *Badā'i'* 5, 38, ll. 8–44, l. 17.

194 *Badā'i'* 5, 42, l. 2.

That he presented his enemy with a huge windfall emerged as a supreme irony of his suspicion.

While al-Ghawrī lingered at Raydānīya, another courier arrived from the viceroy of Aleppo, Khayrbak, who had intercepted a letter to Cairo from Selim and sent it on with his own advice.[195] To everyone's surprise the missive offered peace.

> You [al-Ghawrī] are my father and I ask your pardon. I did not invade 'Alī Dawlāt's lands except by your permission, although he rebelled against me. It was he who instigated the dispute between my father and Sultan Qāytbāy, so that events took their course. This dispute provoked great evil in your realm and his ['Alī Dawlāt's] execution was deserved. As for Sūwār's son, who assumed his place, it is up to you whether he remains in his father's principality or if someone else is installed there. In any case, your pleasure decides the matter. On the merchants who import your Circassians, I have not impeded them although they have found your currency debasements unsettling and have ceased collecting Mamlūks for you. I shall yield up to you the lands I seized from 'Alī Dawlāt. All the sultan desires we shall fulfill.

Al-Ghawrī's officers rejoiced when this missive was read aloud but he was skeptical. The viceroy of Aleppo discounted Selim's professed intentions of good will. This letter was but a ruse to deter the Egyptian monarch while the Ottomans dealt with Ismā'īl and then annexed Aleppo Province unchallenged. Al-Ghawrī heeded the governor's interpretation and brandished this letter as further evidence of Selim's culpability. The expedition would go forward as planned. The sultan's honor had been defamed enough by Selim's arrogance. No more correspondence or omens would dissuade him.[196]

195 *Badā'i'* 5, 45, l. 6.

196 Several incidents occurred while the sultan bivouacked at Raydānīya and when he began his march to Syria. Part of his tent caught fire (*Badā'i'* 5, 46, l. 2), and a violent rainstorm, unusual for the summer season, hampered

Al-Ghawrī entered Ghazza, gateway to Syria, on the fourth of Jumādā I/5 June. Impatient to proceed on toward the provincial capitals, he remained only long enough to receive a formal welcome. Two weeks later, on the eighteenth/19 June, the sultan arrived at Damascus.[197] Despite his misgivings over the prospects of al-Ghawrī's campaign, the governor Sībāy extended all the courtesies befitting his sovereign's status. He ordered a silk tapestry laid along the procession route, and carried the parasol and bird over al-Ghawrī's head as he traversed the town. The throngs beholding al-Ghawrī's entry, his first since his enthronement, made gestures of acclamation, although their true sentiments were certainly more ambivalent. European merchants cast gold and silver coins at the royal entourage. But when the sultan's own recruits broke ranks and jostled around him to pick them up, al-Ghawrī forbade any further gestures that might incite their unruliness. He spent nine days in Damascus, lodged at the Qābūn Pavilion (*masṭaba*) just outside the Bāb al-Naṣr. Electing not to attend Friday prayer at the Umayyad Mosque, he closeted himself with Sībāy, pressuring him to join the campaign with a large contingent. The governor had created an autonomous fiefdom for himself in Damascus, which al-Ghawrī tacitly recognized so long as he declared no open revolt. Sībāy would jeopardize his comfortable position and possibly even his life by committing himself to al-Ghawrī's vendetta. Yet he acquiesced and pledged his combat skills to his sovereign's cause. Unlike his colleague in Aleppo, Sībāy would keep his fealty.

Reinforced by Sībāy's regiment, al-Ghawrī resumed his rapid pace, advancing toward Aleppo via Ḥimṣ and Ḥamā. The sultan entered this bastion of Mamlūk power in the north on Thursday the tenth of Jumādā II/11 July.[198] The viceroy,

---

his advance to al-Ṣāliḥīya (*Badā'i'* 5, 48, l. 4). These events were seen as unlucky by local soothsayers. Ibn Iyās usually discounted such auguries as rank superstition, but this time he gave them credence.

197 *Badā'i'* 5, 51, l. 13; 53, l. 1.

198 *Badā'i'* 5, 56, l. 20; al-Ḥalabī, *Durr*, f. 177b, l. 22.

Khayrbak min Yilbāy, who had so vehemently urged his expedition, extended a second lavish reception complete with formal procession. Al-Ghawrī found two emissaries from Selim awaiting him, one a military judge (*qāḍī ʿaskar*), the other a senior officer.[199] They had arrived at the head of a caravan conveying a vast store of fodder to relieve al-Ghawrī's shortages. How they had learned of his dearth of provisions even while he was on the road could only heighten al-Ghawrī's apprehensions about their ulterior motives. Nonetheless, the sultan received them and accepted their messages with their fodder, although both were compelled to hear his rebuke of their patron for his aggressive posture. The two replied, "Our master has delegated us authority to negotiate whatever solution the sultan [of Egypt] wishes, without our returning for consultation." Al-Ghawrī then read Selim's final letter. "O Sultan my father, I solicit your prayers, but do not intervene between me and the Ṣafavid. I shall not finish with him until I have terminated his authority and obliterated it from the Earth. Do not attempt to arrange a truce between us." Although al-Ghawrī no longer entertained any doubts about Selim's intention to attack him after finishing with Ismāʿīl, he found these words heartening in light of his own strategy. If the Ottoman did indeed plan to strike at Ismāʿīl first, he might well suffer heavy casualties before his encounter with the Egyptians. Poised at Aleppo to take advantage of the outcome, al-Ghawrī's host might inflict a decisive defeat and drive the Ottomans out of southeastern Anatolia as Qāytbāy had done. The sultan thus prevailed upon his deputy dawādār, Mughulbāy, to convey a pledge of neutrality to Selim, who was encamped at Qaysārīya.

While the sultan awaited the Ottoman's response, he reviewed his troops and promoted several officers to the rank of muqaddam. The provincial governors whom he had enlisted in the campaign received special recognition for their service.

[199] *Badāʾiʿ* 5, 60, l. 5; al-Ḥalabī, *Durr*, f. 178, l. 11.

The sultan ordered prayers of supplication day and night in the Great Mosque of Aleppo. All the religious dignitaries were called upon to participate. On Friday, the Shāfiʿī qāḍī of Cairo, Kamāl al-Dīn al-Ṭawīl, preached an eloquent khuṭba in which he quoted ḥadīths extolling the blessings of peace. Yet once again, al-Ghawrī remained reclusive and refused to attend.[200] The sultan made few public appearances in these tense days, emerging only to extract loyalty oaths sworn on the ʿUthmānī Koran and to honor another of Selim's fugitive nephews, Qāsimbak Aḥmad, whom he had brought along from Cairo as a possible hostage for bargaining. Al-Ghawrī had left him temporarily under the custody of the nā'ib of Ḥamā for safekeeping until he ascertained Aleppo's security.

According to some accounts, he also attempted to contact Ismāʿīl again, sending a second pledge of support for the Shah's efforts. When Selim intercepted this message, he flew into one of his choleric tantrums and arrested al-Ghawrī's courier, Mughulbāy, who had just arrived with his master's offer of neutrality.[201] Selim threatened to strip the hapless go-between nude, pluck out his mustache and force him to walk behind his own charger holding a tray to catch its droppings. Dissuaded by his ministers from this barbarity, he nevertheless divested Mughulbāy of his belongings and packed him off on an aged nag to inform his patron of his contempt. Al-Ghawrī found out about the miscarriage of his scheme from a second officer, Kurtbāy, former prefect of Cairo, whom he had sent after releasing the two Ottoman emissaries with ten thousand dīnārs to sweeten the truce offer carried by Mughulbāy. Hearing of his colleague's fate in ʿAynṭāb, Kurtbāy returned immediately.[202] He reported that Selim had altered his original plan and now intended

200 *Badā'iʿ* 5, 62, l. 13; 63, l. 14.
201 al-Ḥalabī, *Durr*, f. 178, l. 15. Ibn Iyās makes no mention of al-Ghawrī's plot, but described Mughulbāy's arrest and humiliation as further evidence of Selim's vulgarity. See *Badā'iʿ* 5, 63, l. 20; 67, l. 22.
202 *Badā'iʿ* 5, 64, l. 7.

to confront al-Ghawrī before dealing with Ismā'īl, tidings confirmed by Mughulbāy when he arrived. The Ottoman was advancing toward Aleppo, occupying several towns that had capitulated without resistance. Thus was al-Ghawrī's fate sealed. He had no choice but to confront Selim, who had told Mughulbāy to deliver the following curt message to his master: "Meet me at Marj Dābiq!"

The Egyptian host departed Aleppo on the twentieth of Rajab/19 August.[203] The Viceroy Khayrbak posed as al-Ghawrī's adviser, claiming his familiarity with Selim's tactics and knowledge of the terrain were crucial. The sultan sent off a packet of missives to Cairo urging his regent to maintain his just rule, admonishing the recruits to behave with some semblance of order until his return, and allowing the Ḥajj if security in the Ḥijāz so warranted. He then headed for the town of Ḥaylān just south of Marj Dābiq, where he would set up his bivouac. Upon receipt of the directives in Cairo, Ṭūmānbāy released prisoners jailed for debt and requested Koran readings in all the city markets. He called on all levels of the populace to pray for victory.[204] The weeks passed as the court in Cairo awaited word of the battle. When it arrived, everyone's worst fears were realized. Al-Ghawrī had ridden toward Ḥaylān with his troops, the governors of Syria, his auxilliary infantry, the four qāḍīs, and all the religious functionaries, the Caliph at his side. He reached his camp site at evening and at dawn inspected the layout of Marj Dābiq.[205]

Al-Ghawrī personally deployed his units as he anticipated Selim's arrival.[206] He required the Caliph to remain on his right, and the 'Abbāsid standard to be held over his head by

203 *Badā'i'* 5, 64, l. 14; 65, l. 4; 68, l. 11.
204 *Badā'i'* 5, 65, l. 20.
205 For an overview of the site's history, see E. Honigmann, "Mardj Dābiḳ," *EI*² 6, 544. The plain is in the vicinity of the town of Dābiq, where important battles had occurred since antiquity.
206 *Badā'i'* 5, 68, l. 15; al-Ḥalabī, *Durr*, f. 179b, l. 1.

his retainers. The sultan left no divine appeal to chance and surrounded himself with forty copies of the Koran, including the 'Uthmānī tome he had relied on so often before. These were now wrapped in yellow silk and borne on the heads of the Prophet's descendants (*ashrāf*). The shaykhs, rectors, and heads of Ṣūfī orders he had impressed into service held aloft banners emblazoned with their shrines' insignia. On the sultan's right flank were gathered Sībāy's regiment, on his left Khayrbak's. At the forefront of al-Ghawrī's own contingent assembled the seasoned veterans, since the Julbān were not battle-tested and could not be relied upon to stand firm.

The battle took place on Sunday, the twenty-fifth of Rajab/24 August.[207] Despite their inferior numbers, the sultan's officers and veterans displayed the mettle that had rendered them redoubtable in the past. Al-Ghawrī's atābak, Ṣūdūn, led the first charge, followed by the governor of Damascus. So ferocious was their initial onslaught, so agile their maneuvering around Ottoman artillery units, that they broke through the enemy's ranks, confiscated seven of his standards, and cut down his arquebusiers. Stunned by the intensity of their attack, Selim called for a truce. "Victory seemed to hover over the Egyptian army, if only this advantage had prevailed." But when the veterans heard al-Ghawrī call upon his recruits to fall back, leaving them to bear the brunt of fighting, they desisted from further assaults. Both Ṣūdūn and Sībāy died on the front lines, leaving their regiments directionless. It was then that Khayrbak, governor of Aleppo, turned the tide decisively for Selim. Having decided months earlier that al-Ghawrī's cause was hopeless, he had entered into secret negotiations with the Ottoman monarch, promising to betray his liege lord during the battle. Taken aback by the unexpected prowess of the Egyptian army, he broke ranks at the first sign of dissension among al-Ghawrī's soldiers and fled away toward Ḥamā with his own troops.

207 *Badā'i'* 5, 69, l. 9–72, l. 18.

Khayrbak's treachery may have cost al-Ghawrī this battle, but it was hardly unforeseen. The Mamlūk institution fostered pragmatic values. Loyalty remained ever flexible according to an individual's power at the moment. Al-Ghawrī had done little in his reign to encourage feelings of profound trust. While Selim himself would subsequently brand Khayrbak "the traitor" (*al-khā'in*), he also rewarded him with high office. Al-Ghawrī's own reaction to this turn of fortune was typical of the mentality he personified so aptly. Upon beholding the dissolution of his ranks, he shouted out, "O Aghās, this is your moment of destiny! Fight on and my share is yours!" No thought about commitment to a nobler cause, political or ideological, crossed his mind in this dark hour. Rather, his instincts turned to money, the instrument of inducement he employed throughout his life. "But no one heeded him, and all around him began to bolt group by group." The sultan then pleaded with the pious mystics and shaykhs surrounding him to "Pray to God the All-High for victory; this is the time for your supplication!" "Yet the sultan found none to aid him." Feeling suddenly faint in the scorching heat and swirling dust, he swayed on his horse.[208] His armorer, the Amīr Timur, rode up and seized the royal standard to keep it aloft. He then advised al-Ghawrī to flee the battle site. As the sultan called for water, he sensed a burning in his heart. His eyesight then dimmed and he suffered a paralyzing stroke. Attempting to wheel his mount around for escape, he fell from the saddle and expired minutes later. Some onlookers alleged that his arteries had ruptured, causing blood to spurt from his mouth. When the Ottoman high command learned of al-Ghawrī's death, they

[208] al-Ḥalabī, *Durr*, f. 179b, l. 10, claims that the sultan's horse, alarmed by cannon-fire, reared up and forced the saddle pommel to strike al-Ghawrī in the groin. His genitals were bruised, causing him to fall in a swoon to the ground. Several of his bodyguards carried him unconscious to a site removed from the battle where he expired. Many rumors, including suicide by poison, circulated as to the circumstances of al-Ghawrī's death. But all that could be confirmed was the disappearance of his corpse.

charged his faltering entourage, scattering them. But several of his retainers managed to cart the body away from the fray for burial since no trace of it was ever found. "It was as if the earth had swallowed him up on the spot. His end set an example for those who reflect on fate." Selim's host did capture all the standards al-Ghawrī's retinue wildly cast away in their rout. The holy Korans fared less well. Seeking to carry the vestiges of their opponent's former glory in triumph, the Ottomans had a use for the standards. Korans, however, signified little worldly power and could always be replaced. Thus they trampled them underfoot, scattering their folios in the dust. Even the 'Uthmānī copy was lost. "So passed the power (*mulk*) of al-Ashraf al-Ghawrī in an instant, as if it had never existed. Glory be to Him whose authority is eternal!"

Although the defeat was devastating, many escaped capture. Only three of al-Ghawrī's muqaddamīn had perished: Ṣūdūn the atābak, Baybars his intendant, and Aqbāy al-Ṭawīl. The governors of Damascus, Ṭarābulus, Ṣafad, and Ḥimṣ had also fallen. Indeed, casualties were highest among officers of all ranks. Numerous veterans also died, since they had participated in the initial charges. But most of the recruits survived to straggle back toward Aleppo. Still, the plain was littered with mutilated remnants of this confrontation. "Corpses lay in heaps, many without heads. Faces of the fallen were smeared with blood and grime, disfiguring their features. Slain horses lay scattered about, their saddles thrown from their backs. Gold-embossed swords, steel-mail tunics, tatters of uniforms were strewn all over. No one took any notice of this booty for the present. They were too preoccupied." Finally, sometime after noon, Selim reined in his troops and proceeded toward al-Ghawrī's camp at Ḥaylān. Seating himself in the former sultan's tent, he confiscated all his baggage. Each enclosure of the fifteen muqaddamīn suffered a similar fate at the hands of Selim's officers. Ibn Iyās summed up his thoughts about this cataclysm in the following lines:

No previous Ottoman ruler had scored such a victory over another king.... No sultan of Egypt had ever been subjected to a disaster like this, dying under his own standard on the day of battle. None ever suffered such a defeat: its like was unprecedented. None lost his baggage and treasury to his enemy. Only Qānṣūh al-Ghawrī endured such a fate. Thus was it written. The sultan and his officers—not a one of them looked to sustain the Muslims' welfare by upholding justice and equity. They now suffered [God's] retribution for their acts, because God empowered the Ottoman so that events took their course. As the verses go:

> Where are the kings whose tyranny sullied the Earth?
> For God has depleted their seats [of power].
> One can but hear of them rather than see them, as a warning.
> For they have left no trace you can behold, save their dwellings.[209]

Aftermath

Confident in his victory, Selim tarried at Ḥaylān, ignoring the survivors of his enemy's army. For their part, the fugitives arrived at Aleppo in their stained uniforms, hoping to find shelter. But the local inhabitants, who nursed feelings of hatred for their "protectors" because of the pillaging and rapine they had inflicted during their billeting, pounced on them with knives and clubs.[210] More recruits died in Aleppo at the hands of those they had abused than at Marj Dābiq. Their amīrs recognized the futility of reprisal and departed for Damascus. There they found a reception only slightly less hostile. Sībāy's regent hesitated to dissolve his ties with Cairo until he had ascertained Selim's intentions, and dared not

209 *Badā'i'* 5, 72, l. 18.

210 *Badā'i'* 5, 73, l. 8; al-Ḥalabī, *Durr*, f. 179b, l. 16.

chance arousing Ṭūmānbāy's wrath. He accordingly granted the survivors sanctuary until they acquired new clothes and mounts for their passage to Egypt.

Selim received the Caliph and three of the senior qāḍīs in Ḥaylān.[211] The Ḥanafī qāḍī, Maḥmūd ibn al-Shiḥna ('Abd al-Barr's son), had decided against surrender and fled with the fugitives. The Ottoman extended full honors to the Commander of Believers and pledged to restore "all his customary prerogatives." Yet he also hinted at his possible return to Baghdād, a prospect the Caliph could hardly relish. In these times, the glories of Baghdād under al-Manṣūr or Harūn al-Rashīd were but faint memories; the town was now an outpost, a shadow of its former grandeur. Selim treated the qāḍīs less hospitably. Chiding their corrupt practices, he upbraided them for winking at al-Ghawrī's vices. All three were placed under surveillance.

When Selim finally entered Aleppo, its populace hailed him as a savior who delivered them from the Mamlūk yoke.[212] The prefect of Aleppo's citadel had escaped with the remnants of al-Ghawrī's army, leaving its gates open in his haste. Selim thus encountered not even a barred door to protect the loot of a lifetime. While his troops waited below, a lame clerk leaning on a cane limped up to the summit to initiate the inventory. Selim had vowed that when he took the stronghold the weakest man in his army would open its vaults. What the aged clerk found overwhelmed him. Totally unattended were all the treasures al-Ghawrī had brought from Cairo for safekeeping. When the clerk reported riches past calculation, Selim's curiosity overrode his arrogance and he ascended to examine them personally.[213] Ibn Iyās listed the astounding sum of one hundred million dīnārs for the bagged coinage, a figure at variance with his earlier estimate (cf. note 194). Whether any preindustrial polity could have amassed such

211 *Badā'i'* 5, 74, l. 3.
212 *Badā'i'* 5, 74, l. 17.
213 *Badā'i'* 5, 75, l. 6.

a quantity of currency, regardless of hoarding, is open to question. But Selim clearly had chanced upon a trove exceeding any his predecessors had acquired. Ibn Iyās dwelt on the ceremonial equipage embossed in gems and precious metal the Ottoman could save or reprocess as he chose. The extent of this treasure and Selim's amazement over its size suggests something about the rustic nature of the Ottoman state prior to its incorporation of Egypt and Syria. Al-Ghawrī had hauled along objects dating back to Saladin's reign and perhaps earlier. Selim expropriated a private fisc that enabled him to defray the enormous cost of subsequent military adventures. The implications of this massive confiscation for the future expansion of the Ottoman State and its cultural transformation have yet to be evaluated fully.

While Selim savored his triumph, fugitives from the disaster began arriving in Cairo.[214] They told tales of wholesale defection to Selim's cause by both civilian and military personnel. When the household of the fallen atābak Ṣūdūn received news of his demise, his family keened the ritual wail of mourning. All eyes now turned to the amīr Ṭūmānbāy. As regent, he had shown himself a man who commanded respect. Although he had delegated to Zaynī Barakāt absolute control over the bureaucracy, he also upheld the commoners' rights while the sultan was away. No one else could shore up the regime's courage in this desperate hour, and when al-Ghawrī's name was omitted from Friday sermons everyone expected Ṭūmānbāy to succeed his uncle.[215]

Ṭūmānbāy showed restraint in these trying days and permitted no vindictive attacks against Anatolians residing in Cairo. Only the estates of officials who had betrayed al-Ghawrī were sequestered and redistributed to loyal survivors who had lost everything. On the seventh of Ramaḍān/4 October, Ṭūmānbāy formally welcomed the grand

214 *Badā'i'* 5, 79, l. 6.
215 *Badā'i'* 5, 81, l. 18.

amīrs returning from Damascus.[216] When they convened their first council since the defeat, all demanded Ṭūmānbāy's accession. Reflecting on the dangers he confronted, since Selim would certainly have business with him, Ṭūmānbāy refused their acclamation. A delegation of amīrs then rode out to the shrine at Kūm al-Jāriḥ, where Abū Sa'ūd, the shaykh whom al-Ghawrī had visited years before, resided. Upon hearing of Ṭūmānbāy's recalcitrance, the shaykh brought out a Koran and compelled the officers to swear their good behavior on it. They then affixed their signatures to a written contract. "They would neither betray nor deceive nor plot against their sovereign.... From this day they would not abuse the masses or treat them unjustly or impose arbitrary measures upon them. They would abolish all al-Ghawrī's oppressive schemes, including the monthly and weekly imposts on shops. The state of affairs prevailing under al-Ashraf Qāytbāy would be restored." The shaykh admonished the amīrs: "If God has allowed the Ottoman ruler to defeat, humiliate, and rule over you, this stems from denunciations by all creation against you on land and sea." The officers replied: "We repent and desist from injustice this very day." Upon receipt of their written pledge, Ṭūmānbāy capitulated and accepted the sultanate. Since Selim was focusing his attention on Iran for the present, the new monarch could exploit the respite for preparations against an invasion.

Thus we depart from this narrative. The Mamlūk State's final months and ultimate defeat lie beyond its scope. Reflecting over al-Ghawrī's fate, one is tempted to speculate what might have been had destiny placed a less impetuous individual than Selim on the throne of 'Uthmān. Were al-Ghawrī's acts so heinous that he undermined the foundation of his regime beyond recovery? Was it indeed a polity awaiting a conqueror? Or, following a miracle, might he have implemented some long-overdue changes in the functioning of this

216 *Badā'i'* 5, 85, l. 1.

inertia-bound state? We cannot know. But the complexities and contradictions exhibited by this remarkable man surely warrant comparison with the legacy of his tradition-oriented predecessor. From such a query, the causes of Egypt's waning as a great power may be sought.

Chapter Four

Closing Reflections

THE foregoing biographies have revealed opposing concepts of royal authority. Al-Ashraf Qāytbāy saw his mission fully within parameters of behavior set by his predecessors long before. Even alleged innovations he adopted under pressure of need never exceeded conceptual limits fixed earlier in the evolution of the Mamlūk regime. Qāytbāy was indeed revered by both military colleagues and civilian clients because they found in his actions the reassurance of proven precedent. In the final analysis, such reassurance outweighed the piety Qāytbāy so genuinely espoused. Qāytbāy reinvigorated an inertia-bound system of military power and bureaucratic procedure. His horizons did not extend beyond principles he inherited from bygone days.

Individuals who wield power according to customary norms of authority invariably invoke praise from those whose interests are enhanced by prolongation of the status quo.

All the chroniclers who judged their rulers' performance belonged to social groups that profited from continuance of the old order in Cairo. In their incessant criticisms of the Mamlūk regime, they frequently railed against surface ills but rarely condemned underlying causes. And when the latter were confronted, the historians offered few alternatives to remedy them. The chroniclers' admiration for Qāytbāy was thus predictable. His dogged heroism and stoic resolve in the face of calamity resonated with their appreciation of a protector's defiance before enemies but humility before God. Qāytbāy radiated the assurance of one whose role demanded custodianship of a system that had worked reasonably well for many decades, and guardianship of a realm that had long stood as a bastion of safety in a turbulent world. Even Ibn Taghrī-Birdī's castigations were provoked by the vagaries of succession at the outset of his reign. That Qāytbāy had not a single new idea about governing his realm not one of his biographers found blameworthy.

Qānṣūh al-Ghawrī, whom most of his contemporaries deemed wanting by comparison, exhibited more than the deficiencies of an uncharismatic personality. Juxtaposed against the myriad cases his critics listed of abuse, corruption, and extraction are an equal number of schemes impressive for their ingenuity. Upon reflection over the stridency of condemnation apparent in Ibn Iyās' obituary of al-Ghawrī, reproduced at the beginning of Chapter 3, one is nonetheless struck by the sultan's shrewd assessment of where individuals adroit in the hoarding of assets stashed—and thus idled—their resources. Although Ibn Iyās lamented at length the decline of Egypt's agrarian, artisanal, and commercial productivity, he never acknowledged the connection between hoarded assets and inactive wealth. While al-Ghawrī warrants no acclaim as even a protocapitalist aware of this linkage, he was driven by practices he perceived as both inimical and irremedial to ponder an assault against the customary patterns of military hierarchy and property control. The alarm such an attempt, however tentative, aroused among al-Ghawrī's peers is palpable on every page or manuscript leaf of contemporary descriptions. Acceptance of their depictions verbatim have induced later historians to echo their tirades as ample proof that a tyrannical regime was haplessly mired in ills of its own making.

My own reading of this superficially dismal record has led me to its qualified revision. At the very least, Qāytbāy's august stature merits rethinking in light of his contemporaries' relief over his preservation of their world, while al-Ghawrī's image as an ogre of avarice calls for reassessment in light of their worries about the implications of his innovations. When al-Ghawrī experimented with artillery, recruited new military units from outside the Mamlūk caste, or manipulated waqfs to pay them, he was denounced for either wasting his time on nonsense or sullying the rights of those whom God had ordained to control society. That these measures, inchoate as they were, might suggest al-Ghawrī's toying with the supplanting of old rights and privileges is never openly admitted by any of his contemporaries. Yet one wonders whether the intensity of their decrying was motivated by subliminal fears of substantive reform, a prospect appealing to no one content with the way things were.

Rarely were al-Ghawrī's actions those of a monarch impelled by noblesse oblige. Nor does our evidence imply a grand design on his part for building a "new Egypt." But necessity is ever the mother of ingenuity, if not invention. Our sources do provide poignant examples of al-Ghawrī's frustration over his incapacity to function as the kind of commander in chief Qāytbāy had been. There are hints embedded in these vivid episodes that al-Ghawrī resented the bankruptcy his predecessor bequeathed him as much as he did Qāytbāy's pious deportment. The piety was odious because of personal aversion or simple jealousy, while the penury was dangerous for the strictures it imposed. Ire is as profound an incentive for change as admiration, perhaps the more since it encourages departure from past precedent. Worship of a precursor promotes replication of his policies, while aversion encourages departure from them.

Thus, as we reflect over these final great reigns of the Mamlūk sultanate, their superficial differences conceal deepper contrasts in political posture and fiscal procurement. The implications of these underlying contrasts, even if but dimly perceived in their own day, prompted the vehemence of adulation or denunciation of the chroniclers who beheld them. However we moderns react to these two careers, they never lacked for vitality. The biographies recapture the flavor of a tumultuous epoch, when the long-standing regional order presided over by the Mamlūks was eclipsed by a new one it could no longer contain. The reigns of these sultans may, in their distinctive ways, be symptomatic of incurable inertia pervading the central Arab lands at the end of the Middle Ages. But though a regime was terminated at Marj Dābiq, its memory was not. Nor did its constituent society lose any of the vigor so apparent in the antics of the characters brought to life in these episodes. Their abiding impact on the vision of generations to come in this part of the world merits our reflection as we contemplate the Middle East today.

BIBLIOGRAPHY OF SOURCES CITED

1. Narrative Sources

Ibn Ḥajar al-ʿAsqalānī. *Inbā' al-ghumr bi-anbā' al-ʿumr*. Edited by Ḥasan Ḥabashī. 3 vols. Cairo 1969–1972 (*GAL* 2, 83).

al-ʿAynī. *ʿIqd al-jumān fī ta'rīkh ahl al-zamān*. Edited by Muḥammad Amīn. Cairo 1987– (*GAL* 2, 65; Suppl. 2, 51).

ʿAbd al-Bāsiṭ. *See* al-Malaṭī.

al-Ba'ūnī. *Al-lamḥa al-ashrafīya wa'l-bahja al-sanīya*. Ms. Paris, B.N., f.a. 1615 (*GAL* 2, 54; Suppl. 2, 67).

———. *Nuzhat al-anām fī ta'rīkh al-Islām*. Ms. Cairo, Dār al-Kutub 1740 Ta'rīkh (*GAL*, 2, 50; Suppl. 2, 49–50).

Badā'ī'. *See* Ibn Iyās.

Ḍaw'. *See* al-Sakhāwī.

al-Ghazzī. *Al-kawākib al-sā'ira bi-manāqib ʿulamā' al-mi'a al-ʿāshira*. 3 vols. Beirut 1979 (*GAL* 2, 291).

al-Ḥalabī, *Durr al-ḥabab fī ta'rīkh aʿyān Ḥalab*. Ms. Vienna, Codex Vinobonensis Palatinus, Mxt. 667 [Flügel 1184] (*GAL* 2, 368).

Ḥawādith. *See* Ibn Taghrī-Birdī.

Ibn al-Ḥimṣī. *Ḥawādith al-zamān wa-wafayāt al-shuyūkh wa'l-aqrān*. Ms. Istanbul, Feizullah 1438 (*GAL* Suppl. 2, 41).

Iʿlām. *See* Ibn Ṭūlūn.

Inbā'. *See* al-Jawharī al-Ṣayrafī.

Kitāb ithbāt dalālāt Muḥammad ibn al-marḥūm al-malik al-Ashraf Qāytbāy. Ms. Istanbul, Topkapı Saray 2960, listed in the catalogue as *Al-kitāb al-saʿīd min taʾrīkh al-maqām al-malik al-Nāṣir*.

Ibn Iyās. *Badāʾiʿ al-zuhūr fī waqāʾiʿ al-duhūr*. Edited by M. Mustafa, H. Roemer, and H. Ritter. Vols. 3–5. Cairo and Wiesbaden 1960–1963. (*Badāʾīʿ*.) Abridged version: *ʿUqūd al-jumān fī waqāʾiʿ al-azmān*. Ms. Istanbul, Aya Sofya 3311. (*ʿUqūd*.)

———. *Nuzhat al-umam fīʾl-ʿajāʾib waʾl-ḥikam*. Ms. Aya Sofya 3500 (*GAL* 2, 295; Suppl. 2, 405).

Jawāhir al-sulūk fīʾl-khulafāʾ waʾl-mulūk. Ms. London, British Museum 6854 (*GAL* 2, 42; Suppl. 2, 53). (*Jawāhir*.)

Ibn al-Jīʿān. *Al-qawl al-mustaẓraf fī safar mawlānā al-malik al-Ashraf*. French translation by H. Devonshire. *IFAO Bulletin* 20 (1922) 2–40 (*GAL* 2, 38; Suppl. 2, 26).

al-Malaṭī, ʿAbd al-Bāsiṭ. *Majmūʿ al-bustān al-nūrī li-ḥaḍrat mawlānā sulṭān al-Ghūrī*. Ms. Istanbul, Aya Sofya 4793.

———. *Al-rawḍ al-bāsim fī ḥawādith al-ʿumr waʾl-tarājim*. Ms. Vatican arabo 728. (*Rawḍ*.)

———. *Al-risāla al-laṭīfa tashtamalu ʿalā dhikrin man waliya Miṣr min al-Salāṭīn*. Ms. Istanbul, Laleli 2044 (*GAL* 2, 54; Suppl. 2, 52).

al-Maqrīzī. *Kitāb al-sulūk li-maʿrifa duwal al-mulūk*. 12 parts in 4 vols. Cairo 1934–1973 (*GAL* 2, 48; Suppl. 2, 36–37).

Nujūm. *See* Ibn Taghrī-Birdī.

Rawḍ. *See* ʿAbd al-Bāsiṭ al-Malaṭī.

al-Sakhāwī. *Al-ḍawʾ al-lāmiʿ fī aʿyān al-qarn al-tāsiʿ*. Edited by Ḥusām al-Qudsī. 12 vols. Cairo 1934. (*Ḍawʾ*)

———. *Al-dhayl al-tāmm ʿalā duwal al-Islām*. Ms. Tūnis, Dār al-Kutub al-waẓīfa 6856 (*GAL* 2, 43; Suppl. 2, 31–32).

———. *Shajarat al-khulafāʾ*. Ms. Istanbul, Aya Sofya 3266 (*GAL*, as preceding).

al-Jawharī al-Ṣayrafī. *Inbāʾ al-haṣr fī abnāʾ al-ʿaṣr*. Edited by Ḥasan Ḥabashī. Cairo 1970. (*Inbāʾ*.)

———. *Nuzhat al-nufūs waʾl-abdān fī tawārīkh al-zamān*. Edited by Ḥasan Ḥabashī. 3 vols. Cairo 1971–1873 (*GAL* Suppl. 2, 41).

al-Suyūṭī. *Badāʾiʿ al-ʿumūr fī waqāʾiʿ al-duhūr*. Ms. Istanbul, Aya Sofya 2987.

Ibn Taghrī-Birdī. *Ḥawādith al-duhūr fī madā al-ayyām wa'l-shuhūr*. Edited by William Popper. University of California Publications in Semitic Philology, vol. 7, nos. 1–4. Berkeley and Los Angeles 1930–1931. (*Ḥawādith.*)

———. *Al-manhal al-ṣāfī wa'l-mustawfī ba'd al-wāfī*. Edited by Muḥammad Amīn. Cairo 1984–.

———. *Al-nujūm al-zāhira fī mulūk Miṣr wa'l-Qāhira*. Edited by William Popper. University of California Publications in Semitic Philology, vols. 5–7, 12, 14, 17–19, 22. Berkeley and Los Angeles 1915–1960 (*GAL* 2, 51–52). (*Nujūm.*)

Ta'rīkh al-malik al-Ashraf Qāytbāy. Ms. Paris, B.N., f.a. 5916 (*GAL* 2, 38; Suppl. 2, 26). (*Ta'rīkh Qāytbāy.*)

Ibn Ṭūlūn. *I'lām al-warā bi-man wulliya min al-Atrāk bi-Dimashq*. Edited by 'Abd al-'Aẓīm Ḥāmid Khaṭṭāb. Cairo 1973. (*I'lām.*)

———. *Mukāfaha al-khillān fī ḥawādith al-zamān*. Edited by Muḥammad Muṣṭafā. 2 vols. Cairo 1962–1964.

'Uqūd. *See* Ibn Iyās.

2. Archival Sources

Amīn: M. Amīn, *Catalogue des documents d'archives du Caire de 239/853 à 922/1516*. Cairo, IFAO, 1981.

DW: Dār al-Wathā'iq al-Qawmīya, Cairo.

AW: Wizārat al-Awqāf, Cairo.

Amīn no. 116. DW 18/11.

Amīn no. 450. AW 104 jadīd (new).

3. Secondary Studies

'Abd al-Rāziq, Aḥmad. *La femme au temps des Mamlouks en Égypte*. Cairo, IFAO, 1973.

———. "Al-Mamālīk wa-Mafhūm al-Usrah ladayhim." *Majallat kullīyat al-āthār* 2 (Cairo, Cairo University, 1977) 188–207.

Allen, W. E. D., and P. Muratoff. *Caucasian Battlefields: A History of the Wars on the Turco-Caucasian Border, 1828–1921*. Cambridge 1953.

Ashtor, Eliyahu. *Histoire des prix et des salaires dans l'orient médiévale*. Paris 1969.

———. "Ḳā'it Bāy." EI^2 4, 462–463.

———. *Levant Trade in the Later Middle Ages*. Princeton 1983.

Ayalon, David. "Aspects of the Mamlūk Phenomenon: A. The Importance of the Mamlūk Institution; B. Ayyūbids, Kurds and Turks." *Der Islam* 53 (1976) 196–225; 54 (1977) 1–32.

———. "Burdjīya." *EI*² 1, 1324–1325.

———. "The Circassians in the Mamlūk Kingdom." *JAOS* 69 (1939) 135–147.

———. "Discharges from Service, Banishments and Imprisonments in Mamlūk Society." In *Israel Oriental Studies*, vol. 2, 25–50. Jerusalem 1972.

———. "L'esclavage du Mamlouk." *Oriental Notes and Studies*, vol. 1. Jerusalem 1951.

———. "The European Asiatic Steppe: A Major Reservoir for the Islamic World." In *Transactions of the Twenty-fifth Congress of Orientalists*, 47–52. Moscow 1963.

———. *Gunpowder and Firearms in the Mamluk Kingdom*. London 1956.

———. "Mamlūkiyāt: A First Attempt to Evaluate the Mamluk Military System." *Jerusalem Studies in Arabic and Islam*, vol. 2, 321–349. Jerusalem 1980.

———. "Preliminary Remarks on the Mamluk Military Institution." In *War, Technology and Society in the Middle East*, edited by V. J. Parry and M. E. Yapp, 44–58. London 1975.

———. "Studies on the Structure of the Mamlūk Army," parts 1–3. *BSOAS* 15 (1953) 203–228; 448–476; 16 (1954) 57–90.

———. "The System of Payment in Mamluk Military Society." *JESHO* 1 (1952) 37–65.

Bacharach, Jere. "African Military Slaves in the Medieval Middle East: The Cases of Iraq (869–955) and Egypt (868–1171)." *IJMES* 13 (1981) 471–495.

Baddeley, John F. *The Russian Conquest of the Caucasus*. London 1908. Reprinted 1969.

Barthold, W. *Turkestan down to the Mongol Invasions*. 3d ed. London 1968.

Bosworth, C. E. *The Ghaznavids*. Edinburgh 1963.

———. *The Medieval History of Iran, Afghanistan and Central Asia*. London 1977.

———. "The Political and Dynastic History of the Iranian World (A.D. 1000–1217)." In *The Cambridge History of Iran*, edited by J. A. Boyle, vol. 5, 1–202. Cambridge 1968.

———. "Recruitment, Muster and Review in Medieval Islamic Armies." In *War, Technology and Society in the Middle East*, edited by V. J. Parry and M. E. Yapp, 59–77. London 1975.

The Cambridge History of China, edited by Denis Twitchett and Michael Loewe, vol. 1, 383–405. Cambridge 1986.

The Cambridge Medieval History, 2d ed., edited by H. Gwatkin and J. Whitney, vol. 1, 215–217, 328–366, 660–665. Cambridge 1964.

Canard, Marius. "Une lettre du Sultan Nāṣir Ḥasan à Jean VI Cantacuzène (750/1349)." *Annales de l'Institut d'Etudes Orientales d'Alger* 3 (1939), 27–52.

———. "Le royaume d'Arménie-Cilicie et les Mamlouks jusqu'au traité de 1285." *Revue des Etudes Arméniennes* 4 (1967) 217–259.

———. "Le traité de 1281 entre Michel Paléologue et le Sultan Qalā'ūn." *Byzantion* 10 (1935) 669–680.

———. "Un traité entre Byzance et l'Egypte au XIIIe siècle et les relations diplomatiques de Michel VIII Paleologue avec les sultans mamlouks Baibars et Qalā'ūn." In *Mélanges Gaudefroy-Demombynes* (Cairo, 1934–1945) 197–224.

Crone, Patricia. *Slaves on Horses*. Cambridge 1980.

Darrag, Ahmad. *L'Egypte sous le règne de Barsbay*. Damascus 1961.

Dictionary of the Middle Ages, edited by Joseph Strayer, vol. 2, 12–13; vol. 6, 352–354. New York 1983; 1985.

Dölger, Franz. "Der Vertrag des Sultans Qalā'ūn von Ägypten mit dem Kaiser Michael VIII Palaiologos." In *Serta Monacensia Franz Babinger*, edited by H. J. Kissling, 60–79. Leiden 1952.

Ehrenkreutz, Andrew S. "Strategic Implications of the Slave Trade between Genoa and Mamlūk Egypt in the Second Half of the Thirteenth Century." In *The Islamic Middle East*, edited by A. L. Udovitch, 335–345. Princeton 1981.

Forand, P. G. "The Relationship of the Slave and the Client to the Master or Patron in Medieval Islam." *IJMES* 2 (1971) 59–61.

Al-Ghaytānī, Jamīl. *Al-Zaynī Barakāt*. 3d ed. Cairo 1985. English translation by Farouk Mustafa. New York 1989.

Hewson, Robert H. "Circassians." In *The Modern Encyclopedia of Russian and Soviet History*, edited by J. L. Wiecynski, vol. 7, 134. Gulf Breezes, Florida, 1976.

Holt, P. M. *The Age of the Crusades: The Near East from the Eleventh Century to 1517*. London 1986.

———. "Ḳānṣawh al-Ghawrī," *EI*² 4, 552–553.

———. "The Position and Power of the Mamlūk Sultan." *BSOAS* 38 (1975) 237–249.

———. "Qalawun's Treaty with Genoa in 1290." *Der Islam* 57 (1980) 101–108.

———. "The Structure of Government in the Mamlūk Sultanate." In *The Eastern Mediterranean Lands in the Period of the Crusades*, edited by P. M. Holt, 44–61. Warminster 1977.

———. "Three Biographies of al-Ẓāhir Baybars." In *Medieval Historical Writing in the Christian and Islamic Worlds*, edited by D. O. Morgan, 19–20. London 1982.

———. "The Treaties of the Early Mamluk Sultans with the Frankish States." *BSOAS* 43 (1980) 67–76.

Honigmann, E. "Mardj Dābiḳ," *EI*² 6, 544.

Humphreys, R. Stephen. "The Emergence of the Mamlūk Army." *Studia Islamica* 45 (1977) 67–100; 46 (1977) 147–182.

Inalcik, Halil. "The Socio-Political Effects of the Diffusion of Firearms in the Middle East." In *War, Technology and Society in the Middle East*, edited by V. J. Parry and M. E. Yapp, 195–217. London 1975.

Irwin, Robert. "Factions in Medieval Egypt." *JRAS* (1986) 228–246.

———. *The Middle East in the Middle Ages: The Early Mamluk Sultanate, 1250–1382*. London 1986.

Jomier, J. *Le mahmal et la caravane égyptienne des pèlerins de la Mecque, XIIIe–XXe siècles*. Cairo, IFAO, 1953.

Kazemzadeh, Firuz. "Russian Penetration of the Caucasus." In *Russian Imperialism from Ivan the Great to the Revolution*, edited by T. Hunczak, 239–263. New Brunswick 1974.

Khowaiter, A. *Baibars the First*. London 1978.

Labib, S. *Handelsgeschichte Ägyptens im Spätmittelalter (1171–1517)*. Wiesbaden 1965.

Lambton, A. K. S. *Continuity and Change in Medieval Persia*. Albany 1987.

———. *Landlord and Peasant in Persia*. London 1953.

Lapidus, Ira M. *Muslim Cities in the Later Middle Ages*. Cambridge 1967.

Manz, Beatrice Forbes. *The Rise and Rule of Tamerlane*. Cambridge 1989.

Minorsky, Vladimir. *Medieval Iran and its Neighbors*. London 1982.

Mordtmann, J., and L. Menage. "Dhū'l-Ḳadr." *EI*² 2, 239.

Morgan, D. O. *Medieval Persia, 1040–1797*. New York 1988.

Newhall, Amy Whittier. "The Patronage of the Mamluk Sultan Qā'it Bāy, 872–901/1468–1496." Ph.D. Diss., Harvard University, 1987. Ph.D. abstr. no. 8711525.

Parry, V. J. "La manière de combattre." In *War, Technology and Society in the Middle East*, edited by V. J. Parry and M. E. Yapp. London 1975.

Petrovič, Djurdjica. "Fire-arms in the Balkans on the Eve of and after the Ottoman Conquests of the Fourteenth and Fifteenth Centuries." In *War, Technology and Society in the Middle East*, edited by V. J. Parry and M. E. Yapp, 164–194. London 1975.

Petry, Carl F. *The Civilian Elite of Cairo in the Later Middle Ages*. Princeton 1981.

———. "Class Solidarity vs. Gender Gain: Women as Custodians of Property in Later Medieval Egypt." In *Women and Middle Eastern History: Shifting Boundaries in Sex and Gender*, edited by Nikki Keddie and Beth Baron, 122–142. New Haven 1991.

———. "Geographic Origins of Academicians in Cairo during the Fifteenth Century." *JESHO* 23 (1980) 119–141.

Pipes, Daniel. *Slave Soldiers of Islam: the Genesis of a Military System*. New Haven 1981.

Popper, William. *Egypt and Syria under the Circassian Sultans 1382–1468 A.D.: Systematic Notes to Ibn Taghri-Birdi's Chronicles of Egypt*. University of California Publications in Semitic Philology, vol. 15. Berkeley and Los Angeles 1955.

Rabie, Hassanein. "Ḳalāwūn." *EI*² 4, 484–486.

Saddeque, S. F. *Baybars the First of Egypt*. Dacca 1956.

Salibi, K. S. "Listes chronologiques des grands cadis de l'Egypte sous les mamlouks." *REI* 25 (1957) 81–125.

Schimmel, Annemarie. "Kalif und Kadi im spätmittelalterlichen Ägypten." *Die Welt des Islams* 24 (1942) 1–128.

Sergeant, R. B. *The Portuguese off the South Arabian Coast*. London 1963.

Sobernheim, M. "Ḳā'itbey." *EI*¹ 2, 663–664.

———. "Ḳānṣūh." *EI*¹ 2, 720–721.

Sourdel, D. "Ghulām." *EI*² 2, 1079–1085.

Spuler, Berthold. *Iran in frühislamischen Zeit*. Wiesbaden 1952.

Thorau, Peter. *Sultan Baibars I. von Ägypten*. Wiesbaden 1987. Translated by P. M. Holt as *The Lion of Egypt: Sultan Baybars I and the Near East in the Thirteenth Century*. London 1992.

Wansbrough, John. "The Safe-Conduct in Muslim Chancery Practice." *BSOAS* 34 (1971) 20–35.

Wiet, Gaston. "Baibars I." *EI*² 1, 1124–1126.

———. "Barḳūḳ" *EI*² 1, 1050–1051.

———. "Les biographies du Manhal Ṣāfī." *Mémoires de l'Institut d'Égypte* 19 (1932).

———. "Deux princes ottomans à la cour d'Egypte." *BIE* 20 (1938) 137–150.

———. *L'Egypte arabe*. Vol. 4 of *L'Histoire de la nation égyptienne*, edited by Gabriel Hanotaux, 589–636. Paris 1937.

Winter, Michael. *Society and Religion in Early Ottoman Egypt: Studies in the Writings of 'Abd al-Waḥḥāb al-Sha'rānī*. New Brunswick 1982.

Woods, John. *The Aqqoyunlu: Clan, Confederation, Empire*. Minneapolis 1976.

INDEX